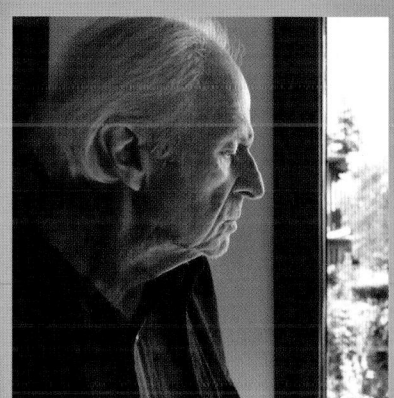

Dedicated to Ralph Angus McQuarrie
(June 13, 1929 – March 3, 2012)

Battle Milk 3

Conceptually Unpasteurized and Creatively Fortified

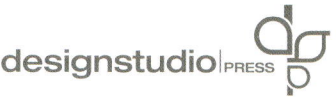
designstudio|PRESS

Designed by

transitcreative

transitcreative.com

Copy Editor: Jessica Hoffmann
Book Design: Michael Long/Transit Creative

Published by Design Studio Press
8577 Higuera Street
Culver City, CA 90232
Website: www.designstudiopress.com
E-mail: info@designstudiopress.com

Printed in China.
First edition, July 2013

10 9 8 7 6 5 4 3 2 1

ISBN: 978-1-933492-70-4

Library of Congress Control Number: 2013935806

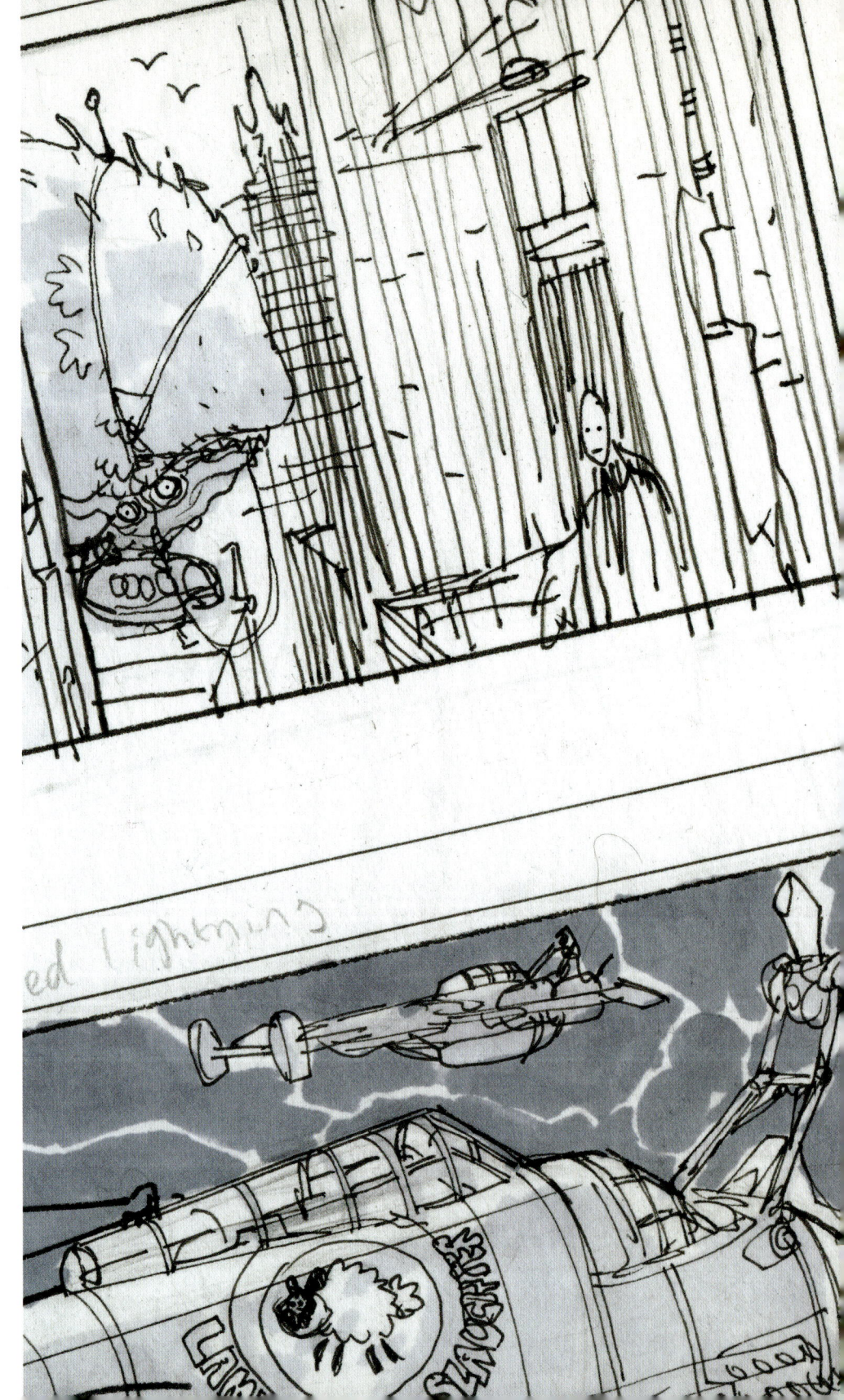

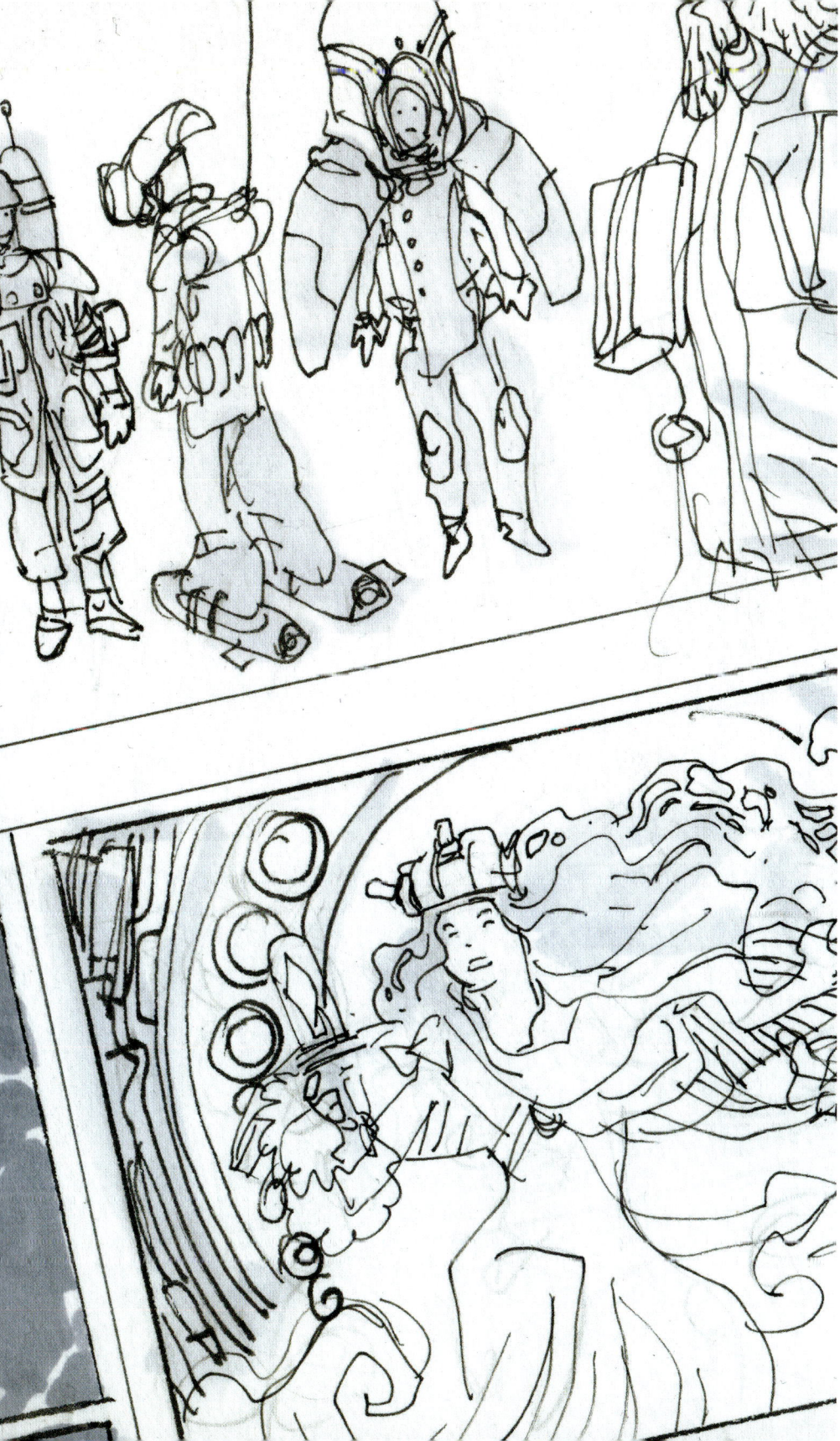

CONTENTS

FOREWORD

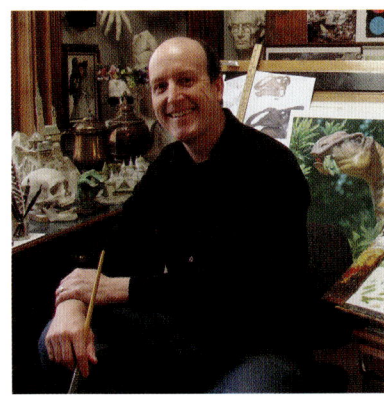

In 1581, when Galileo sat listening to a sermon in a cathedral in Pisa, he was only half listening. The other half of his brain floated up to the chandelier hanging from the ceiling. As the priest droned on, he watched the chandelier swinging back and forth in a light breeze. He timed the motion against his pulse and noticed that each oscillation took the same amount of time, regardless of how far it swung. Before the sermon was over, his imagination worked out the principle of the pendulum, which later revolutionized clockwork.

Galileo was my excuse when I sketched designs for kites in my notebook margins in eighth-grade algebra. Out the high windows I could see a band of blue sky and drifting clouds. Looking in that direction had gotten me scolded, so I kept my head down and drew kites instead: box kites, Marconi kites, string climbers, camera slings, and shutter releases. Whenever I got ahead on my equations, I sketched more construction diagrams.

After school, when my homework was completed, I checked the sky. If it was calm, I beelined to the workshop to saw up sticks and to stretch string and paper. If the wind was up, I bicycled to the schoolyard with my newest kite, which still smelled of glue and hope. Sometimes the day ended well, with a kite that climbed to become a speck against the sky. Other times it ended in disaster. Many of my kites died tangled in trees and wires. Or worse, one time my dad's camera fell 300 feet to the schoolyard pavement when the cigarette fuse burned through its tether instead of the shutter release.

I suffered from Galileo Syndrome later, when I finished college and started working as a commissioned illustrator. After a day spent painting archaeological scenes for *National Geographic*, I set aside a few precious evening hours to paint my own worlds. At my little drafting table in the basement, with snow piling up outside the window, and the steam pipes hissing just above my head, I let my paintbrush take me to cities on waterfalls and parades with dinosaurs. That was what got me into all that trouble with *Dinotopia*.

Each of the artists in *Battle Milk Volume 3* has been diagnosed with an incurable case of Galileo Syndrome. They do a stellar job at their concept art during the day, mind you, throwing their hearts into it, and contributing inspiration to some of the most famous movies and games. But during those spare moments waiting for meetings, or when they're commuting back home from work, their minds are already dancing across cirrus clouds. When they get home and the kids are in bed and the dishes are washed, these artists are hard at work setting sail across their own galaxies.

Before they asked me to write this foreword, I was already a fan of the *Battle Milk* series having picked up a copy of the last edition. I have cherished it on my inspiration bookshelf. They have let me peek at the stuff in this volume. I don't know how it is possible, but this edition surpasses the last, and it takes the viewer into whole new landscapes. I send my warm wishes and hearty congratulations to all of the daydreamers and margin doodlers represented herein—and to you, the reader, for buying this ticket to the wild half of their brains. You're in for a rollicking ride.

James Gurney

James Gurney
Rhinebeck, NY
February 2013

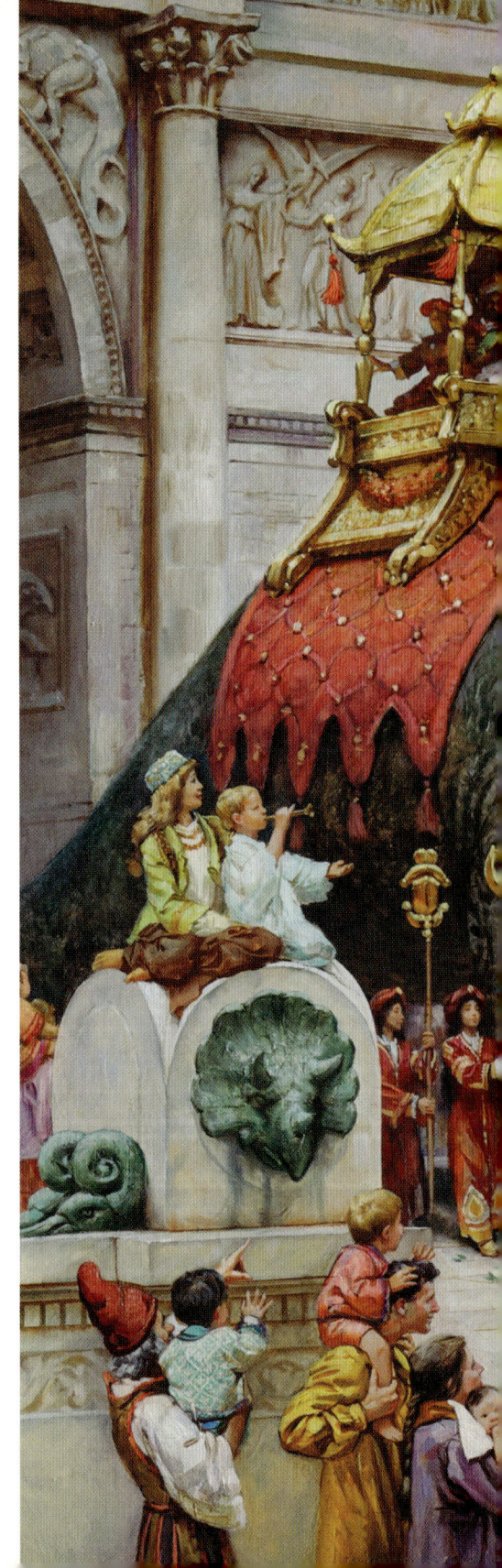

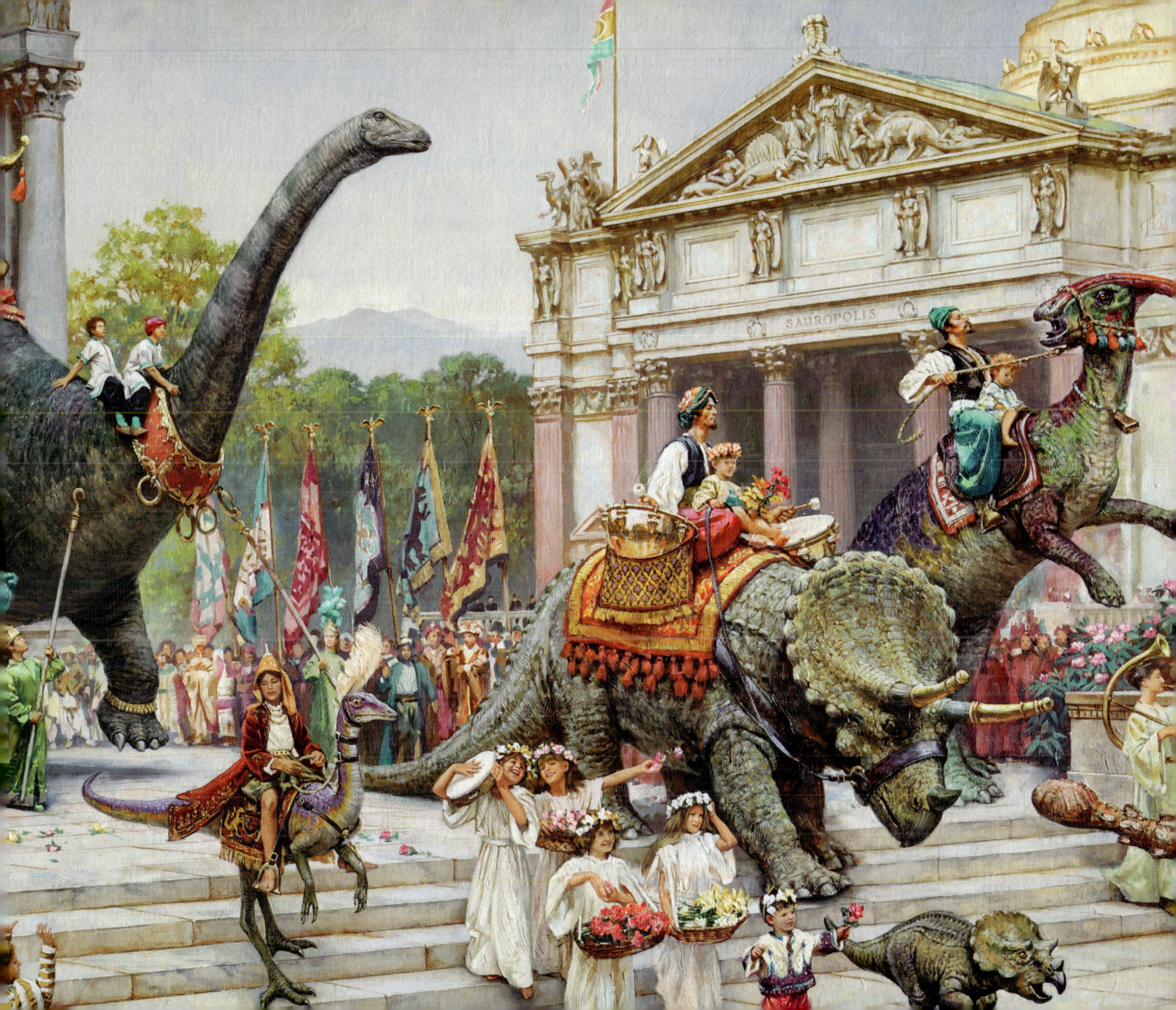

CHRISTIAN ALZMANN

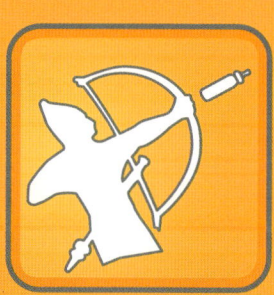

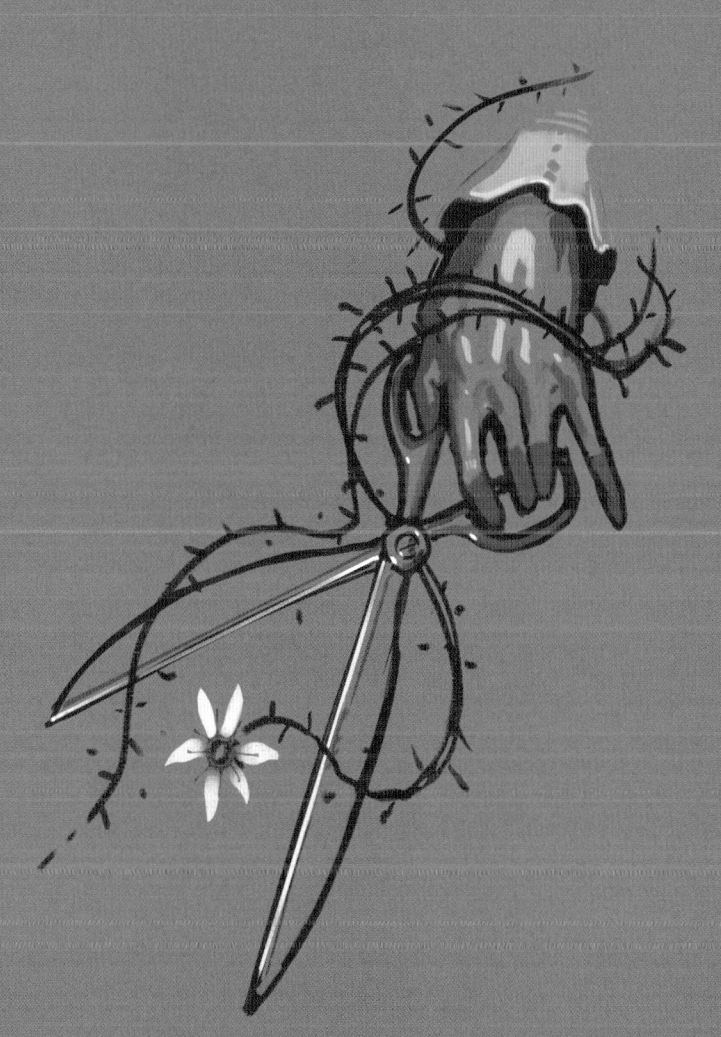

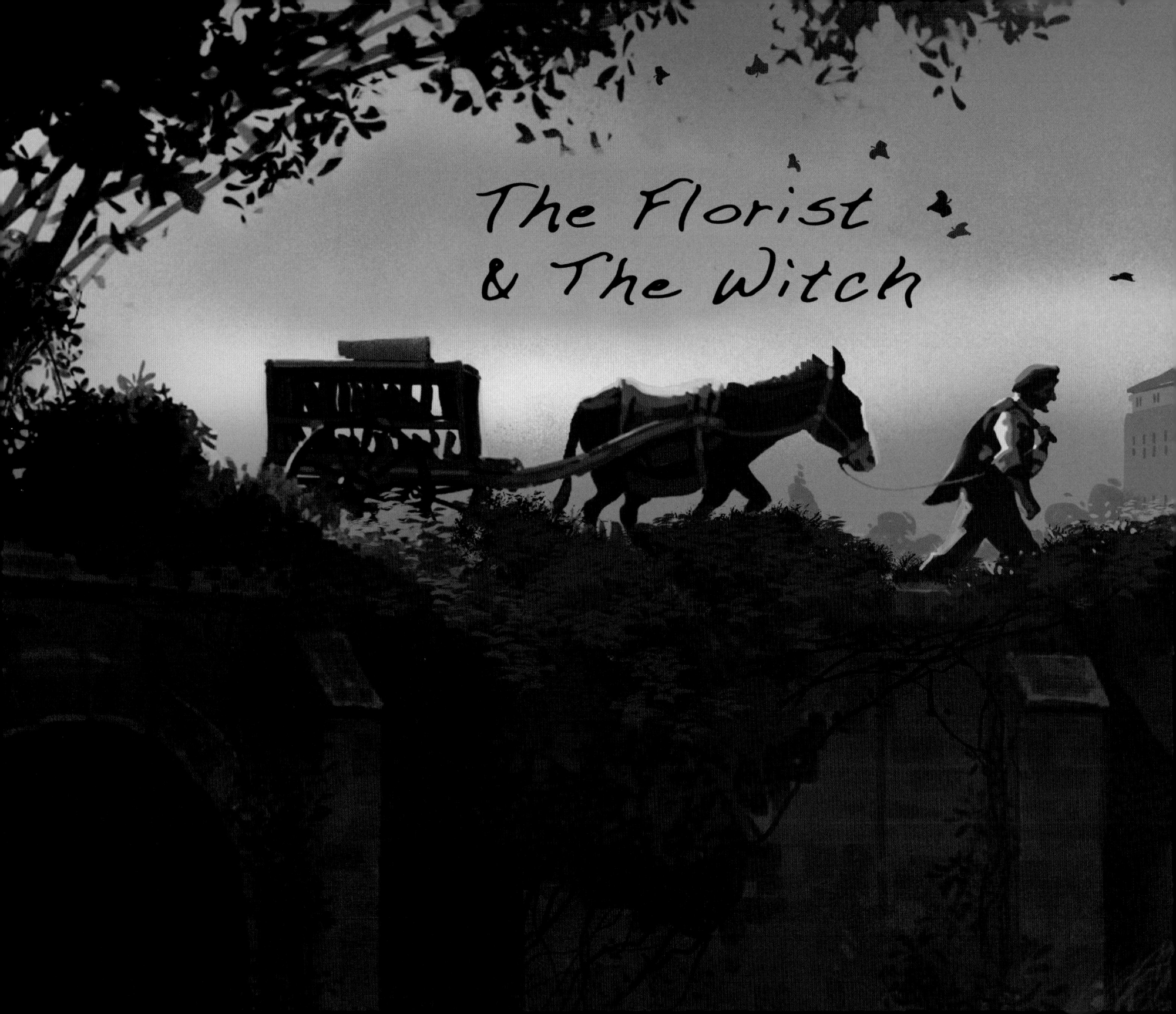

The Florist
& The Witch

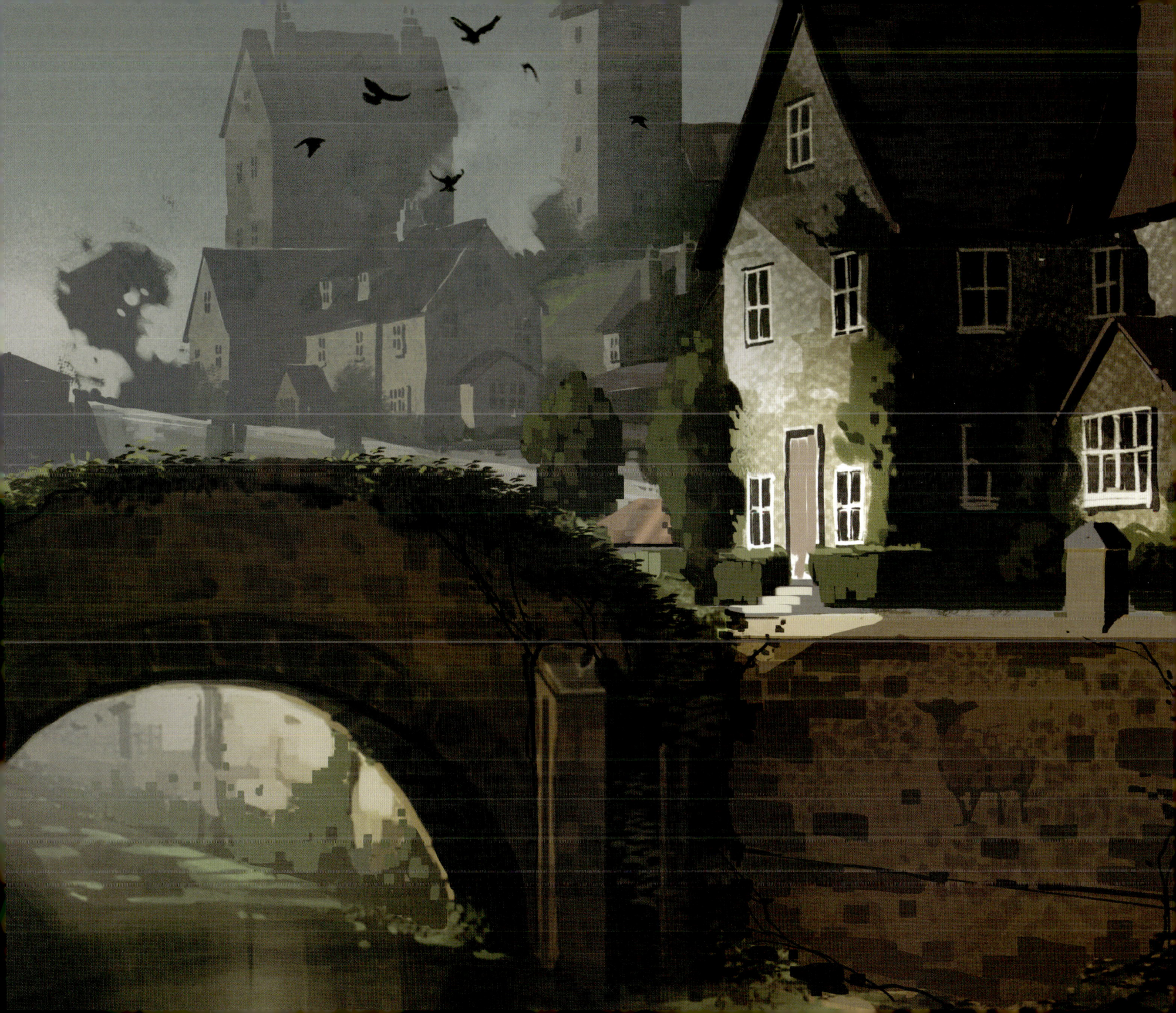

One day a new visitor came to the town of Faybury. The visitor was a traveling bookseller who knew someone in town and needed flowers for a visit. Since his whole life was based on the sale and trade of his books, he offered the florist a rare book that could help the future of his business.

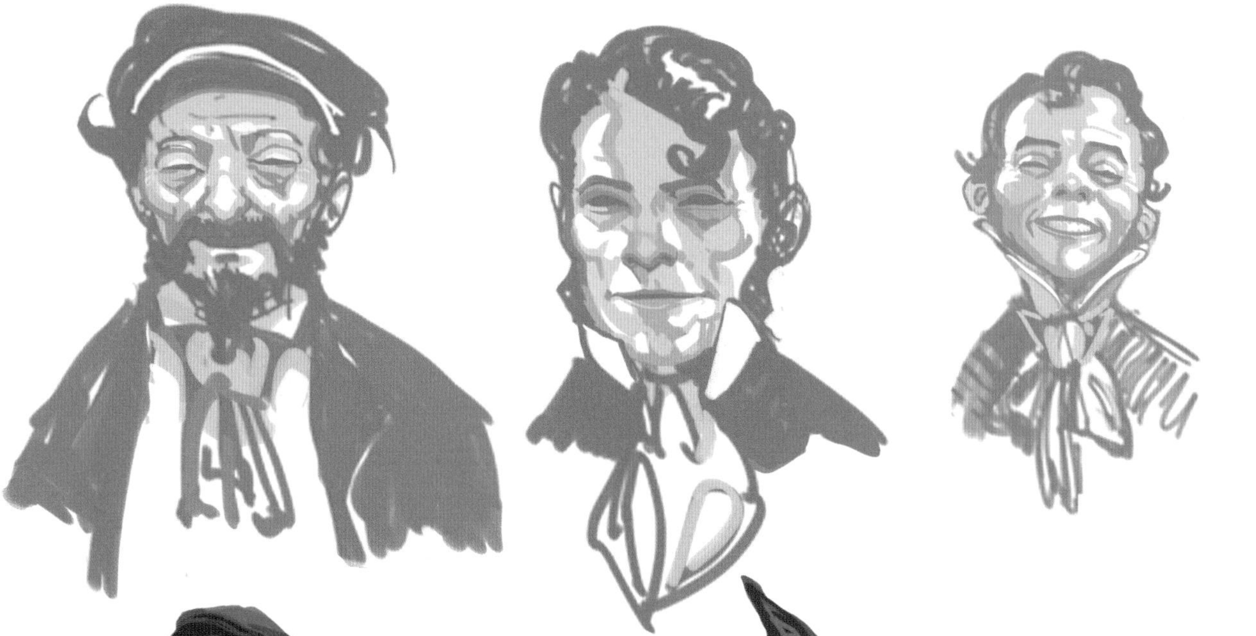

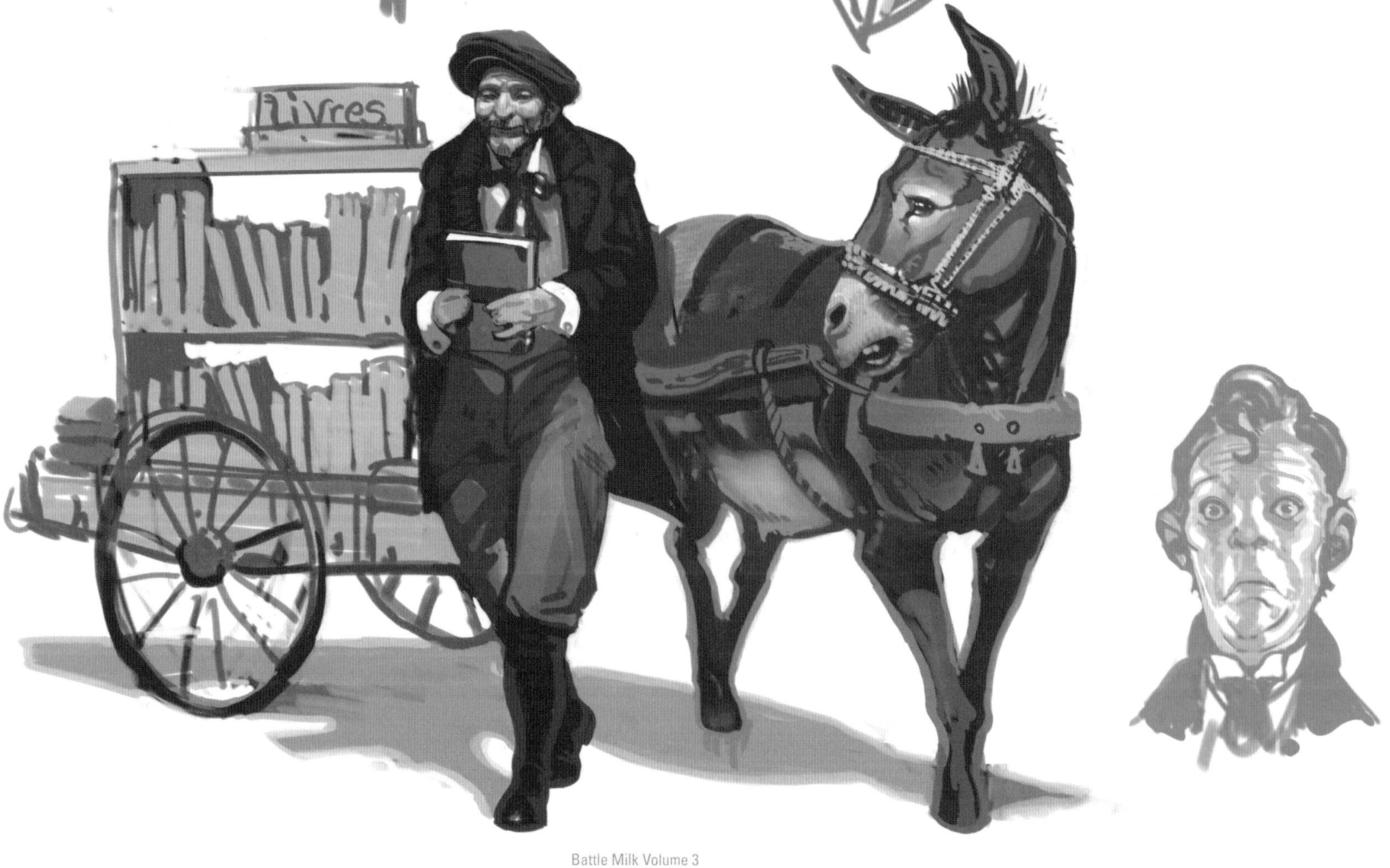

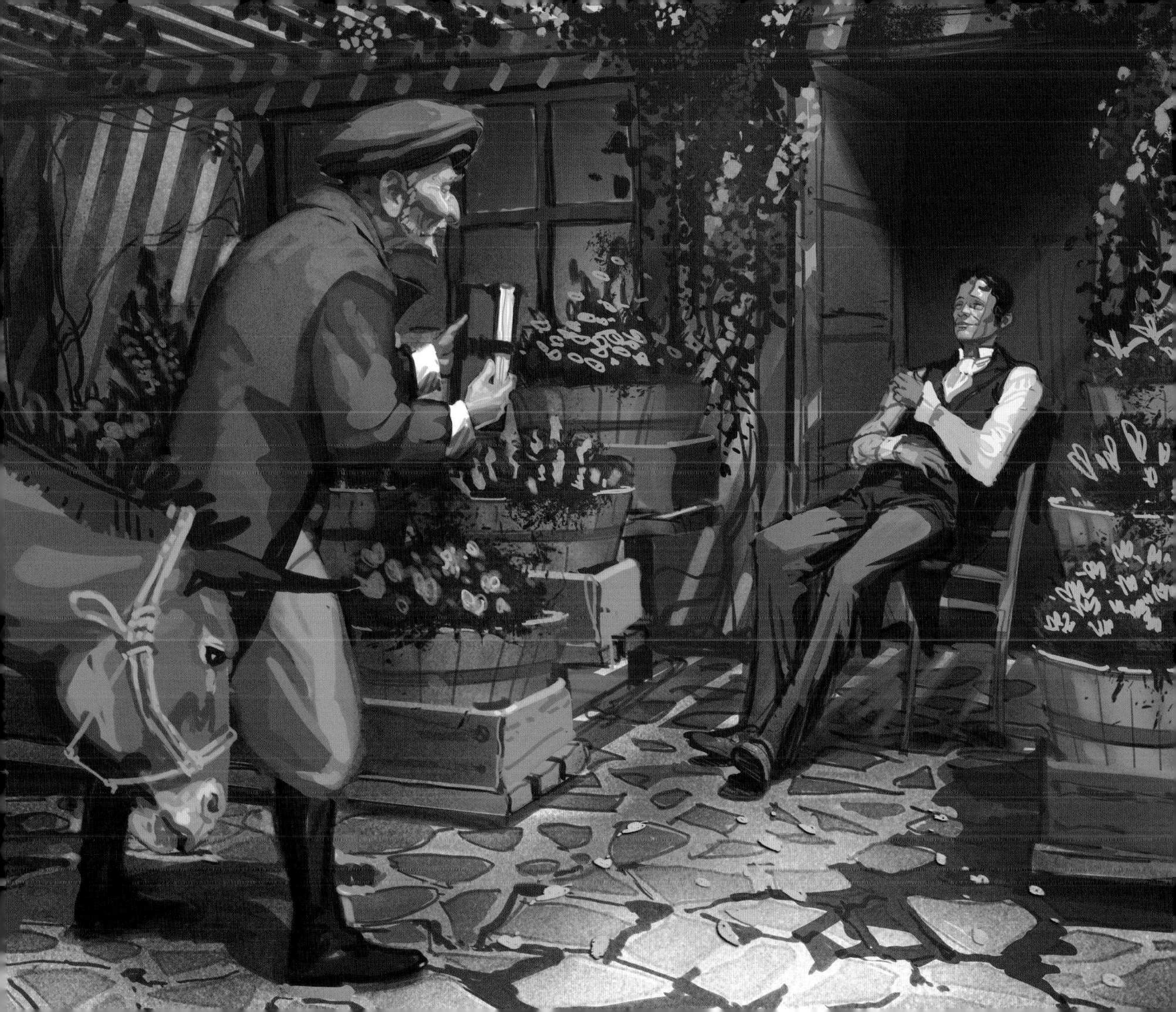

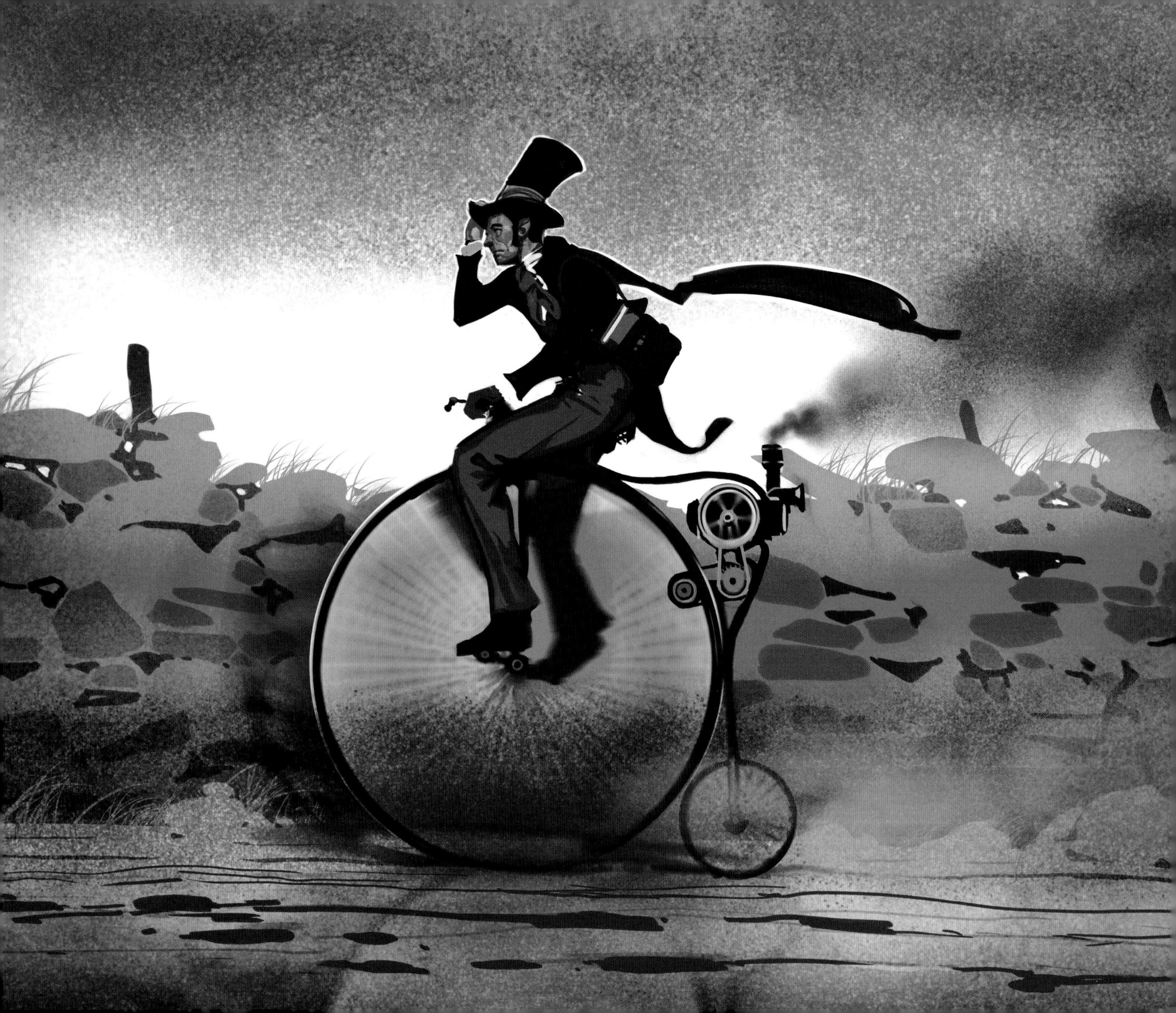

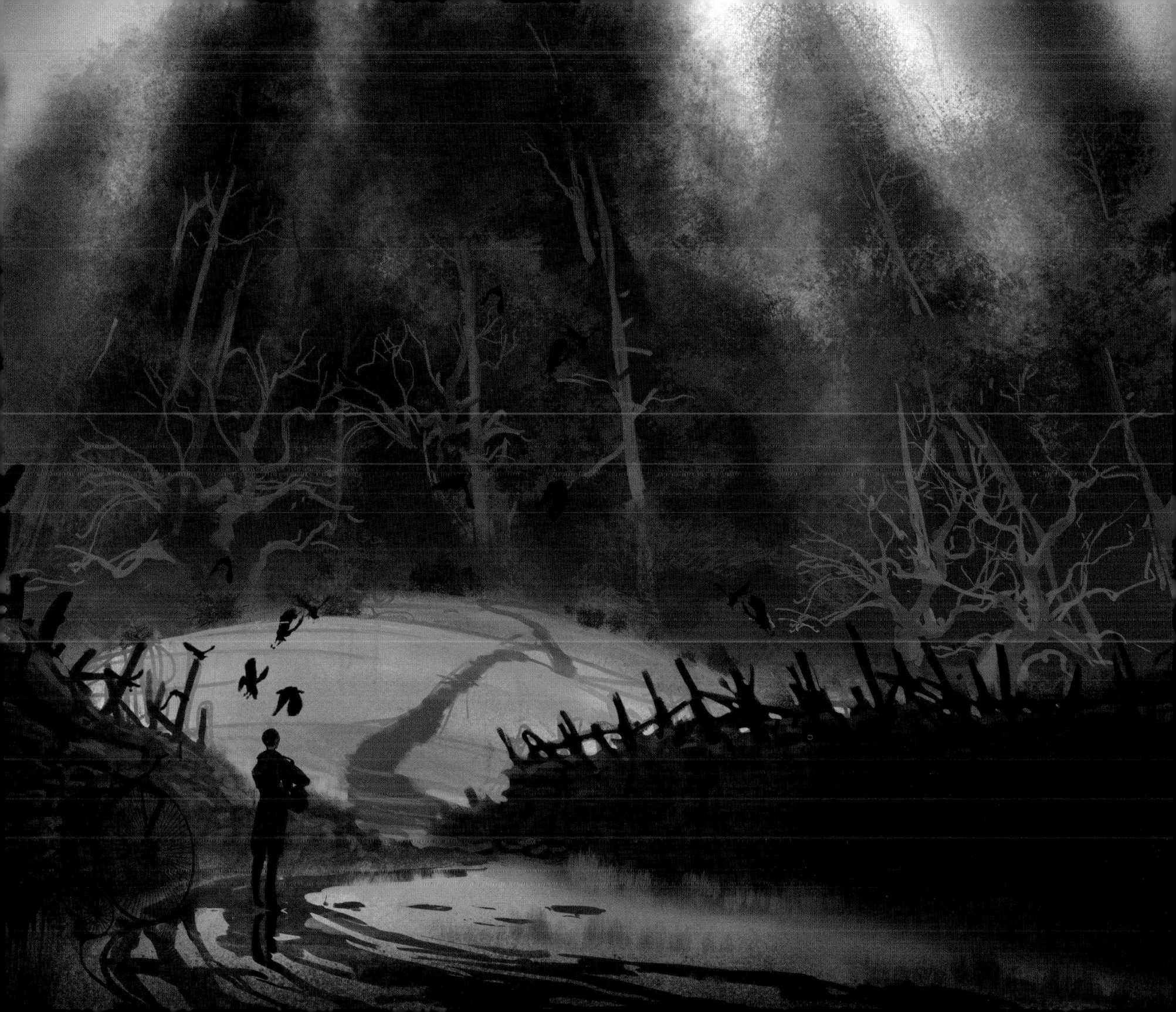

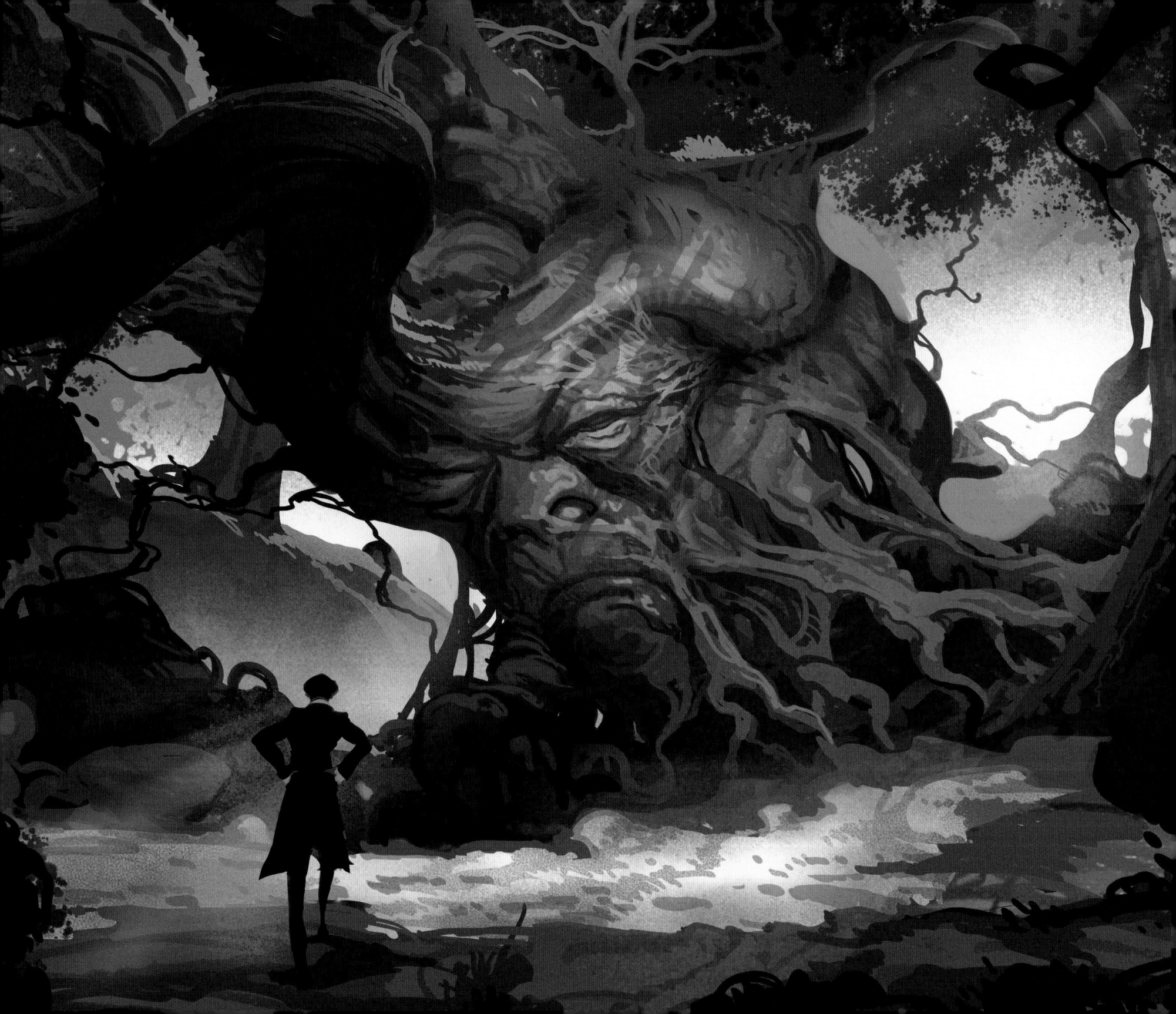

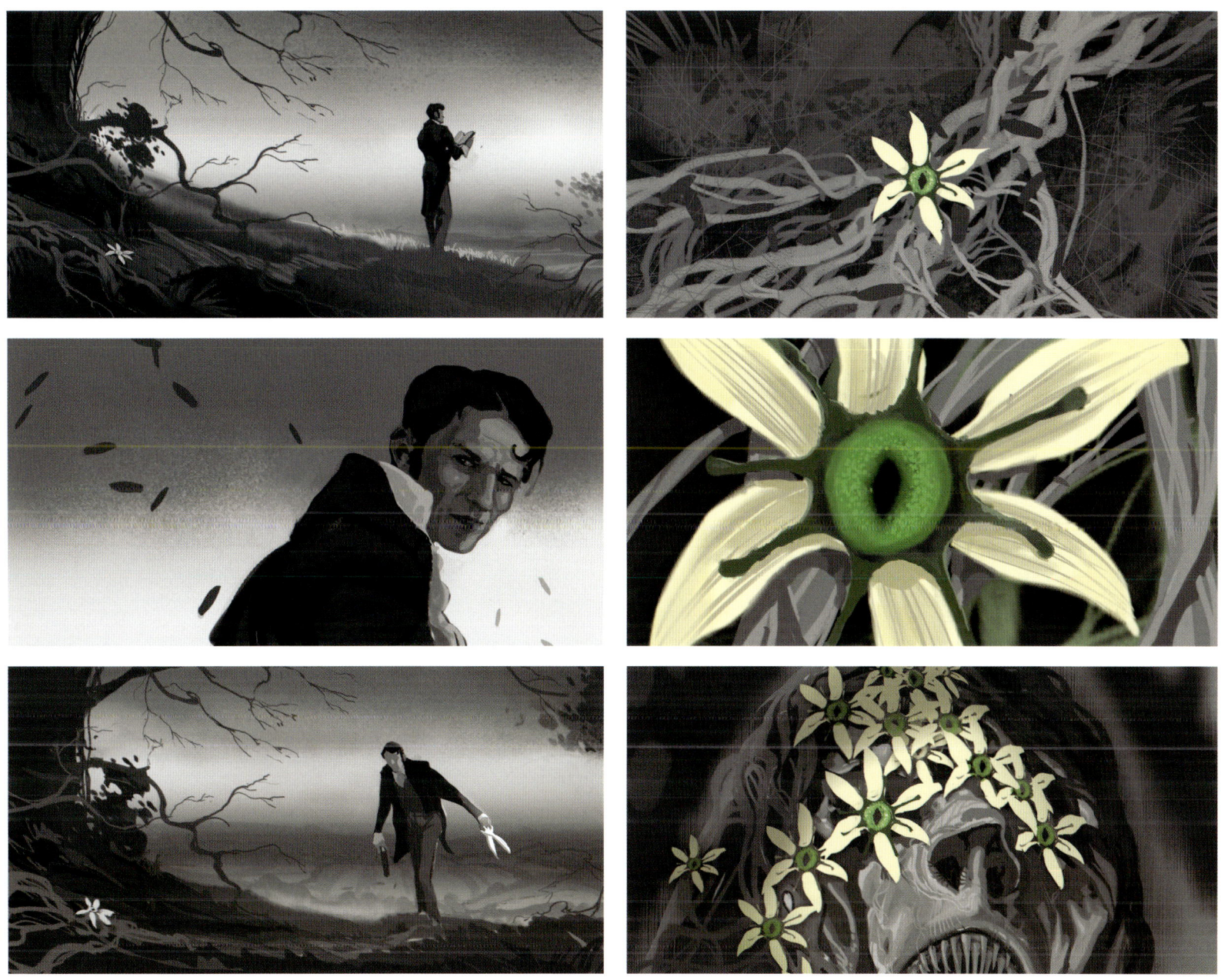

The witch, an old fairy fooled by her hate for the world of men, has learned to use the forest to lure helpless victims into her web. The florist, with the help of his new book, finds his way into the deep forest, into parts that haven't been seen by modern men. The rare flower that he's searching for is the eyes and ears of the spiteful witch herself.

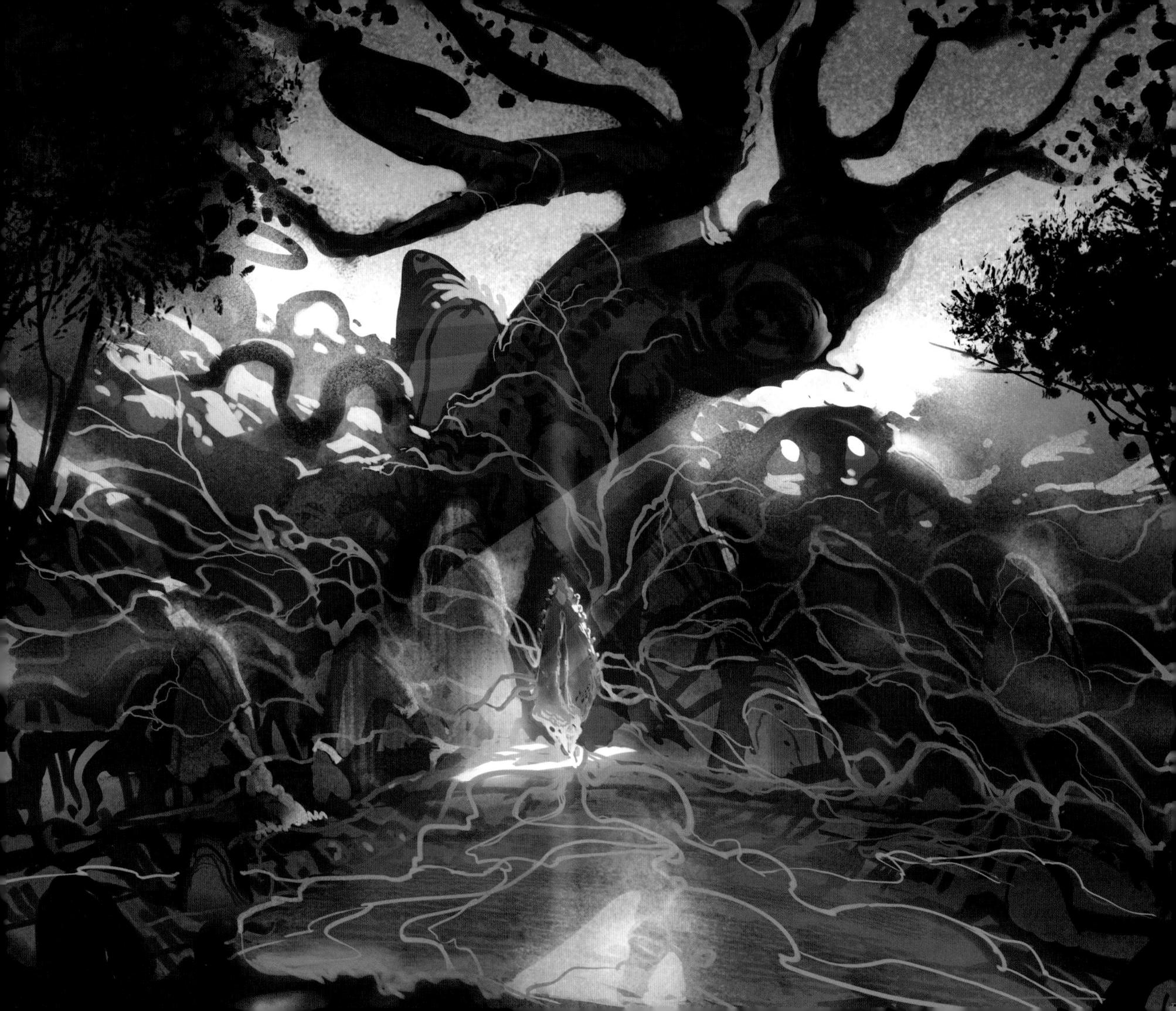

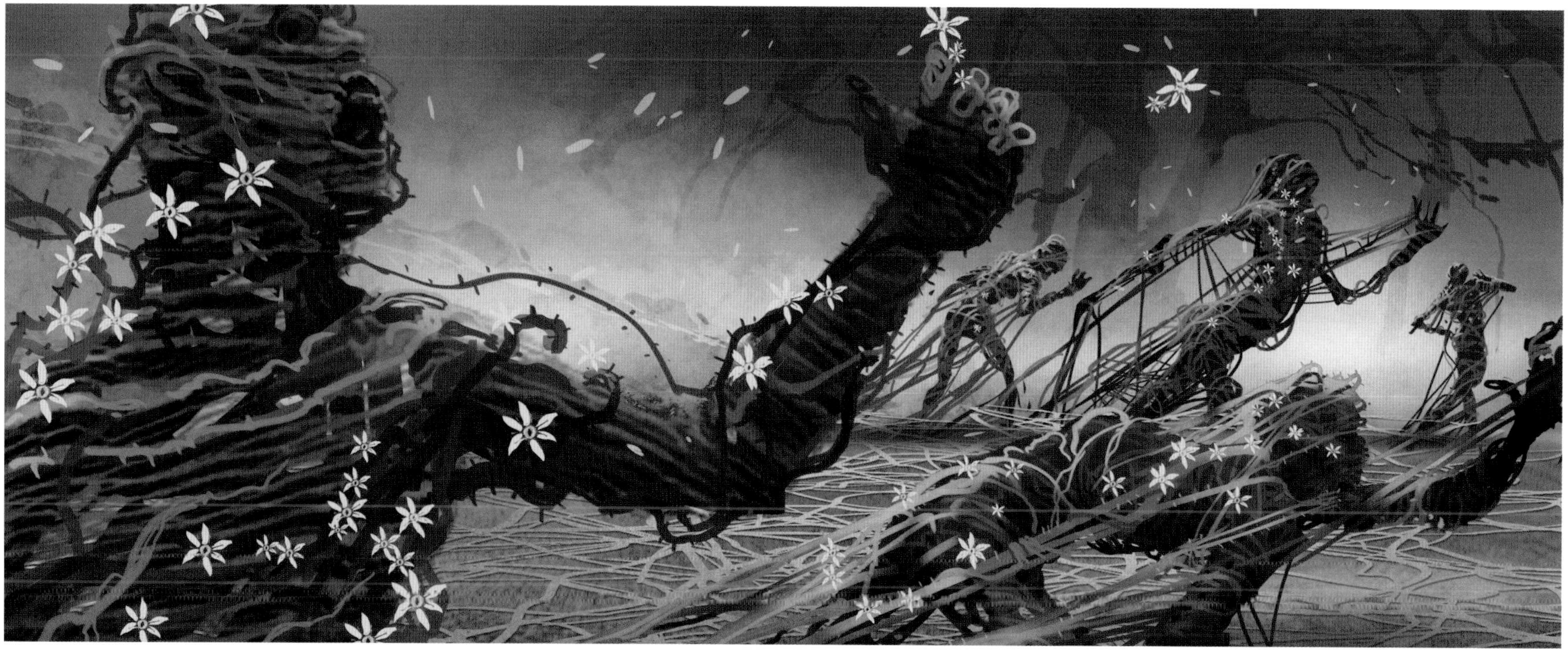

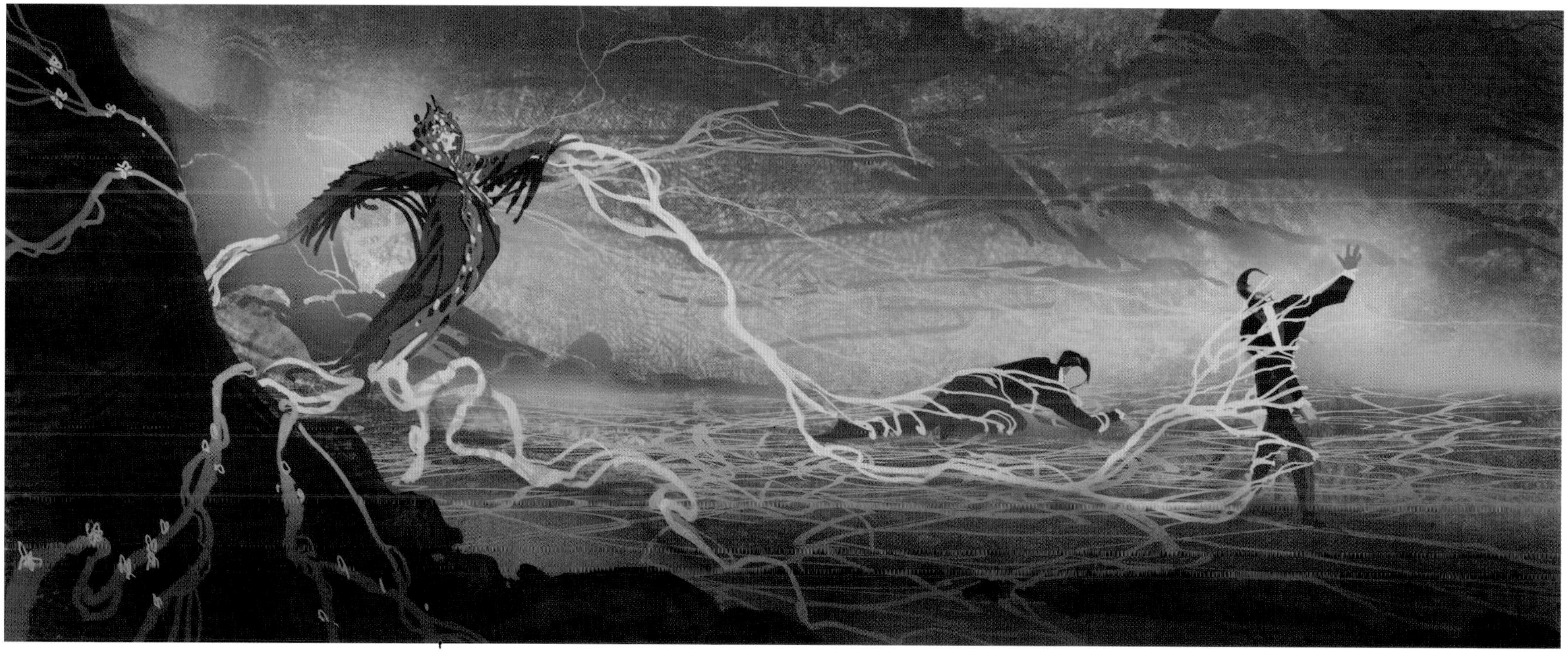

Christian Alzmann

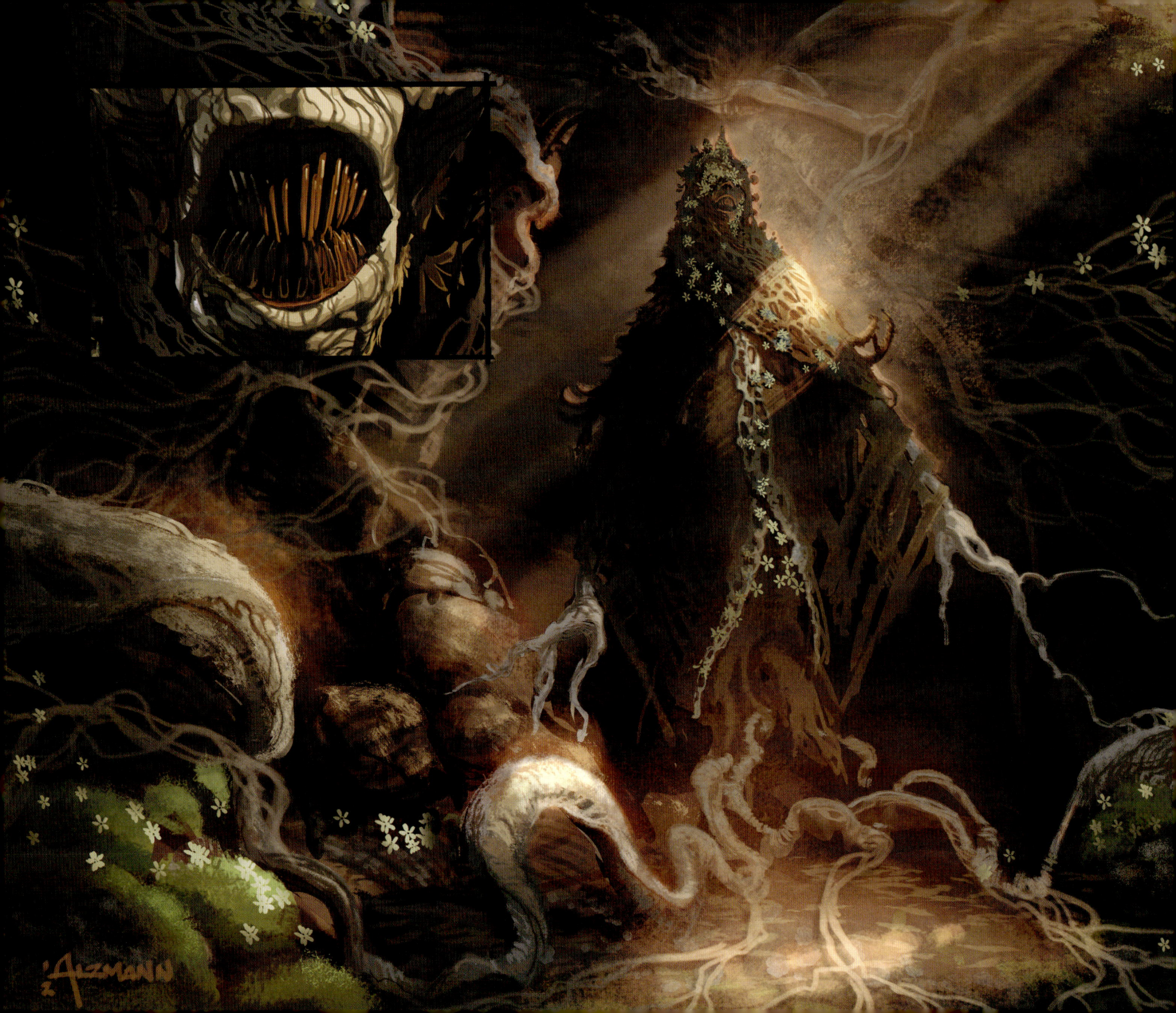

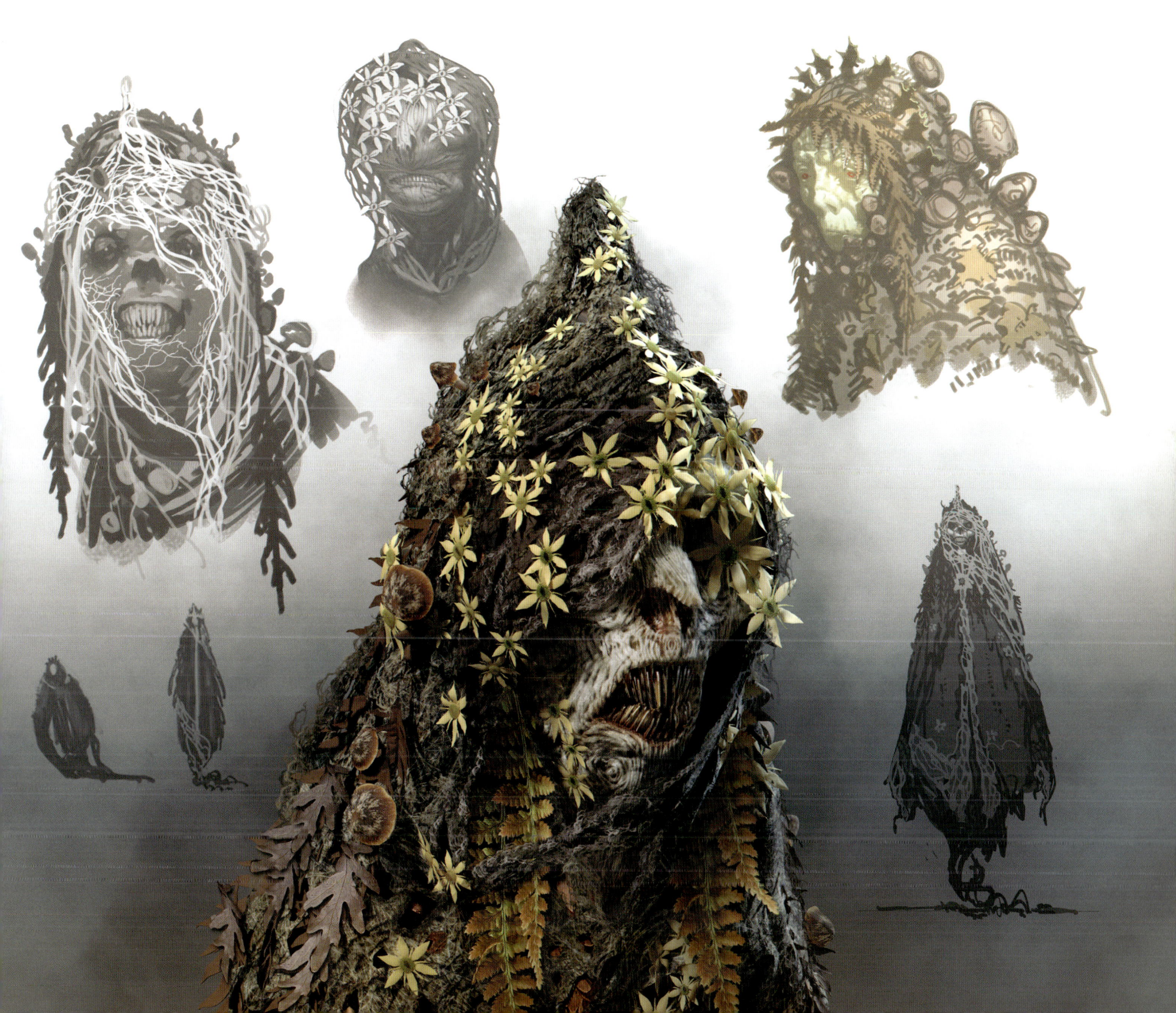

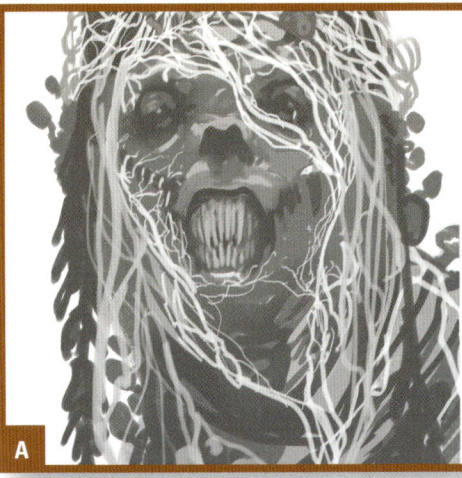

A. The first thing I do is draw—nothing precious; it's just about coming up with a variety of ideas and shapes. I'm looking for a personality. At this point all that I knew was that she was a forest queen gone bad.

B. (Right). I usually start in ZBrush with a simple sphere. In this case I used Dynamesh, which is great for shape exploration.

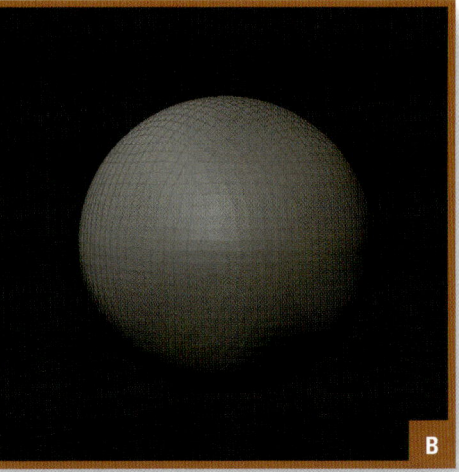

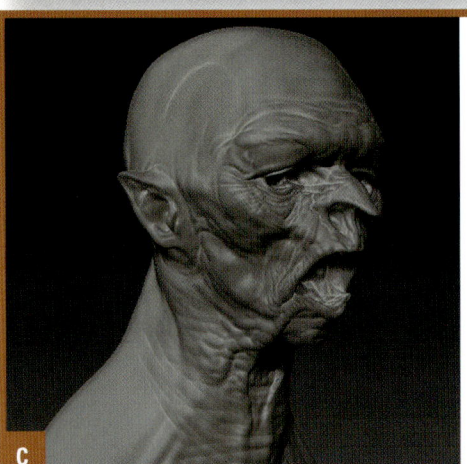

C. With Symmetry on, I start modeling the forms, making sure the large forms are dominant over the smaller ones. Never let the wrinkles or flesh detail dominate the skeletal forms. Those surface forms always need to accentuate the larger ones. Eventually I'll model all of the pieces (e.g., eyes and teeth) as separate SubTools.

D. Here I have the teeth and eyes sculpted and I'm experimenting with color. It's actually faster to throw some color on in ZBrush since you can paint it in symmetry. I will export this basic color as a texture map to be applied later in modo.

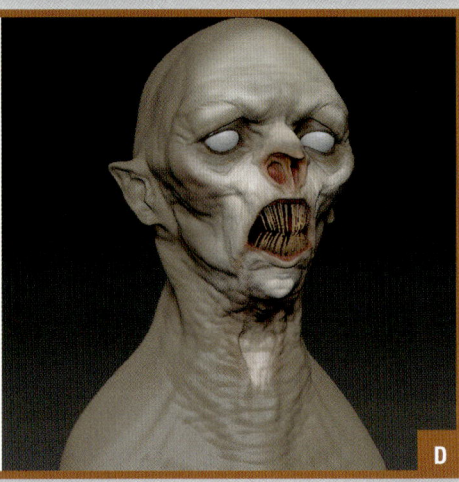

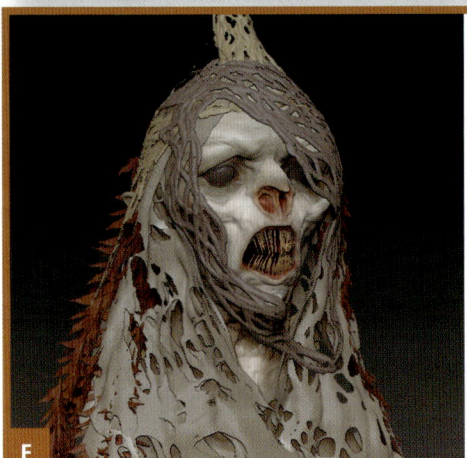

E. I created a lot of her layers of clothing by pulling out a sphere, painting masks, and then using the Extract tool to get the positive and negative shapes from it.

F. After all that work, I really just felt like covering it up. I came up with the concept of flowers for eyes after the original sketch. The idea that she is connected to all of these flowers in the forest gives her potency.

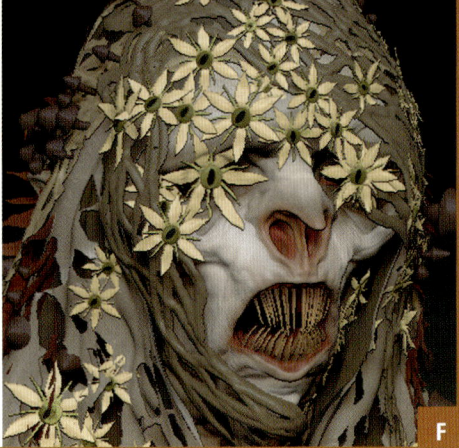

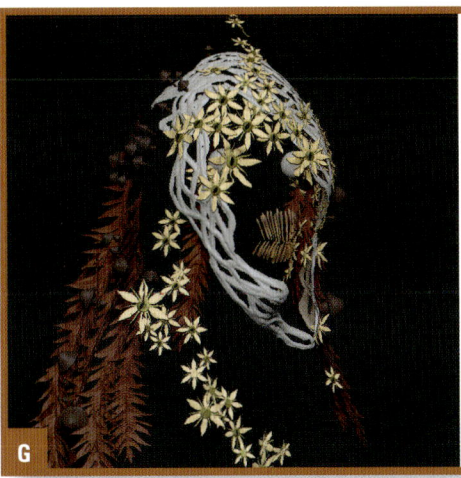

G. I made a lot of these pieces as separate SubTools so that when I bring everything into modo using GoZ they are all separate meshes and they can each get their own rendered materials very easily.

H. In modo I create a simple lighting setup using two directional lights. One will be the brighter key light, and the one on the other side will be a rim light. I create a plane and give that a light-emitting material and put that above her to mock a blue-sky fill light.

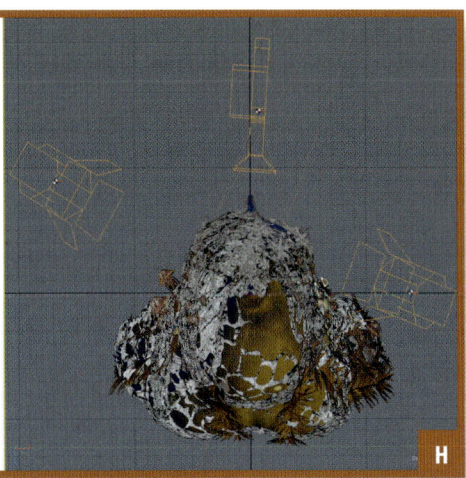

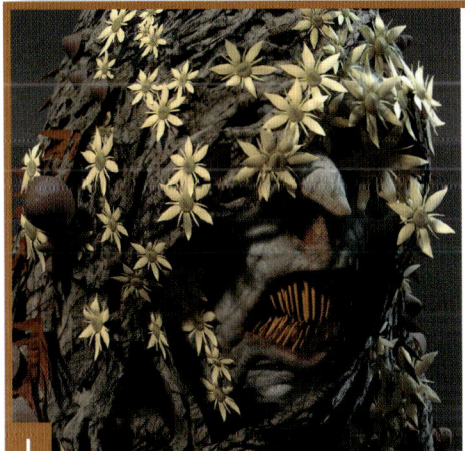

I. Here is the first render I got. I'll render usually about 3K across. I'm usually not too fussy about it because I can paint it up and add to it in Photoshop.

J. At this point I can take some photo textures and apply them on top of the different rendered elements that make up her face. Separate meshes and separate materials means I can have an alpha channel that will clearly define each piece and each texture. Once I have done this in Photoshop I project those textures back onto the model in modo from the render camera and use it for some extra displacement and color.

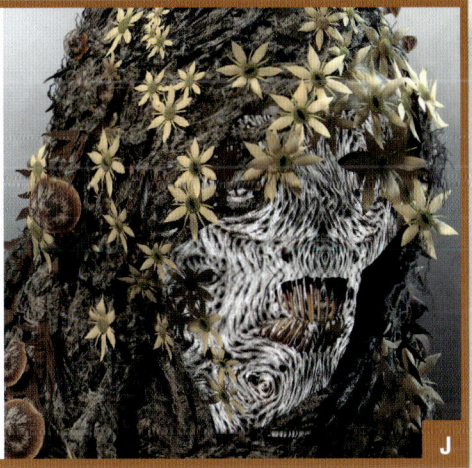

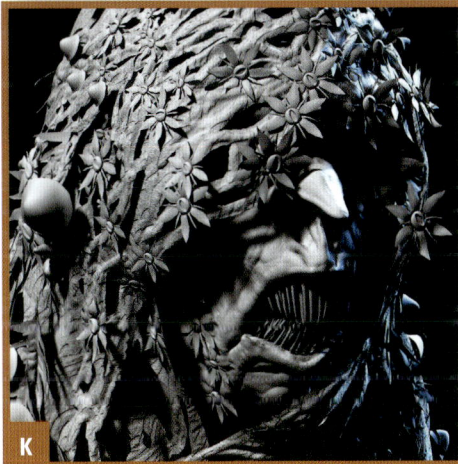

K. Among the benefits of rendering in 3-D are the passes you can render along with your final pass. This pass is just the lights and their color. Other passes I use sometimes are Ambient Occlusion and Reflection Occlusion. These can be dropped in as a layer in Photoshop and mixed in or out as you wish.

L. There is always some paint added in Photoshop to clean up things like edges as well as some other elements like the vertical fern leaves. I also paint in the smoky gradient background.

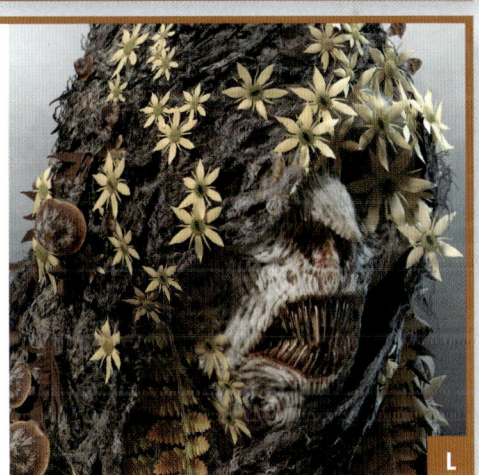

DAVID LE MERRER

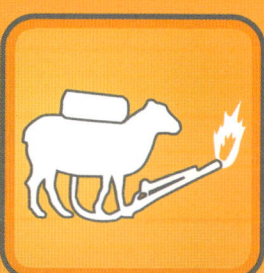

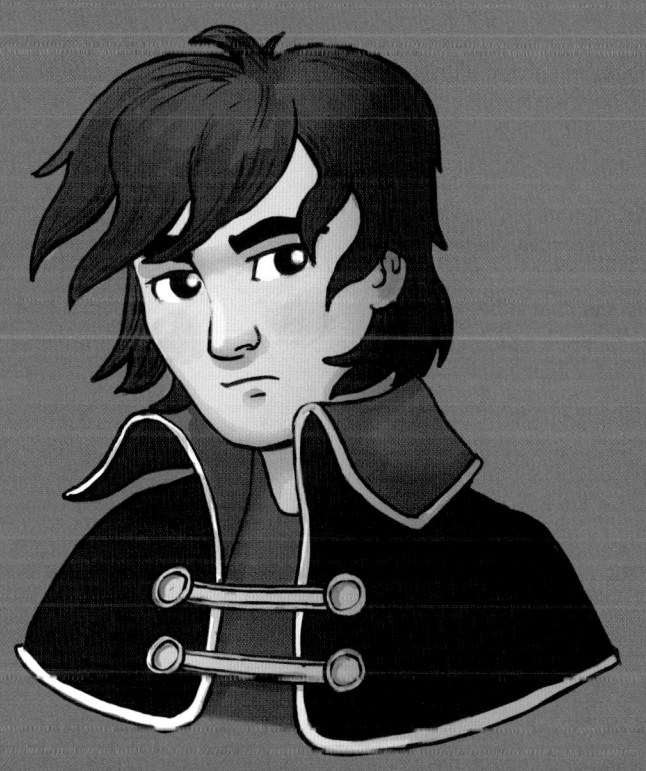

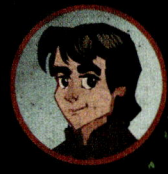

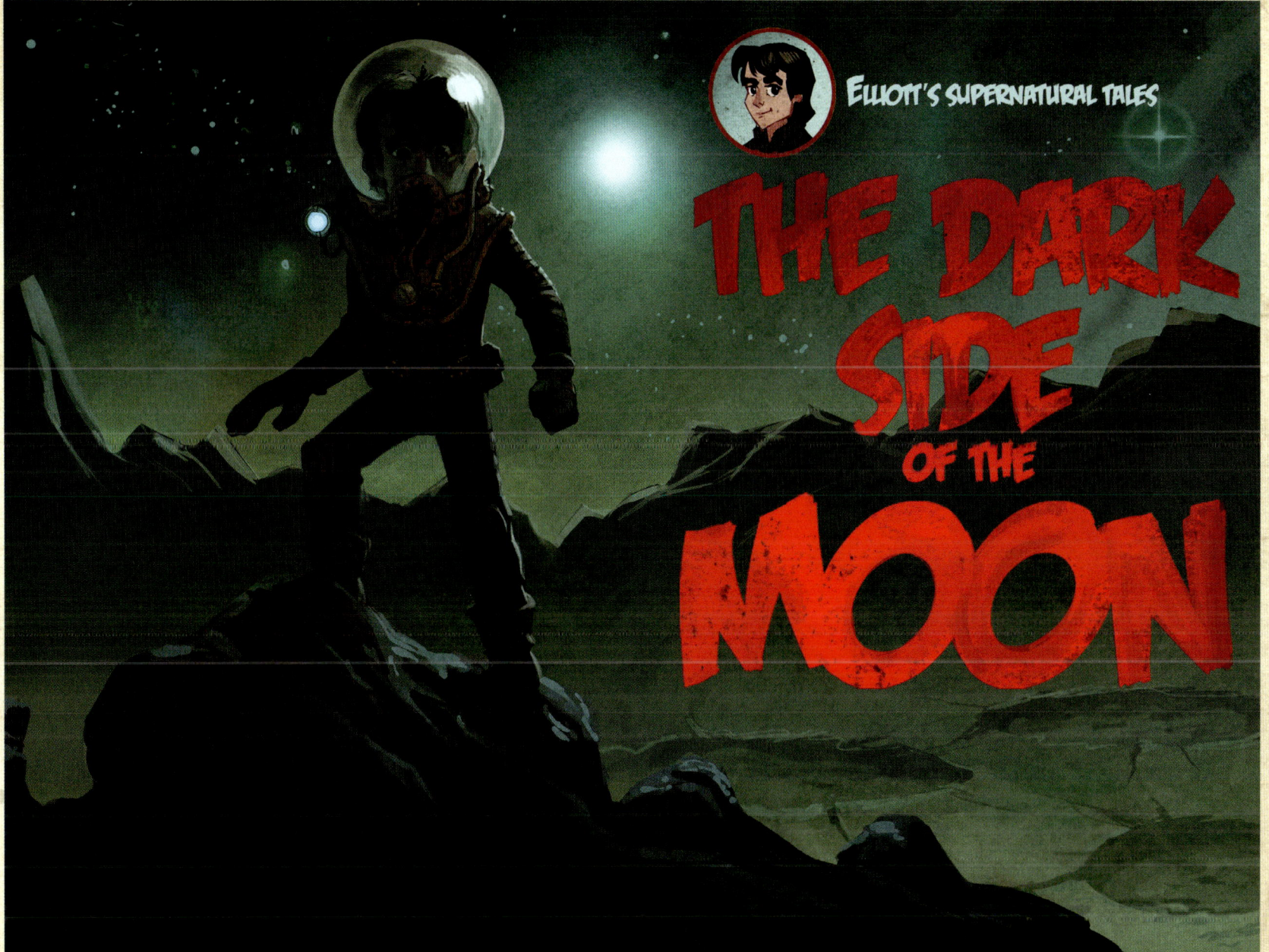

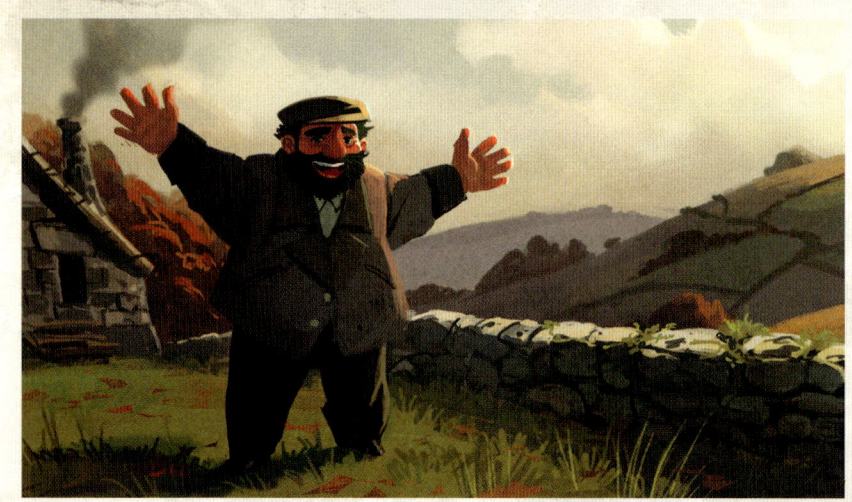

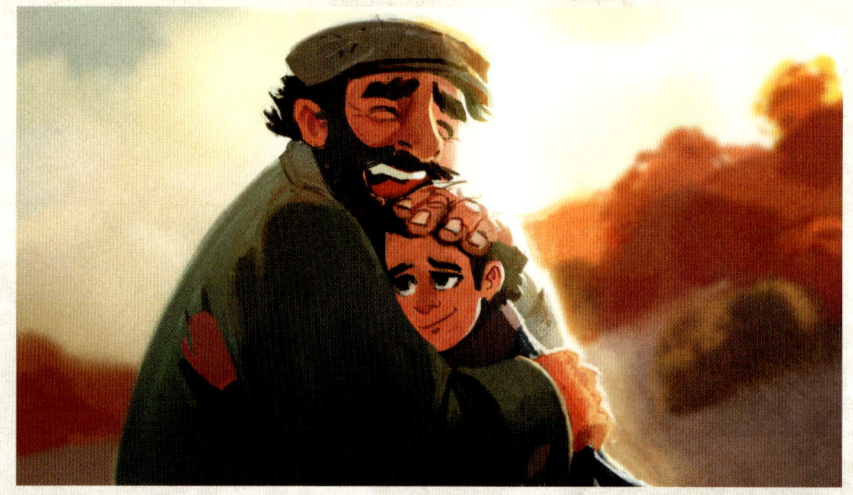

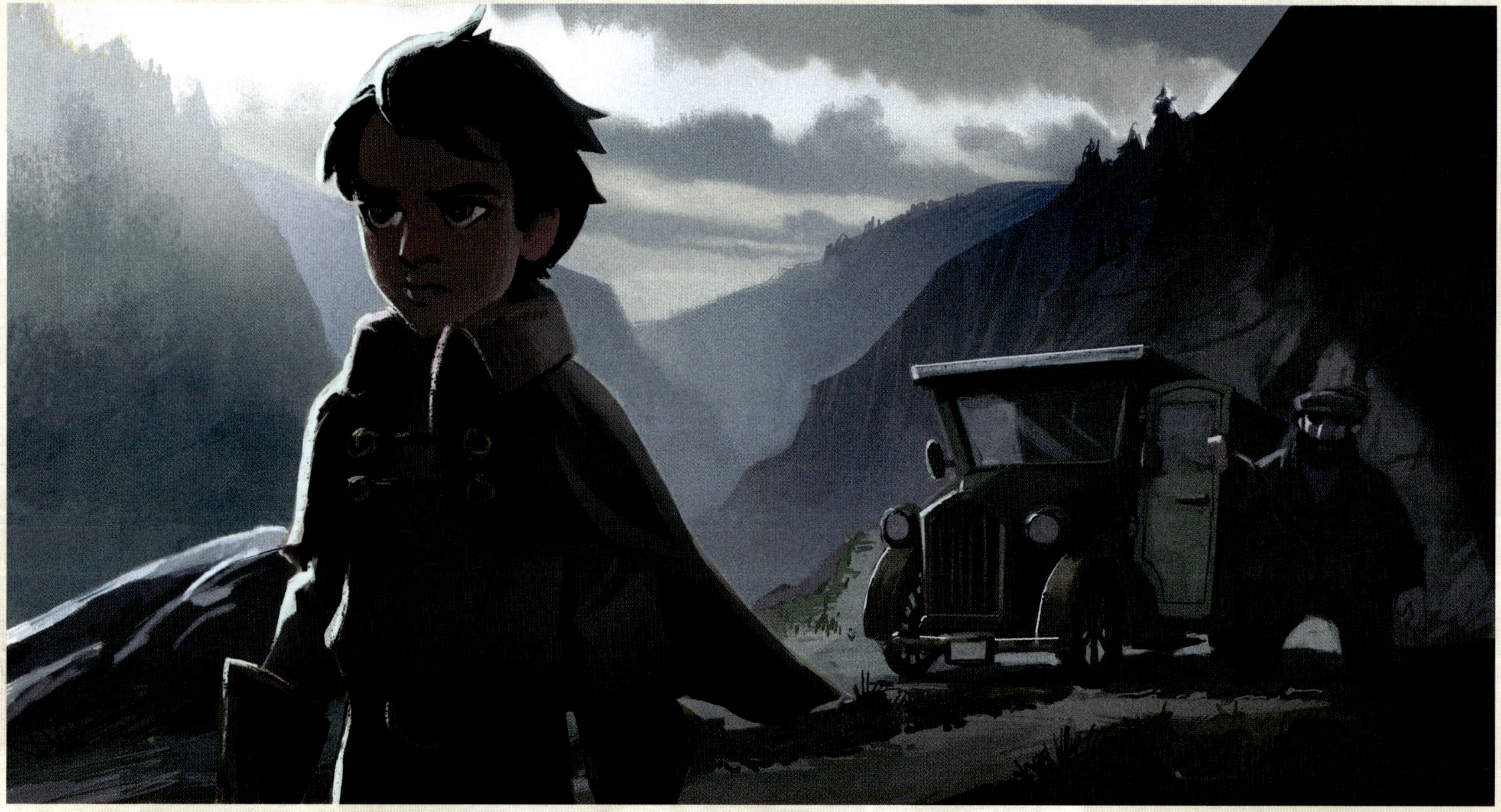

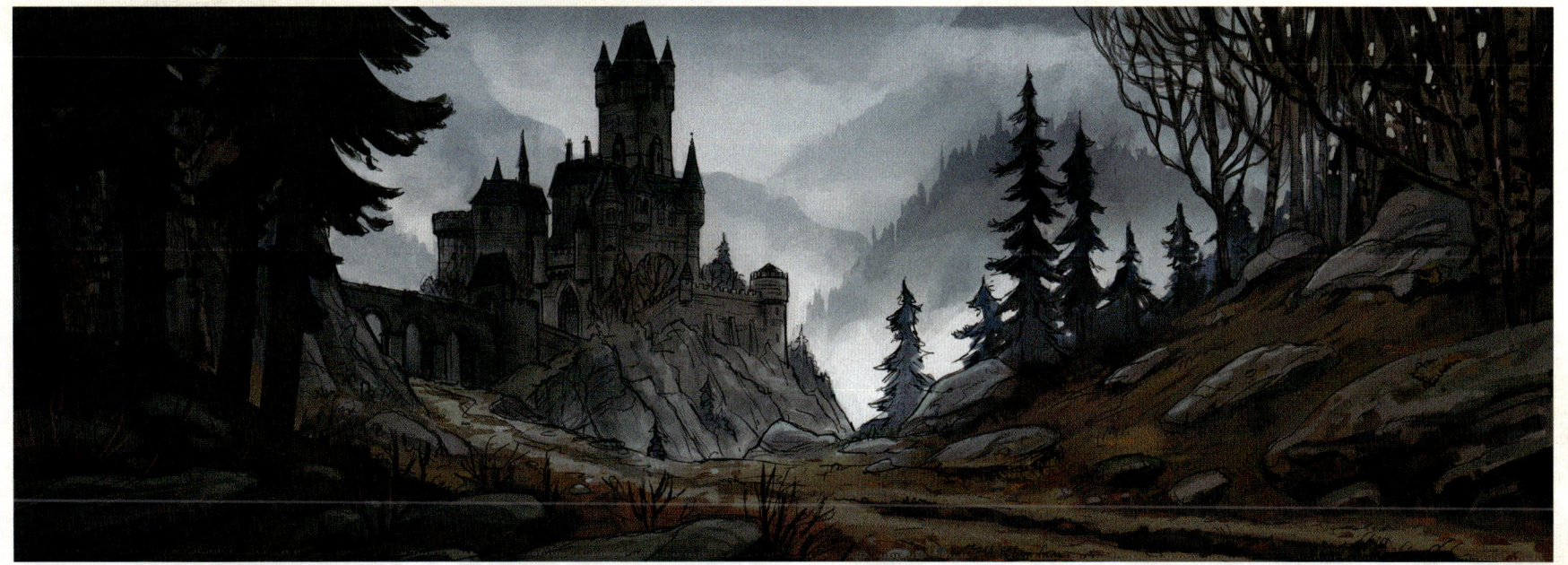

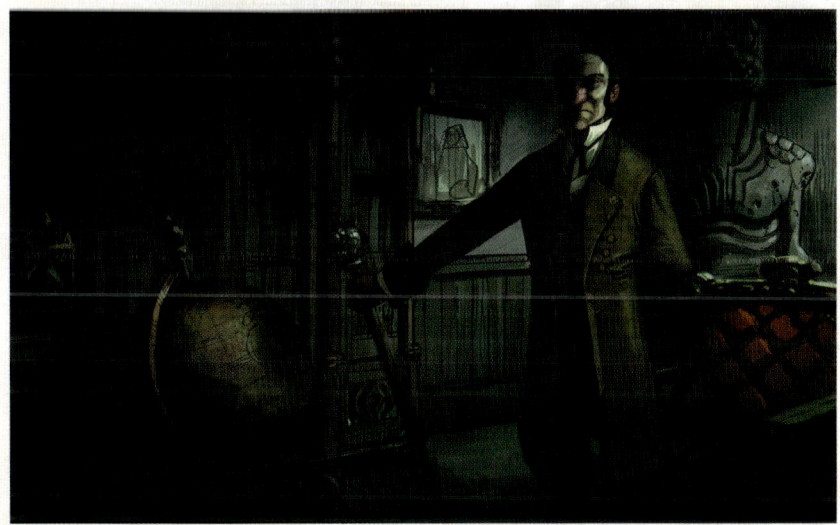

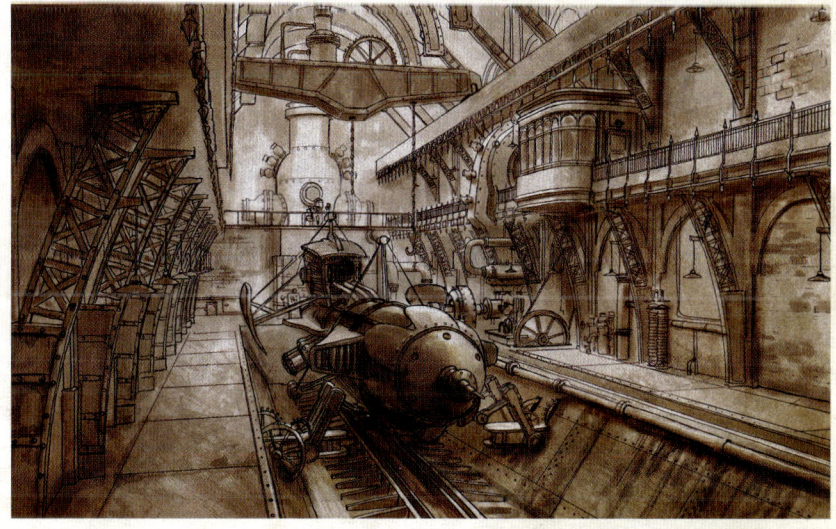

Left: Elliott is meeting with his old friend.

Top: Manor Finkelstein, somewhere in Europe.

Above: Baron Finkelstein, 1866.

Above: *The Drakkhen*, a mysterious ship parked in Manor Finkelstein's hangar. A lot of villagers living nearby saw lights during the night without understanding where they came from. This ship is using steam technology mixed with an unknown source of energy.

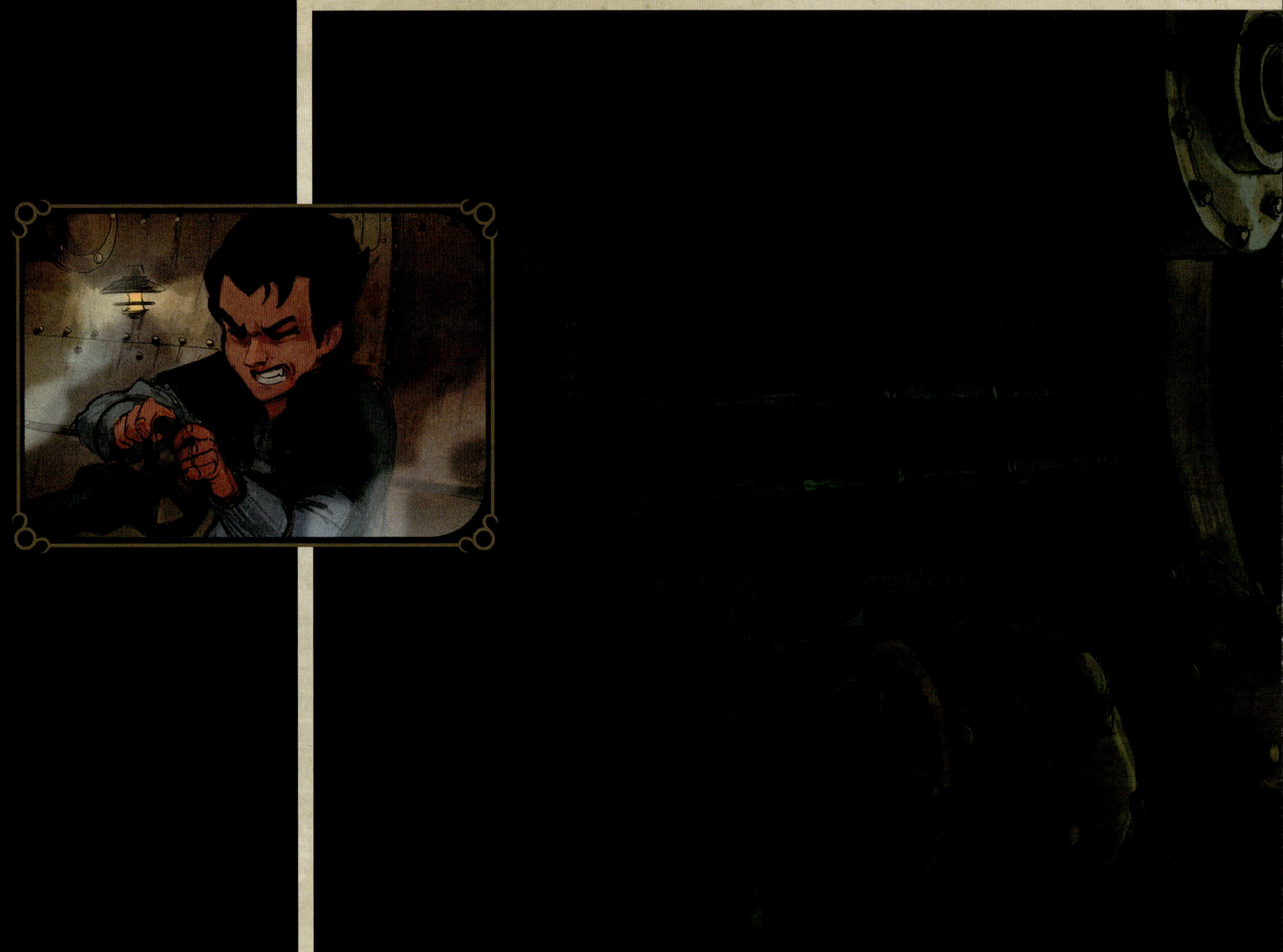

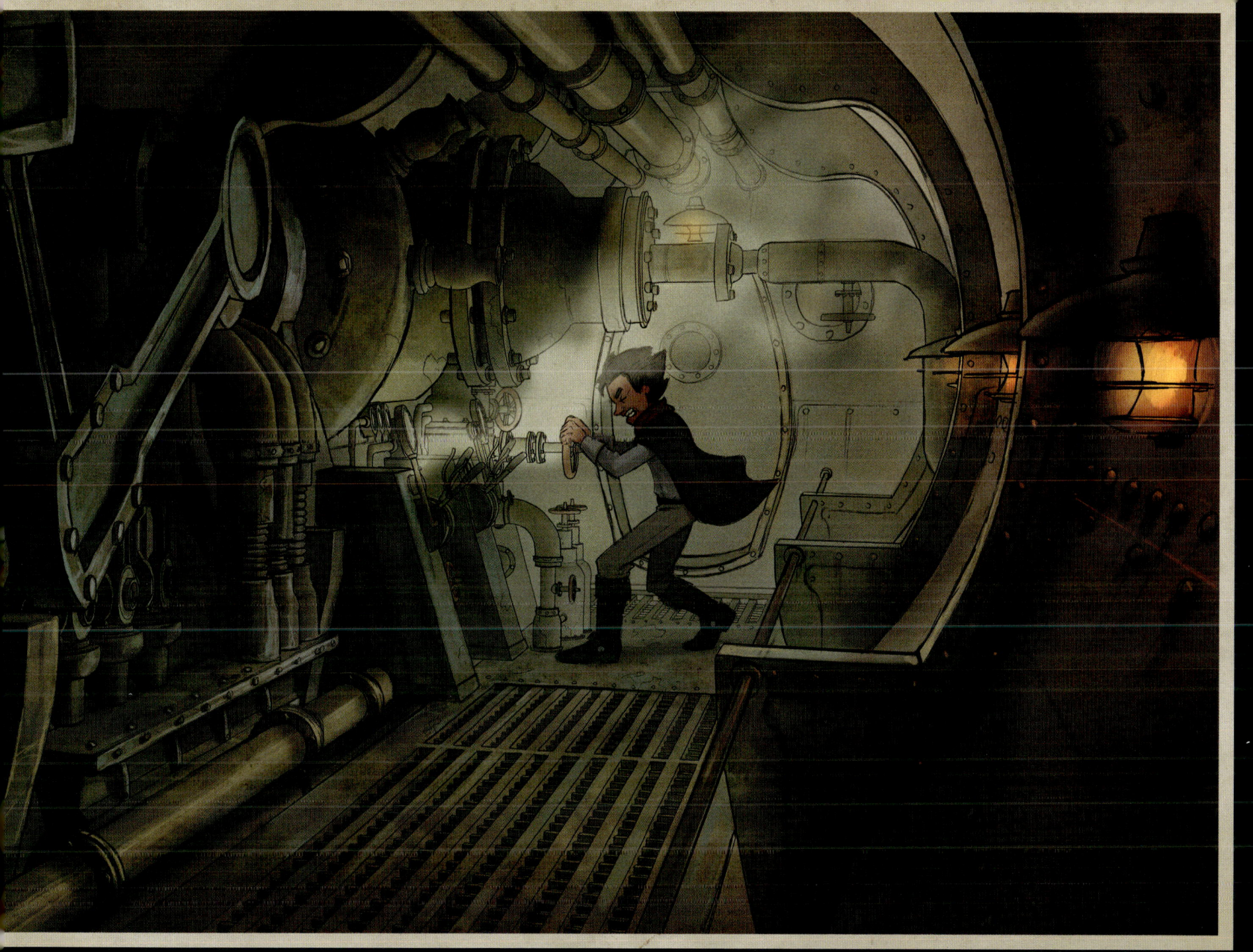

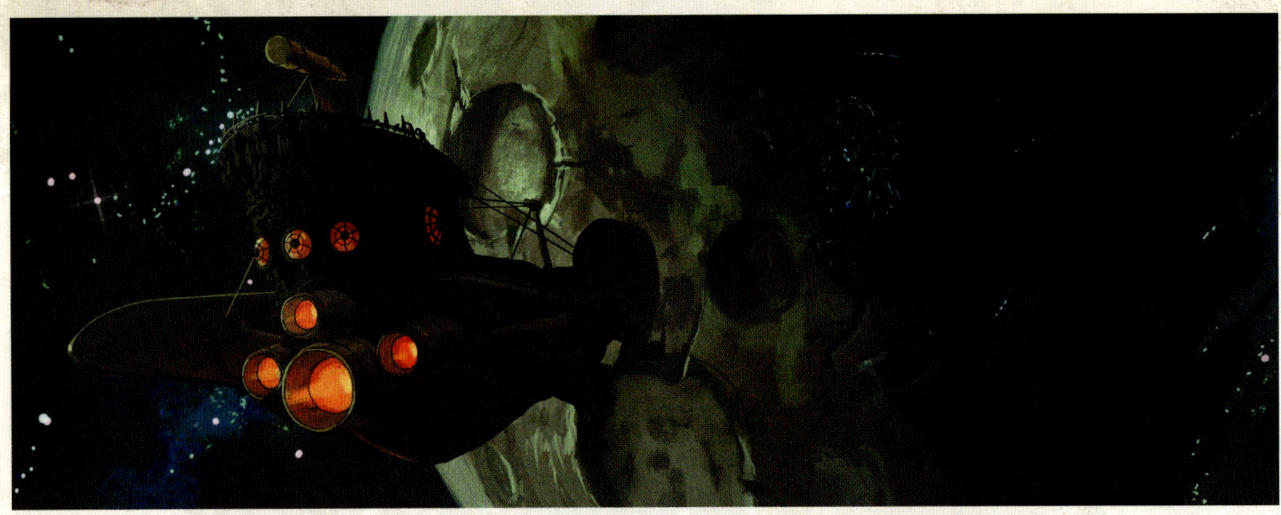

Left: Elliott approaches the moon in his ship. He discovers that the unseen part of it, from the Earth, is a city-like machine. Is it an artificial satellite?

Below and right: What secrets hold the dark side of the moon? What are those machines here for? Who built them? If the moon is an artificial satellite, for what purpose has it been placed in the Earth's orbit?

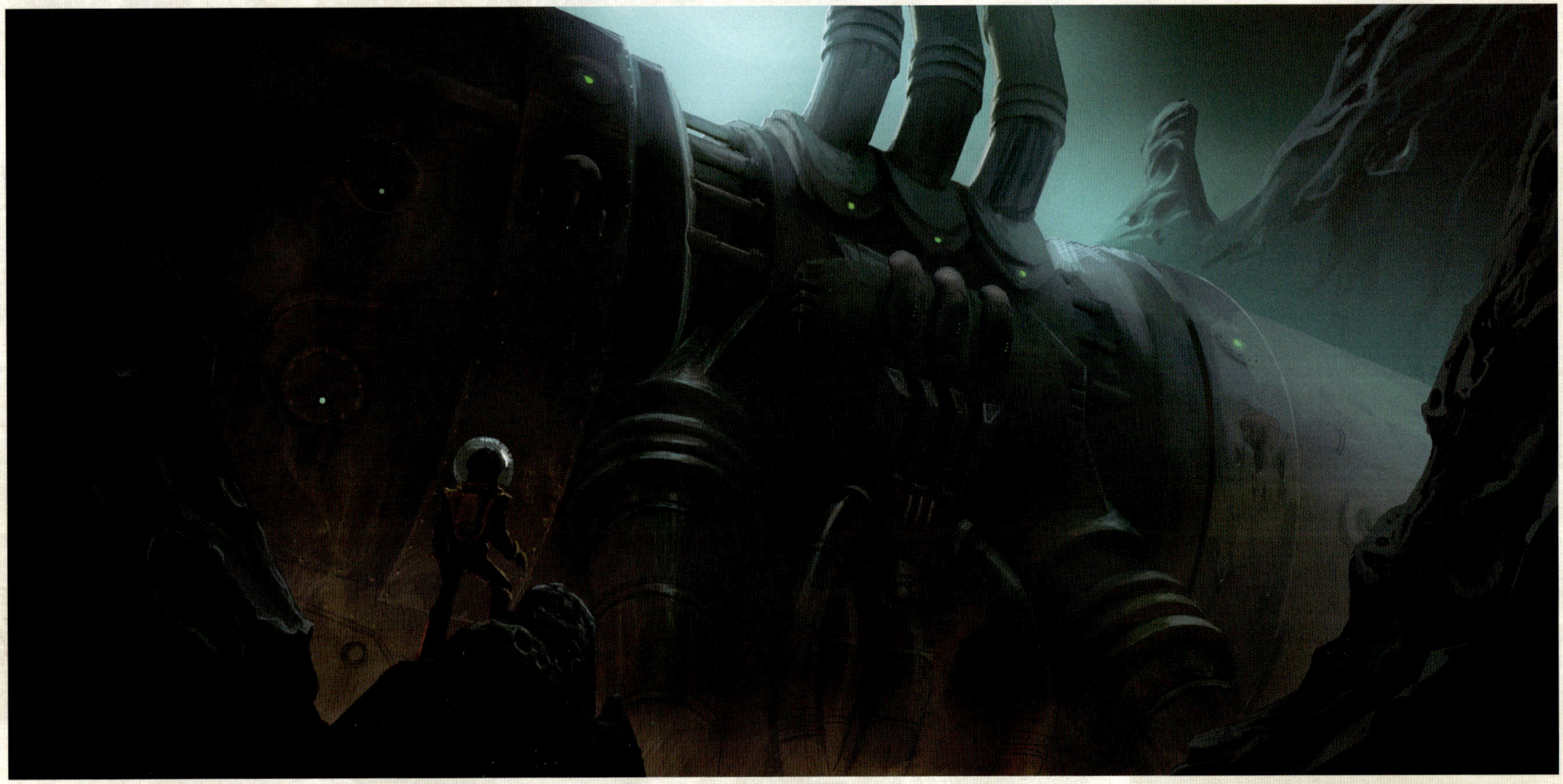

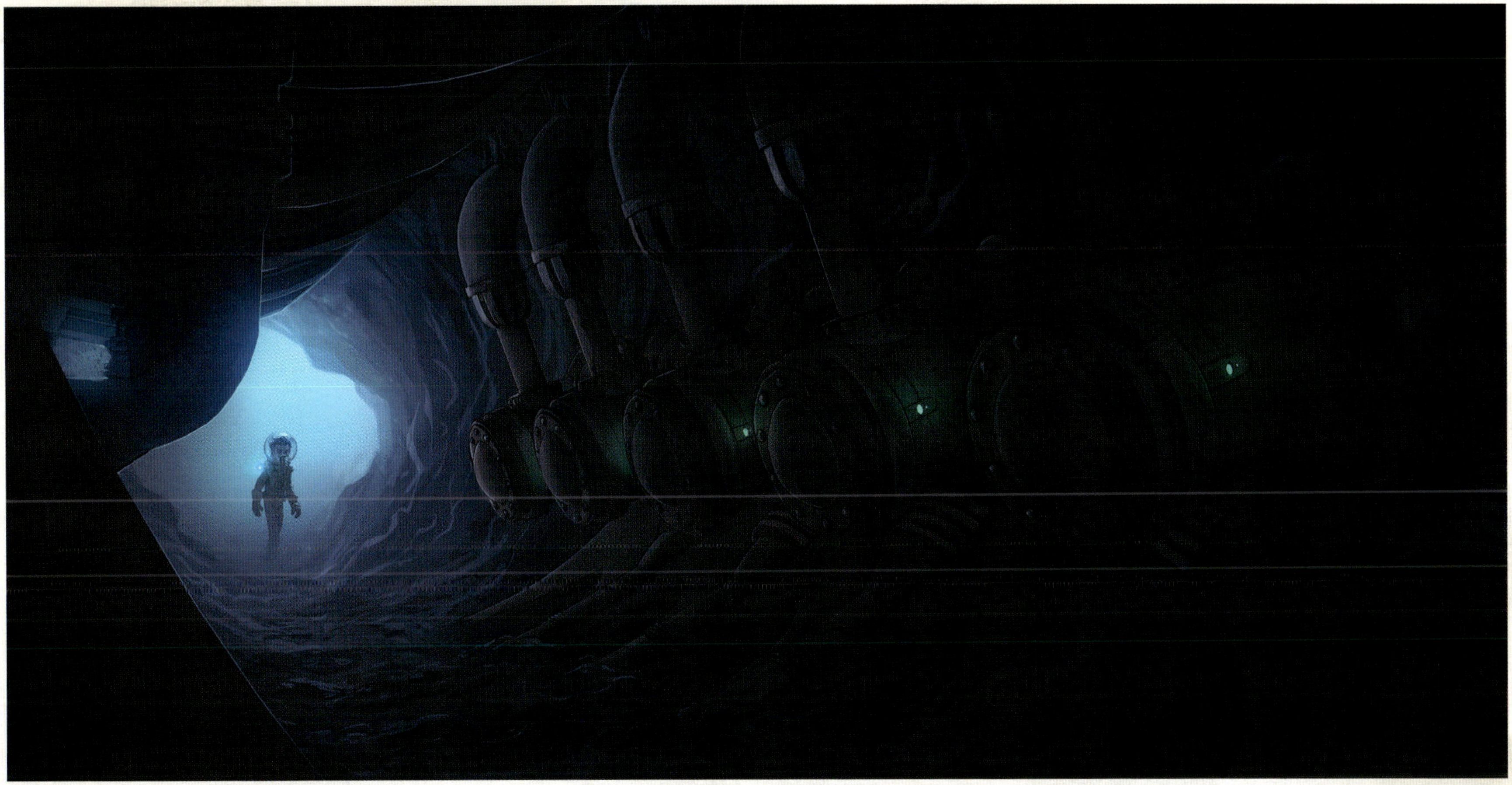

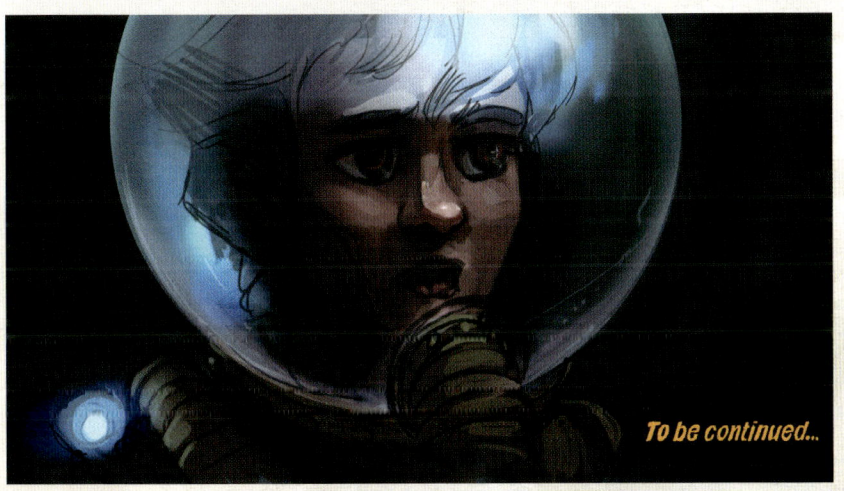

To be continued...

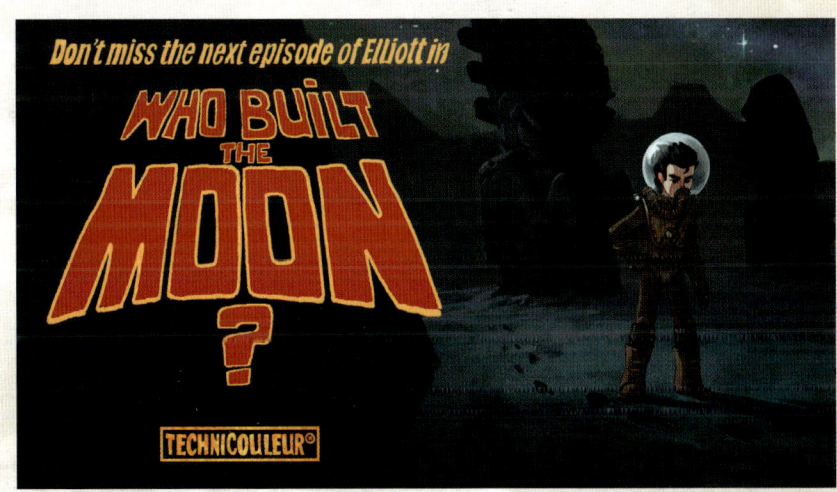

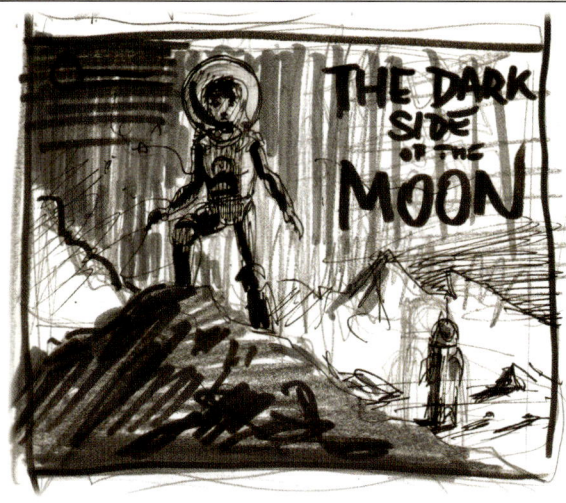

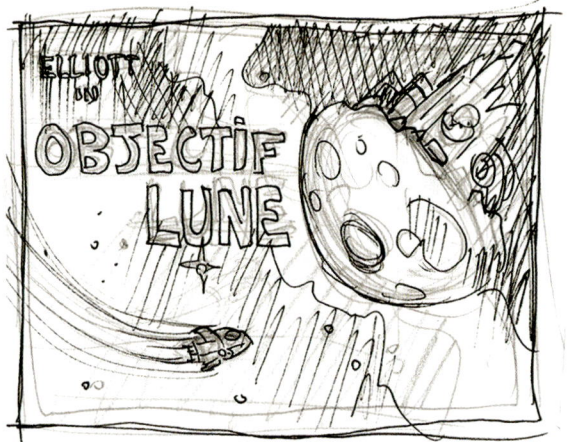

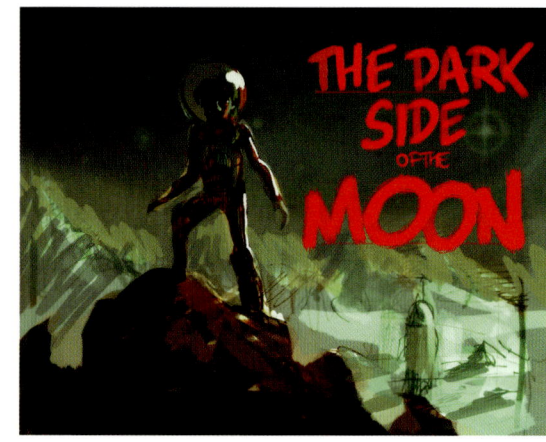

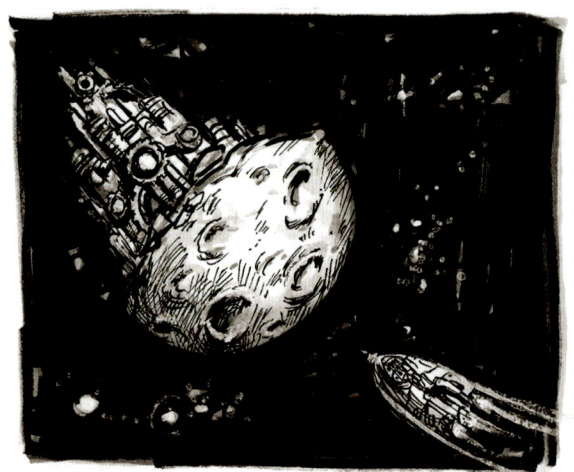

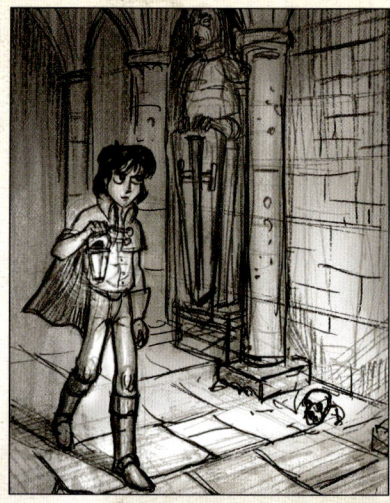

Left : Sketches for the posters, inspired by old sci-fi movies.

Bottom left : Color sketch for Finkelstein's manor. I opted for the darker, gloomier version.

Below : Elliott wandering in the manor's crypt, looking for the mysterious ship.

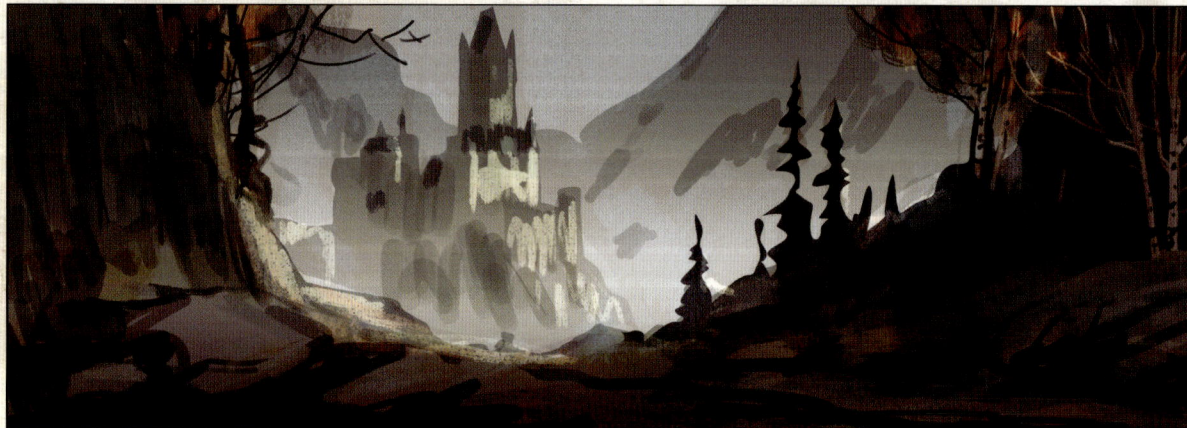

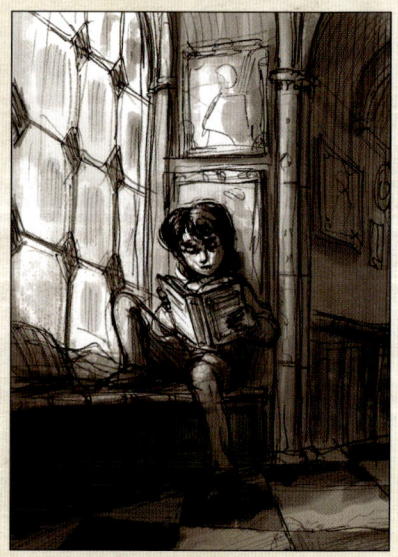

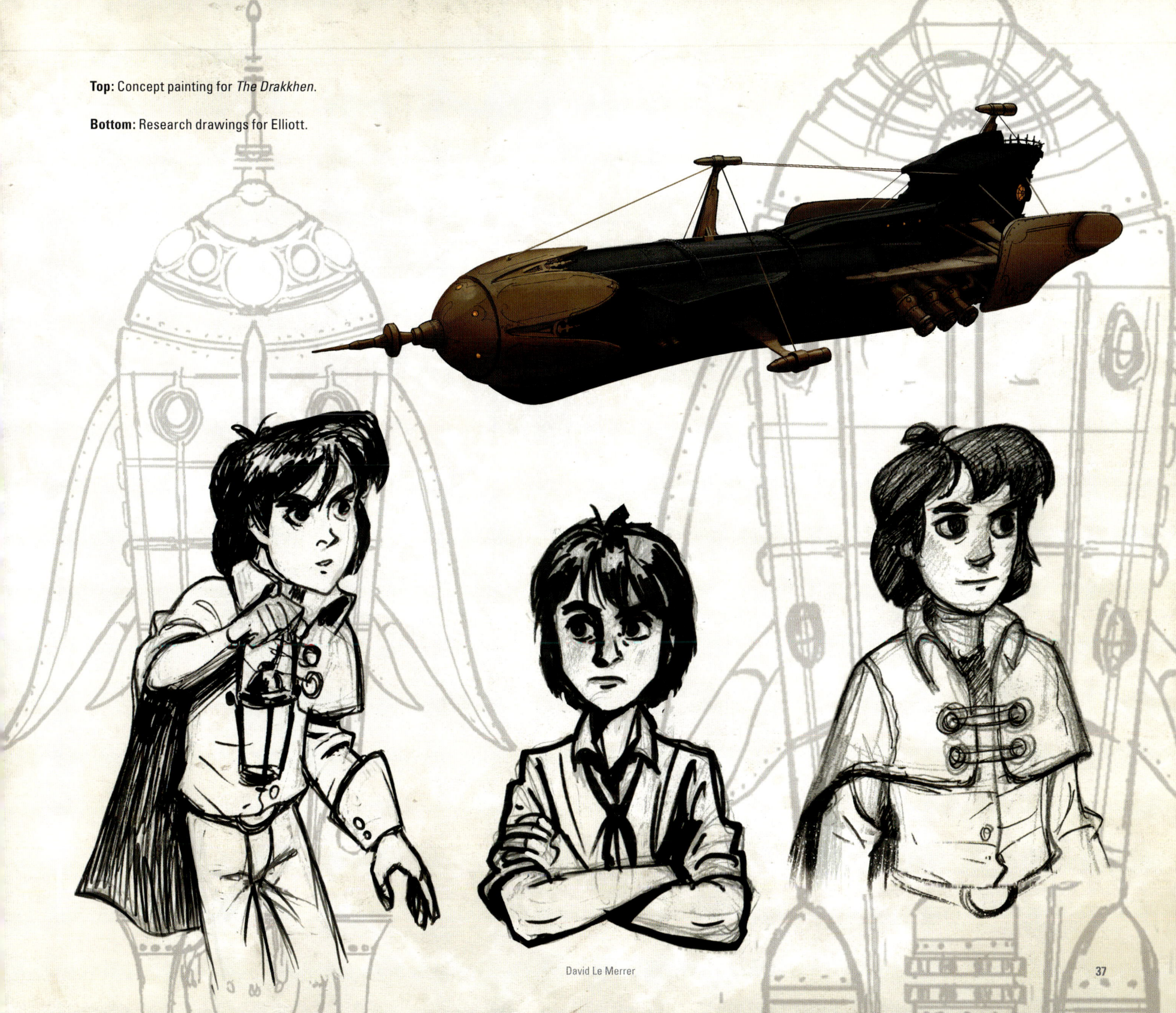

Top: Concept painting for *The Drakkhen*.

Bottom: Research drawings for Elliott.

David Le Merrer

Left page: Exploration for the lizard/reptilian creatures. Although they have more advanced technology than humans, I didn't want them to look too "techy," so I went for a more "medieval" look. I have always liked the Gamorrean piglike creature in *Star Wars*.

Right page: Poster for the last moon episode.

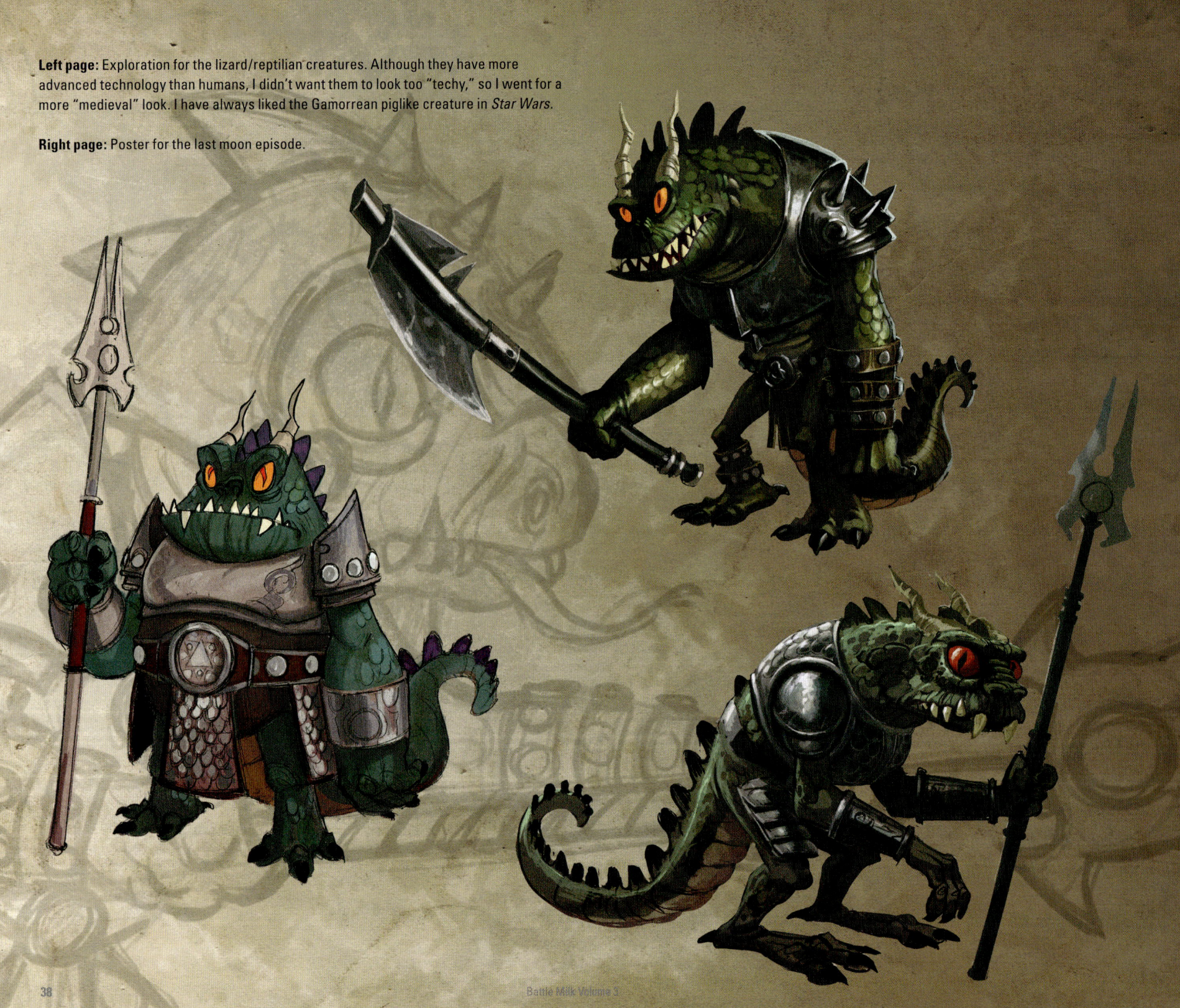

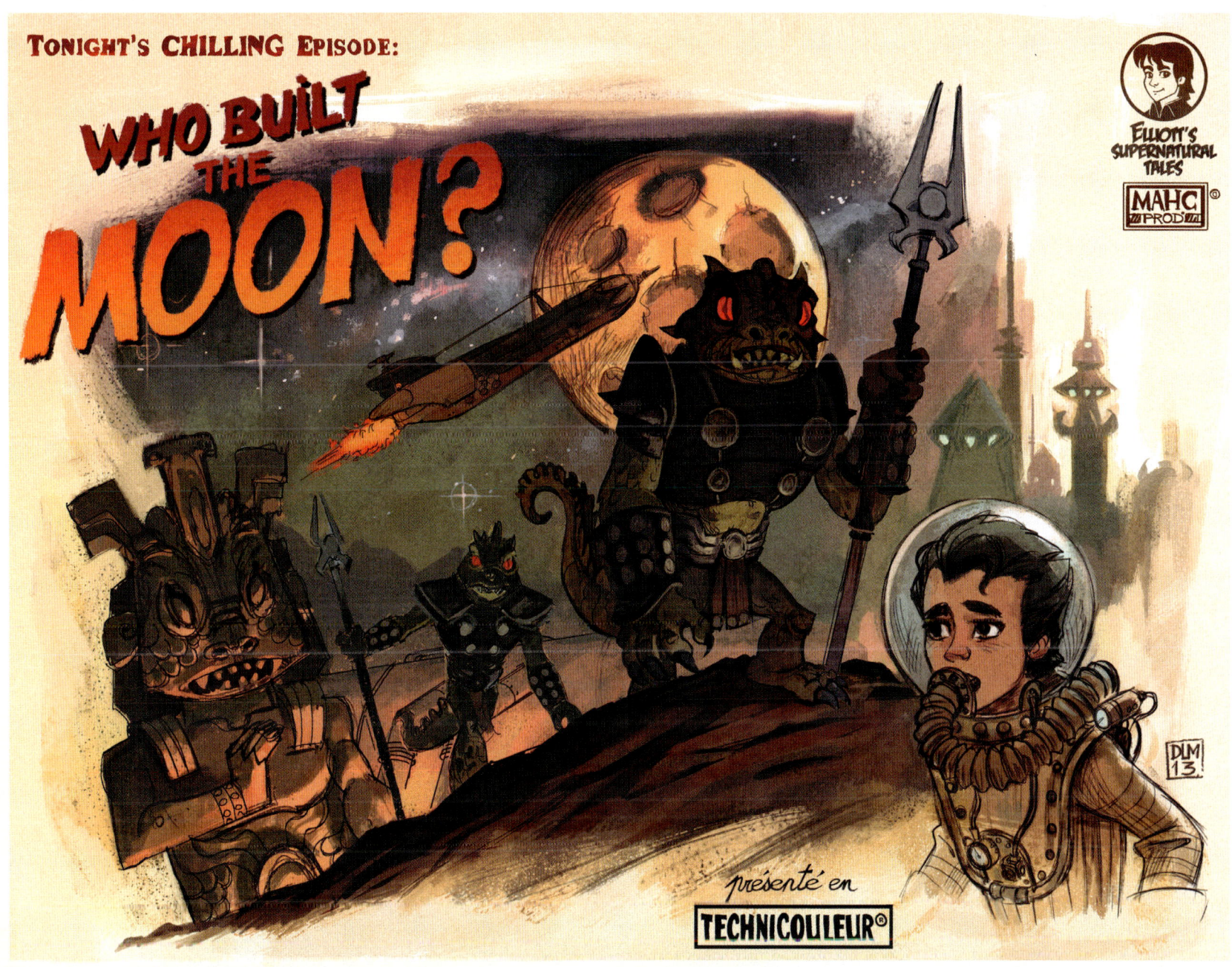

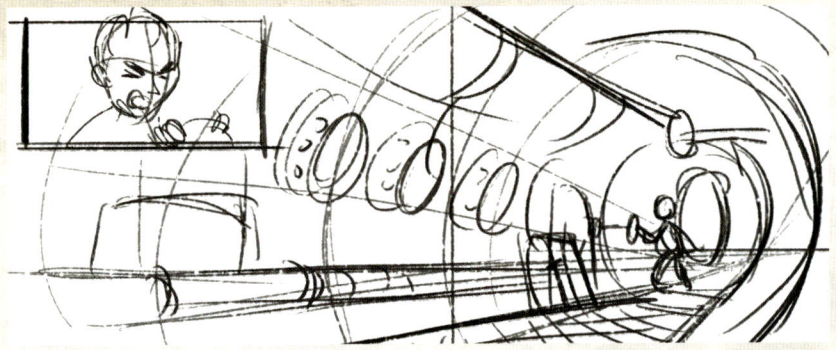

Step 1: Idea Sketch

I started with a small sketch to get the right composition and feel.

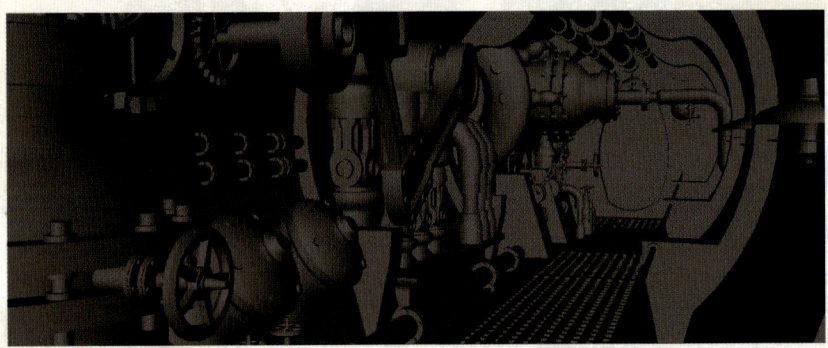

Step 2: 3-D Maya Build

I learned Maya last year. I think it's a great tool, especially if you have a lot of perspective involved. Plus, I am going to reuse this 3-D set for future images, so no need to redraw it, just move around the camera, choose your composition, click "Render," and done!

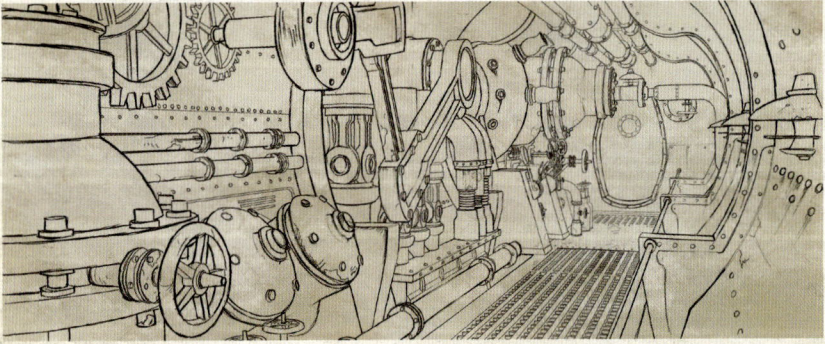

Step 3: Line Drawing

Line drawing on top of the 3-D render. If it doesn't follow the render exactly, it doesn't matter. I like irregularity in drawing; it makes it more "alive." I added a "multiply" layer to have a first feel of metal and rust.

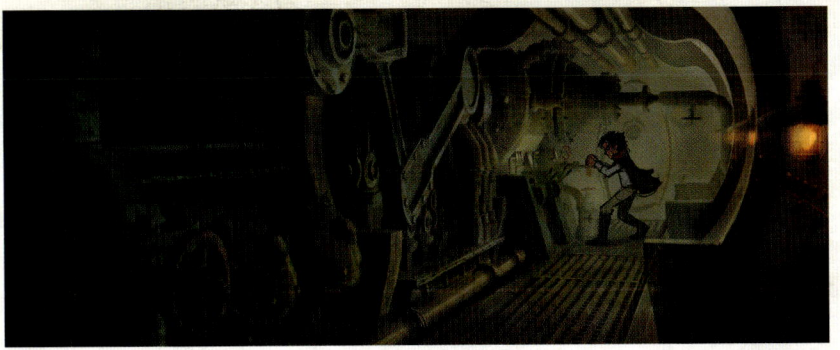

Step 4: Color Pass

I wanted to have a very rusty metallic environment for this image, so I chose warm colors with a hint of blues. I left the background without too much value and tone, so that the character could "pop up" from it; plus, this adds a steamy feel.

The character is here in a very rough color sketch.

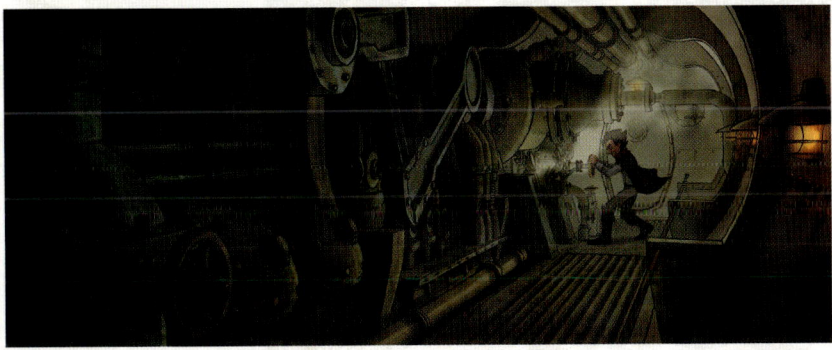

Step 5: Refinement

Here, the character is done. I added a "multiply" layer in the line drawing. I also painted some steam coming out of the pipes.

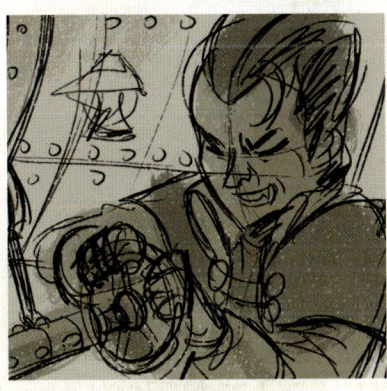
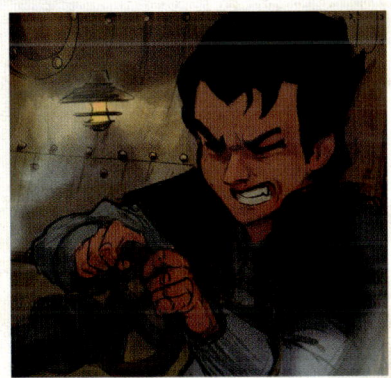

Concept sketch for the insert image and the final version.

JACKSON SZE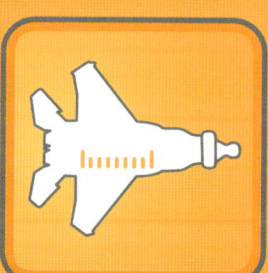

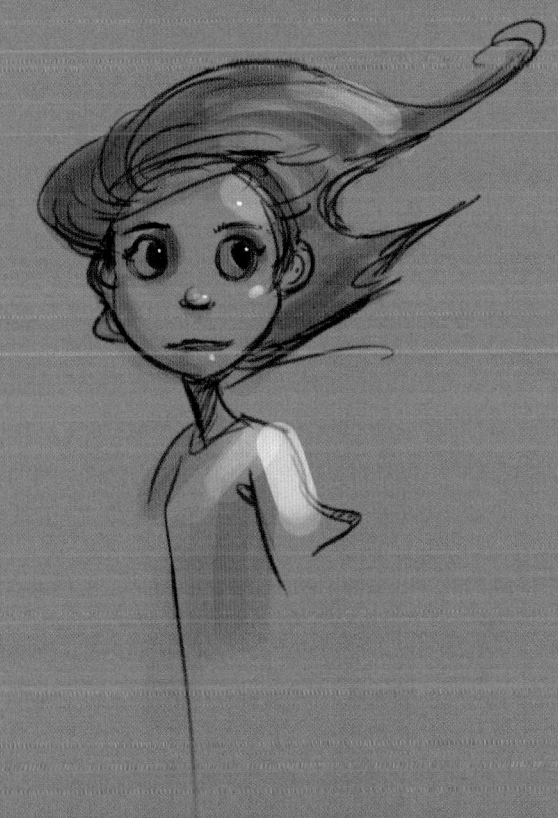

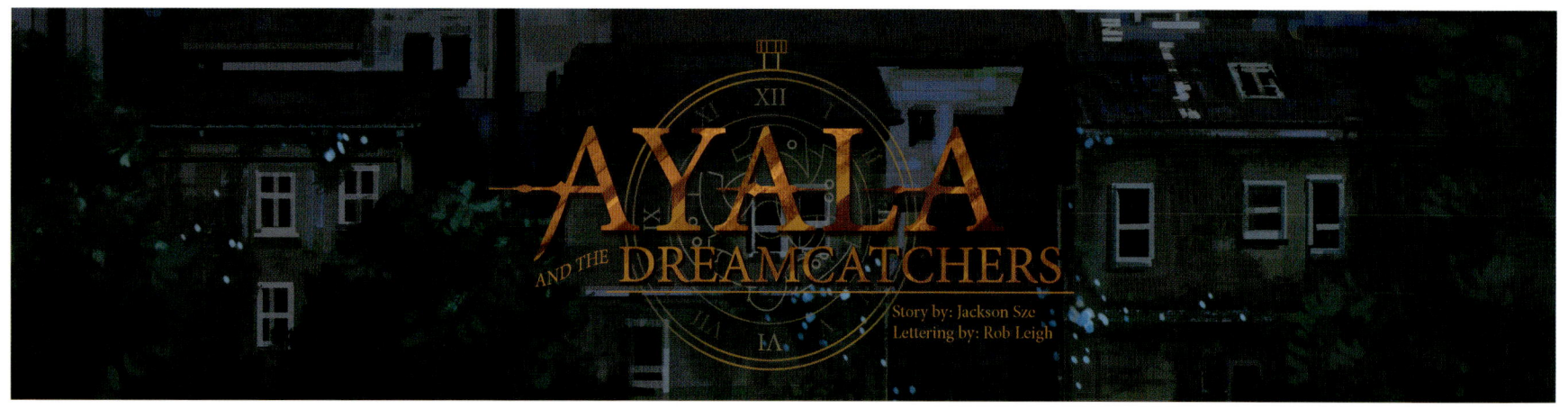

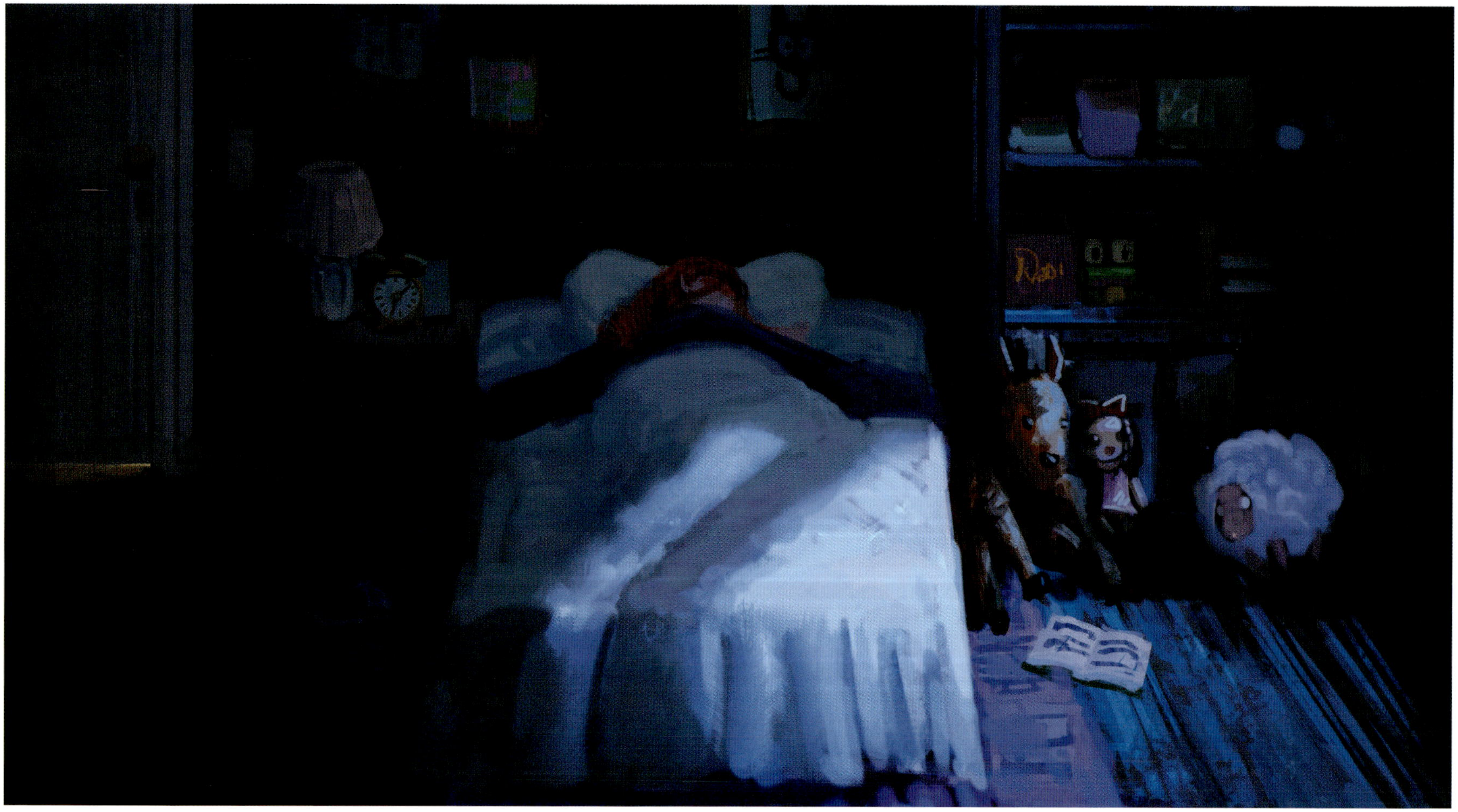

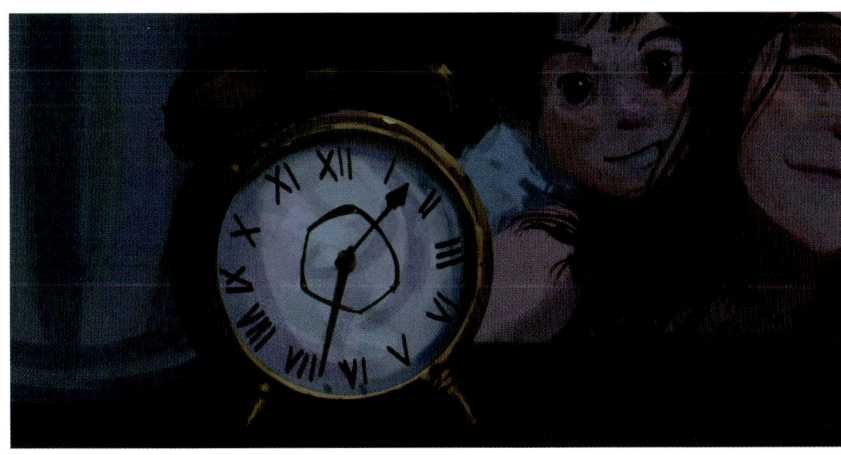
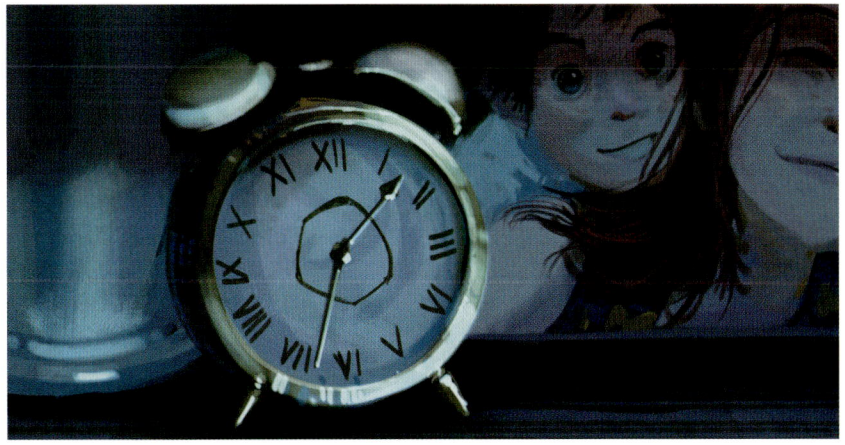
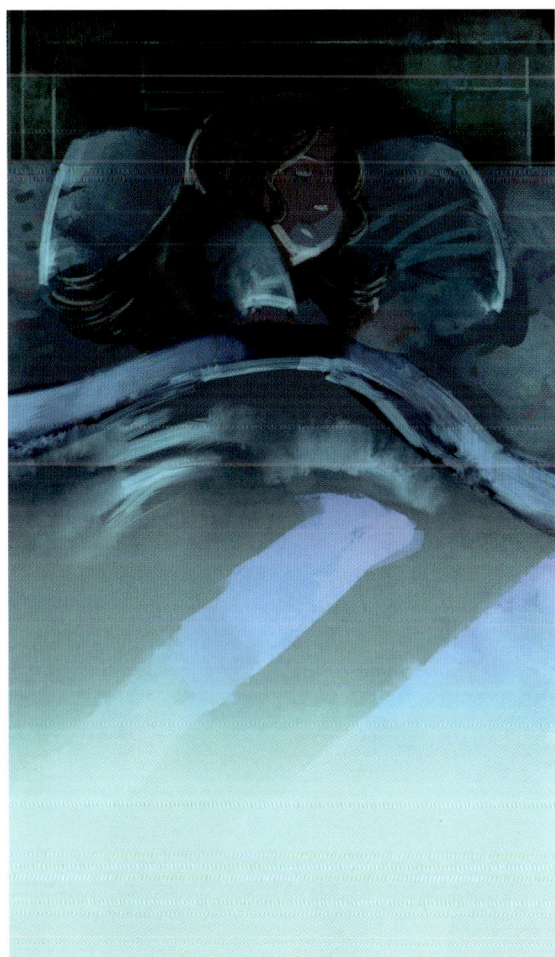
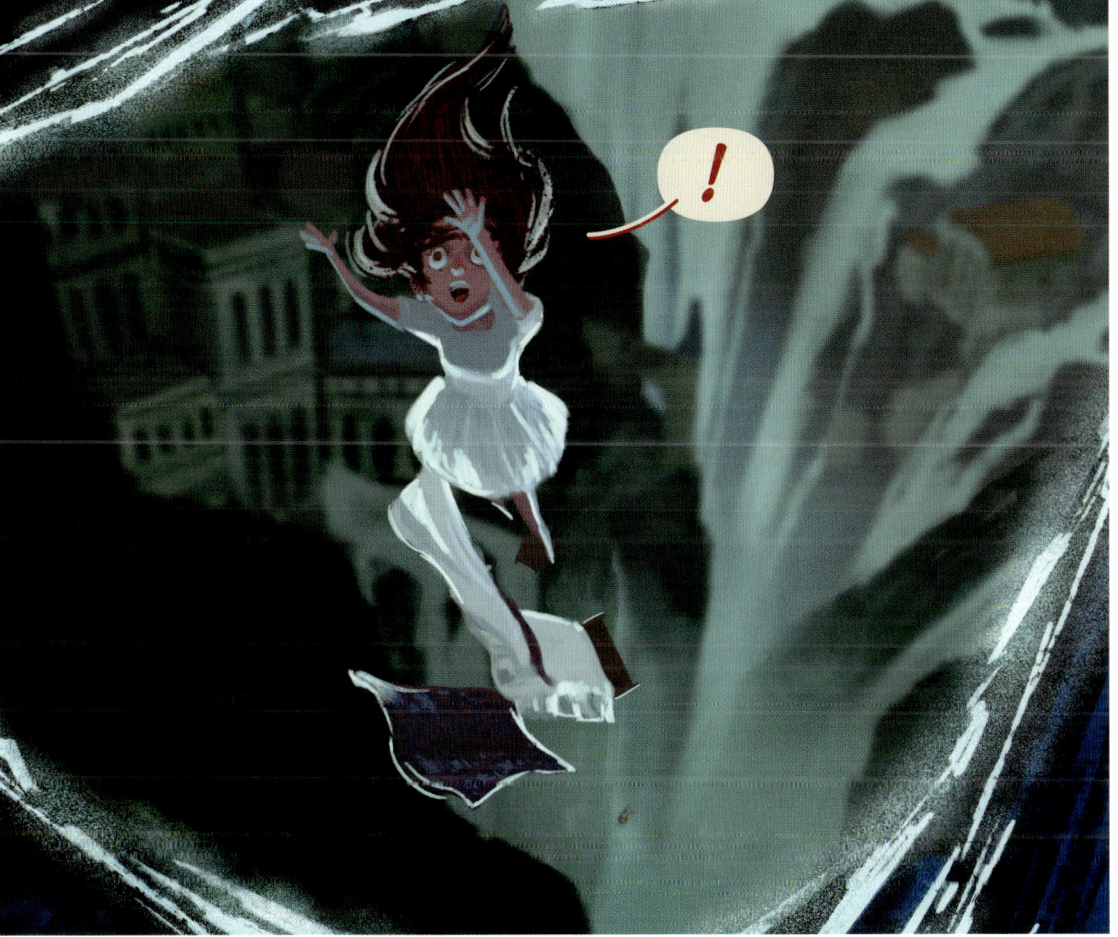

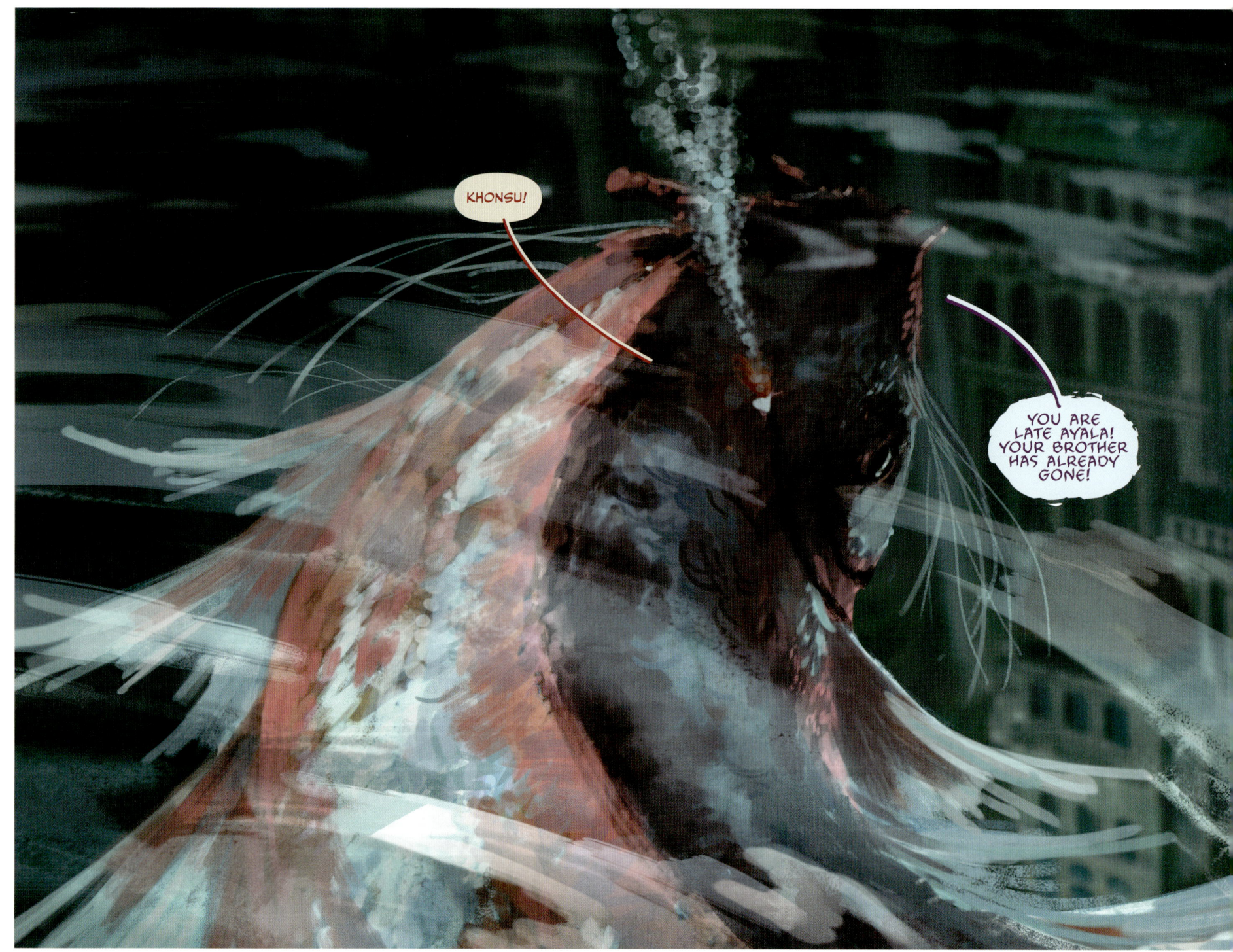

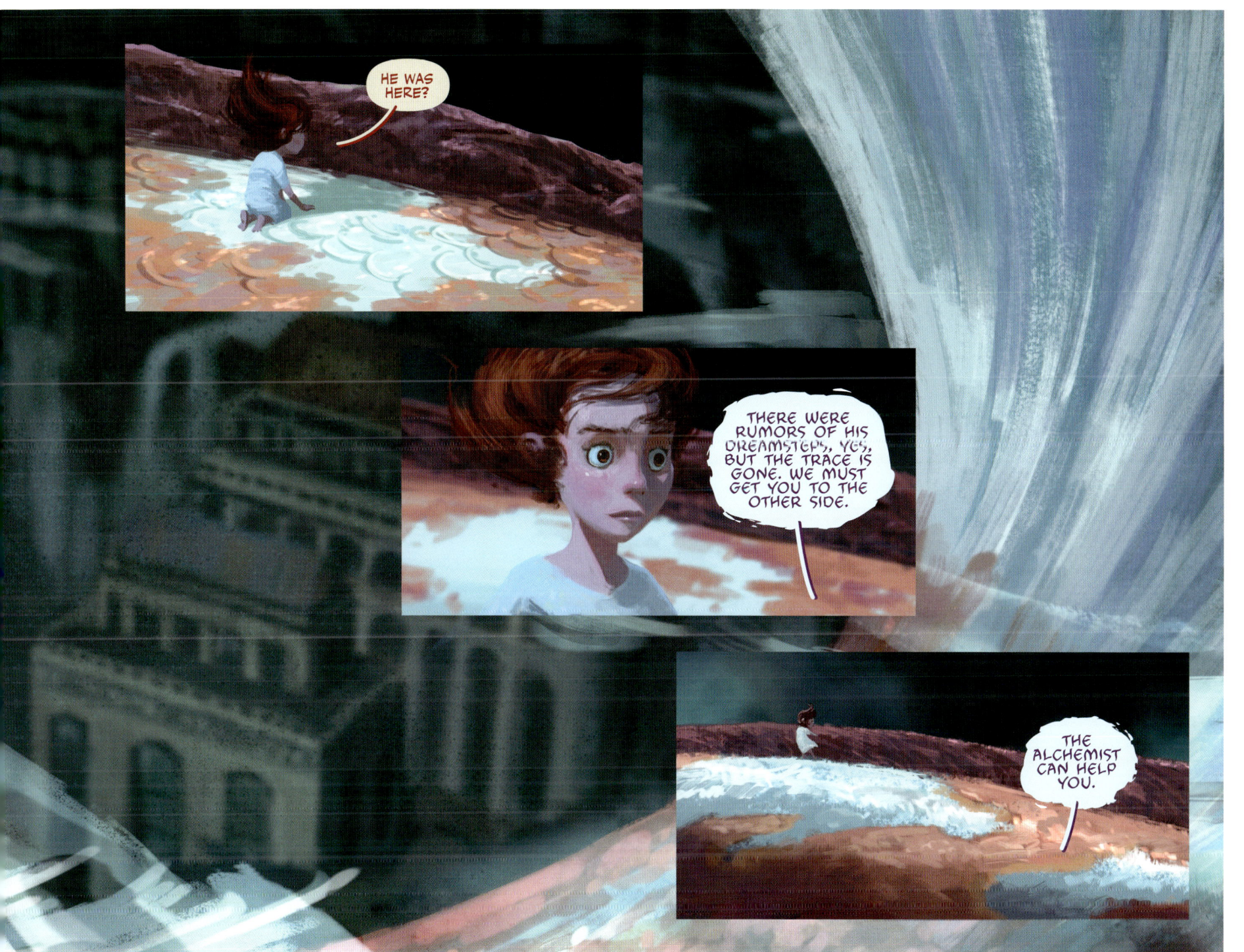

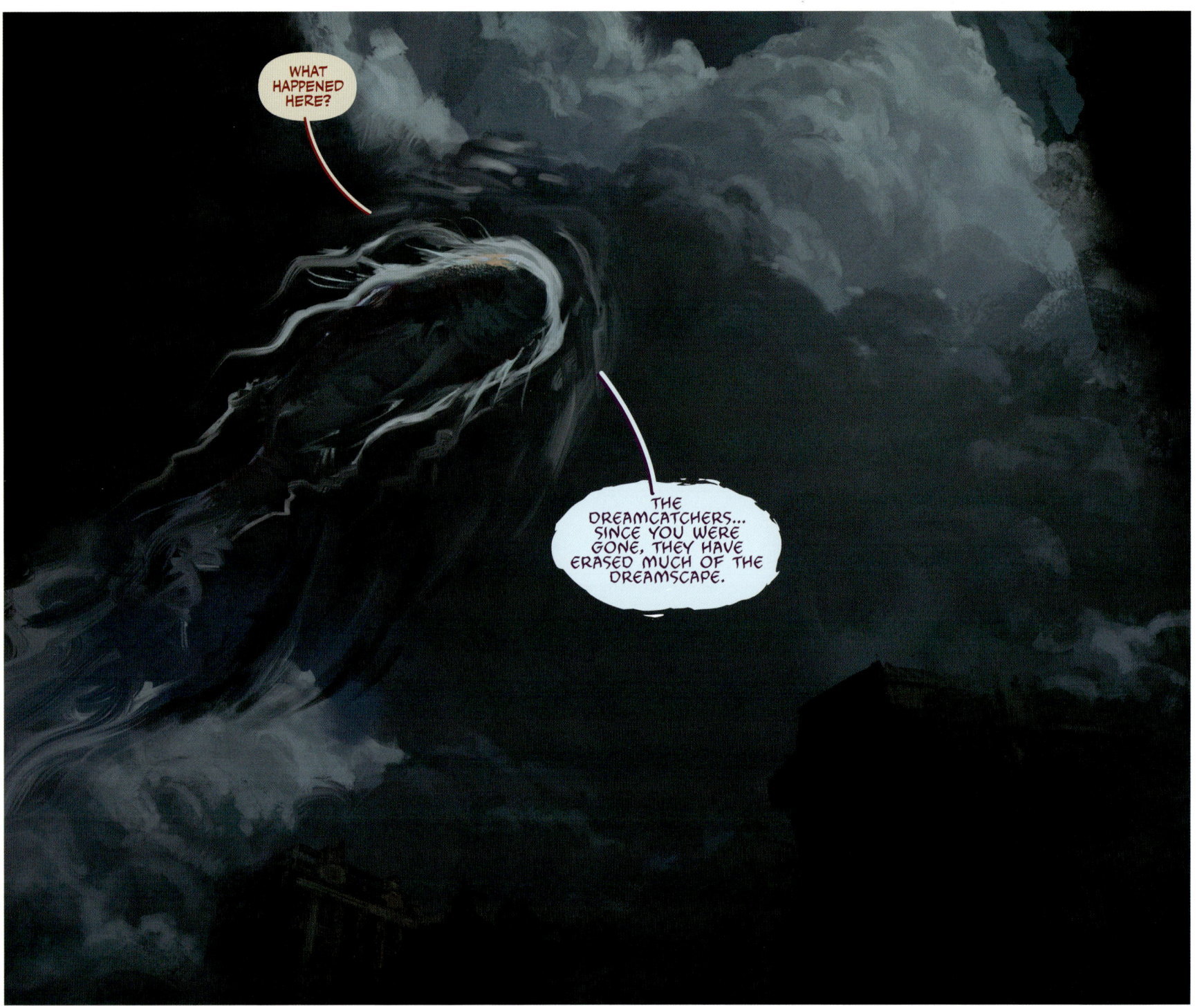

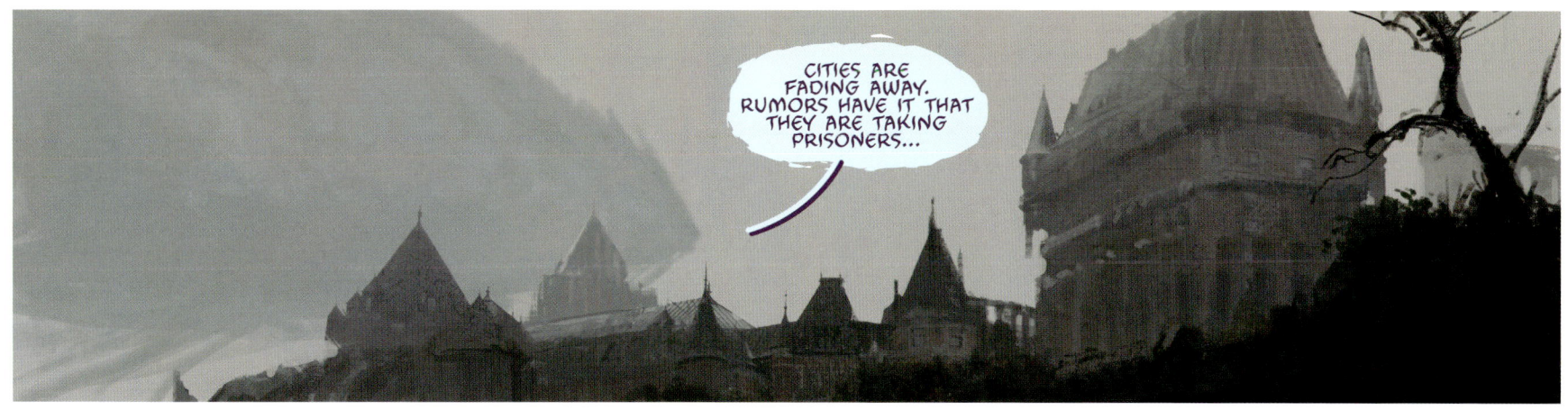

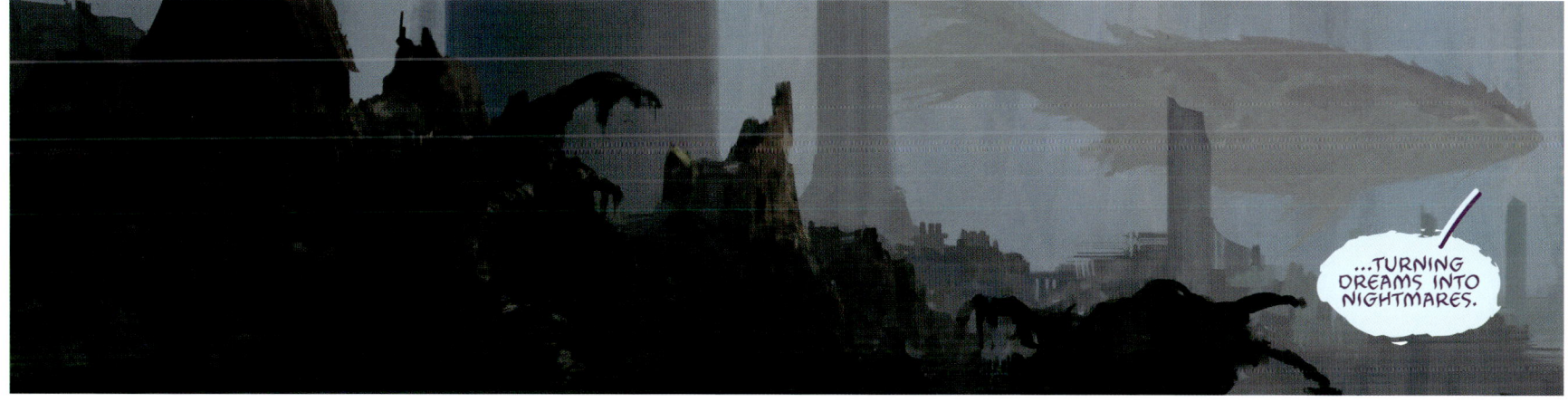

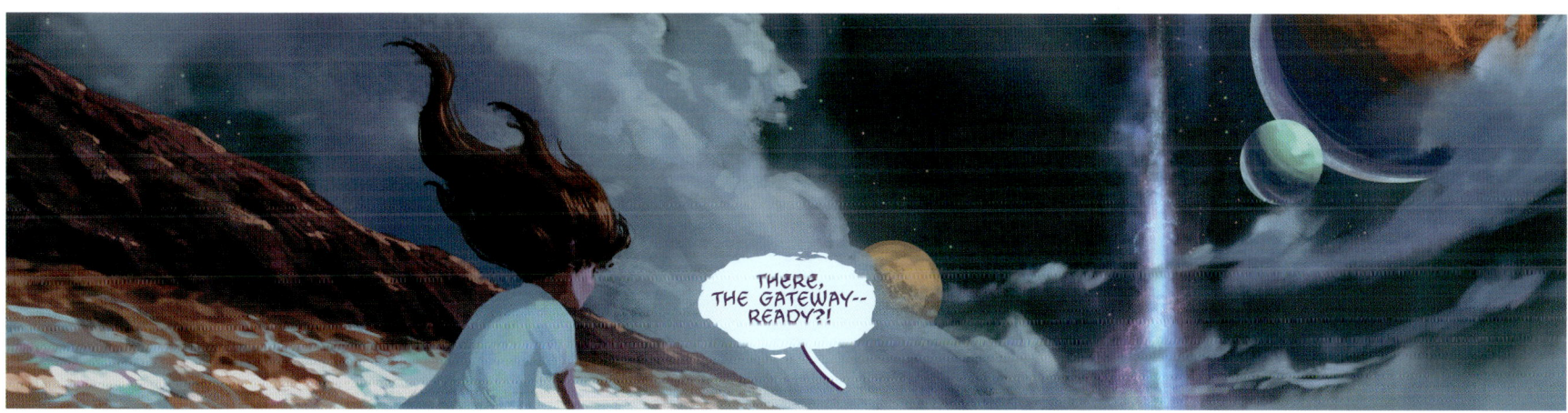

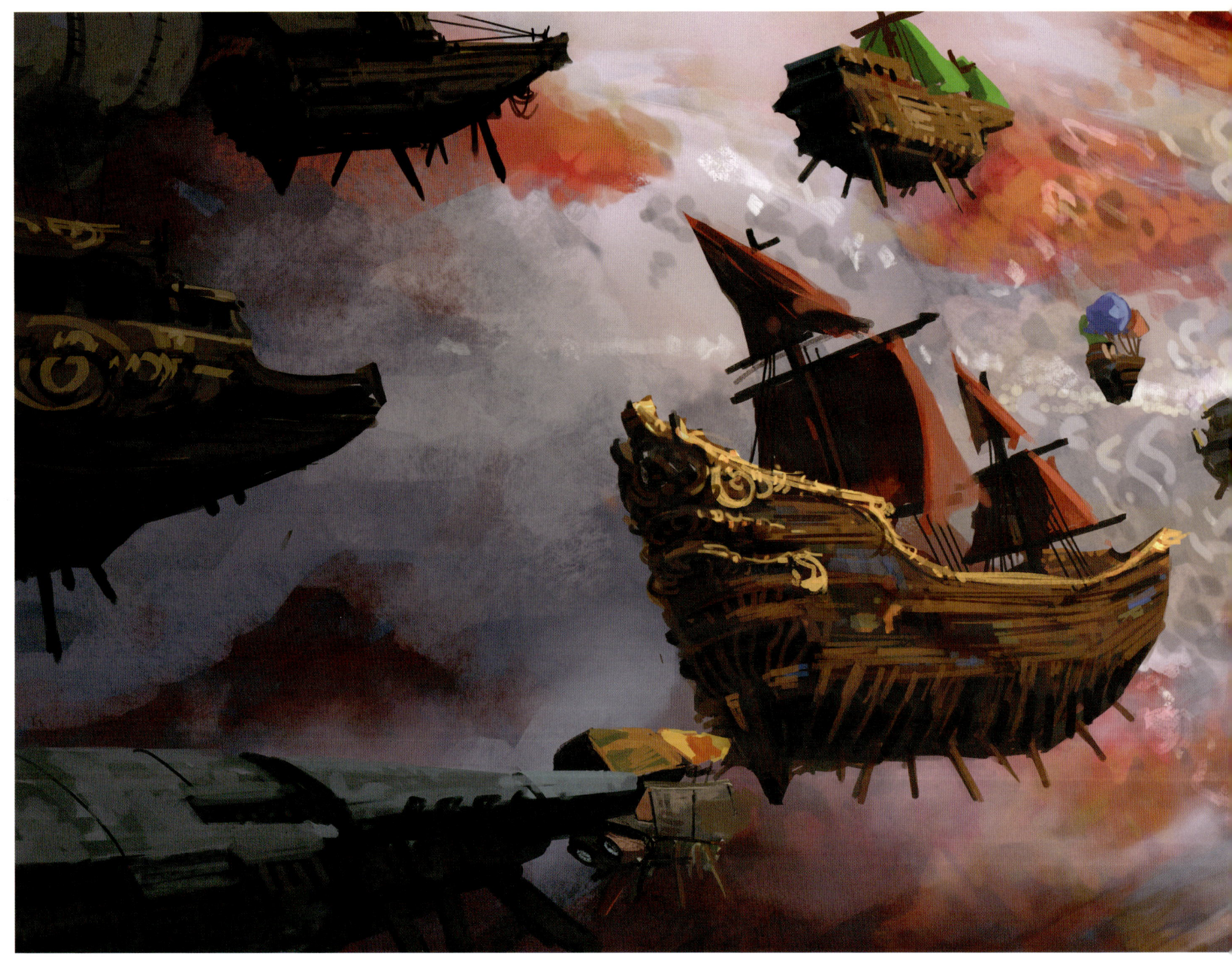

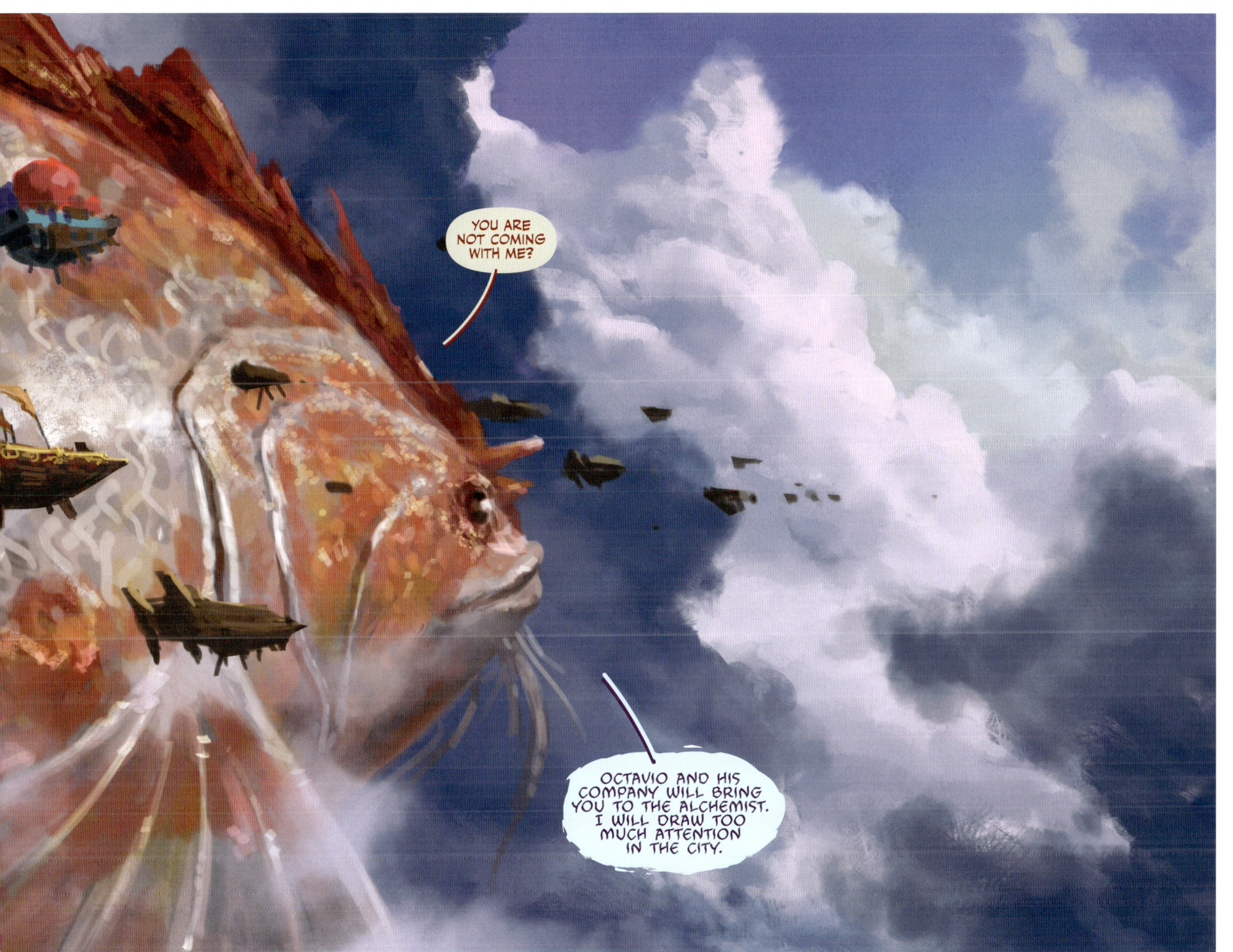

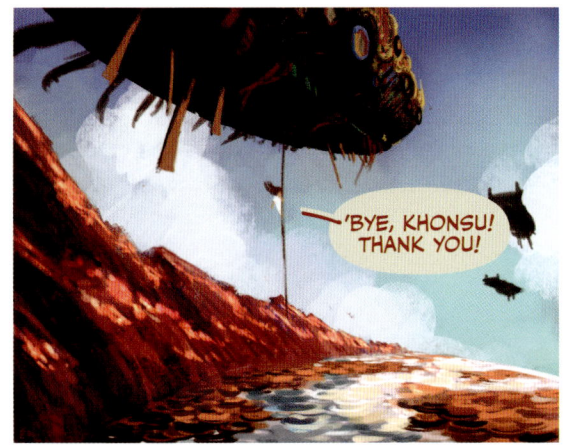

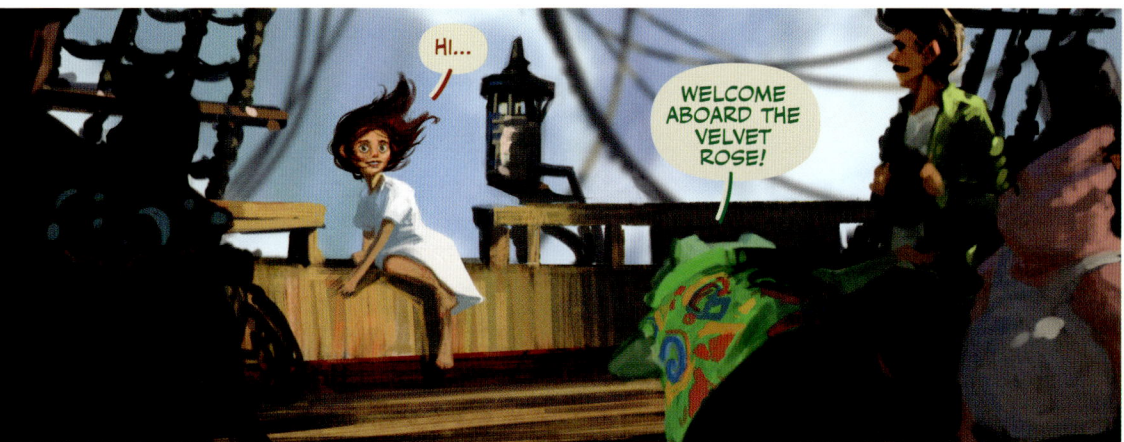

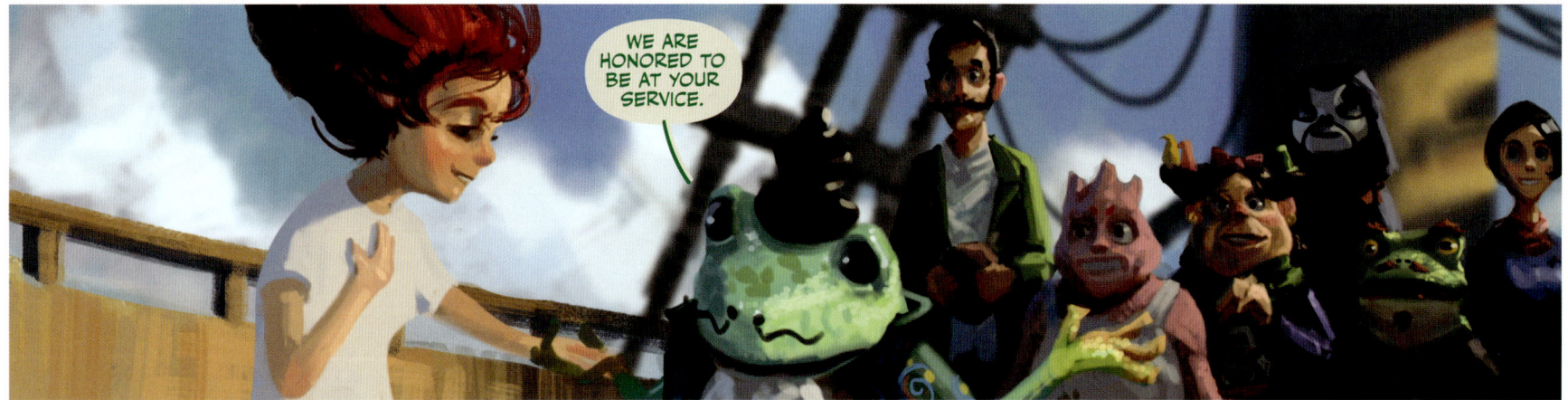

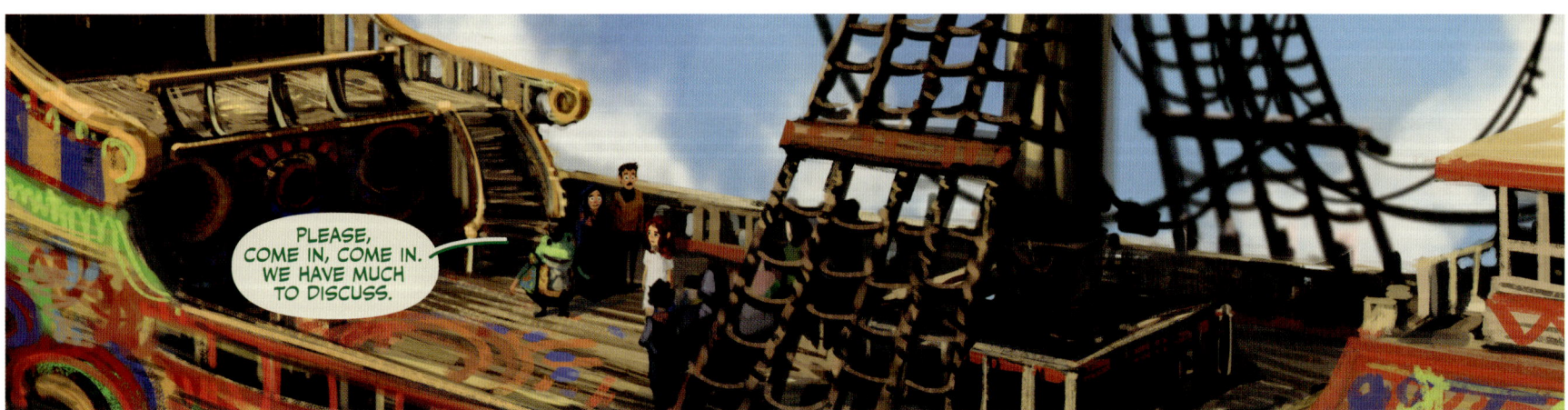

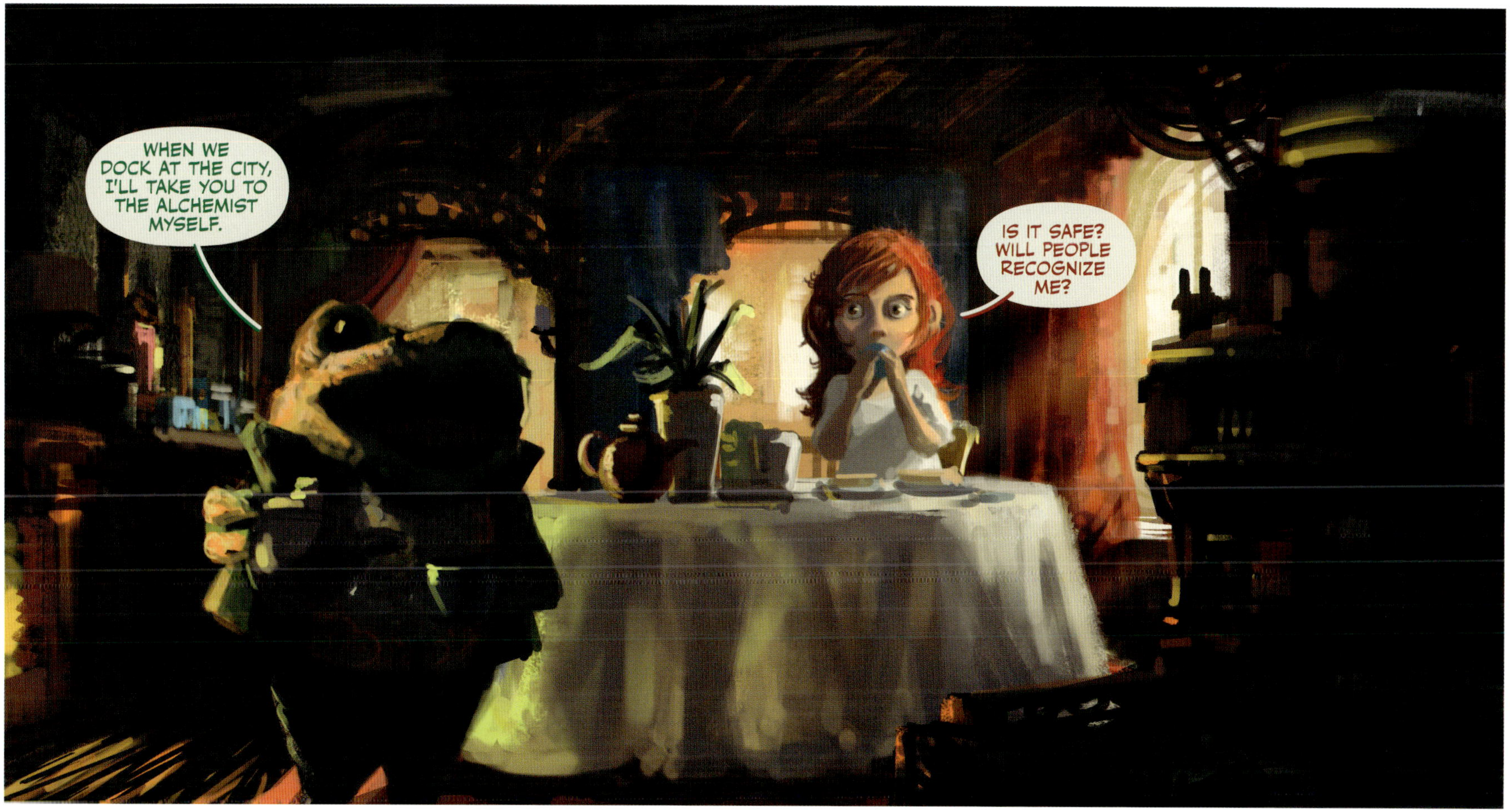

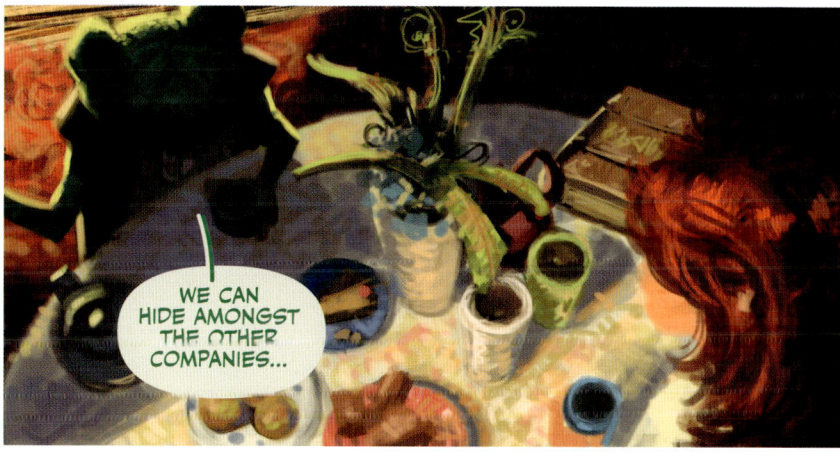
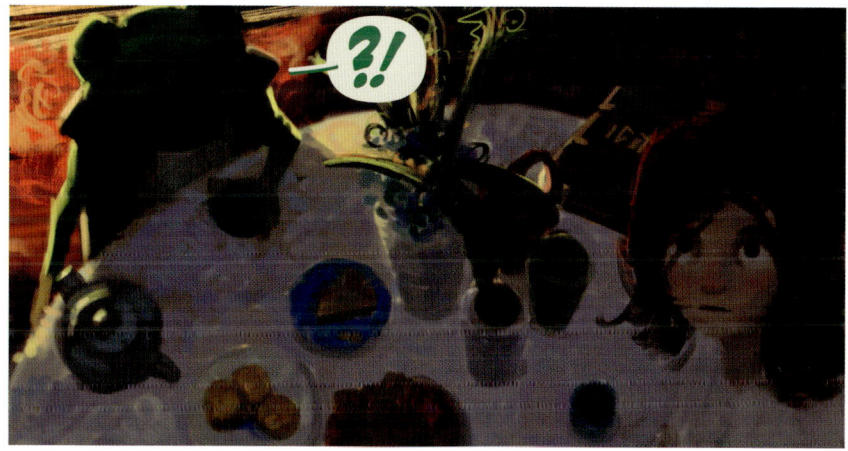

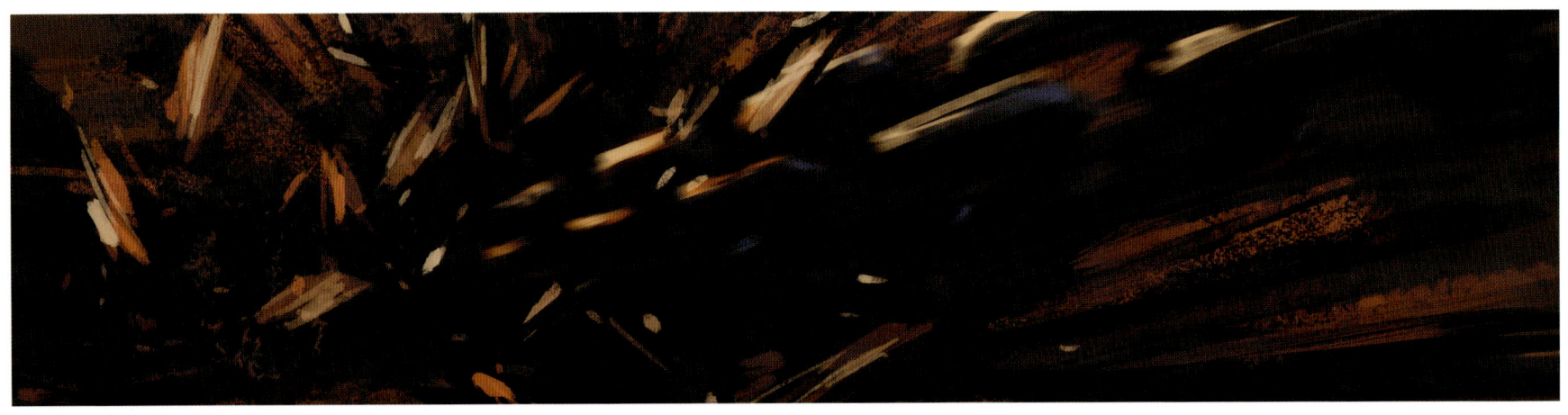

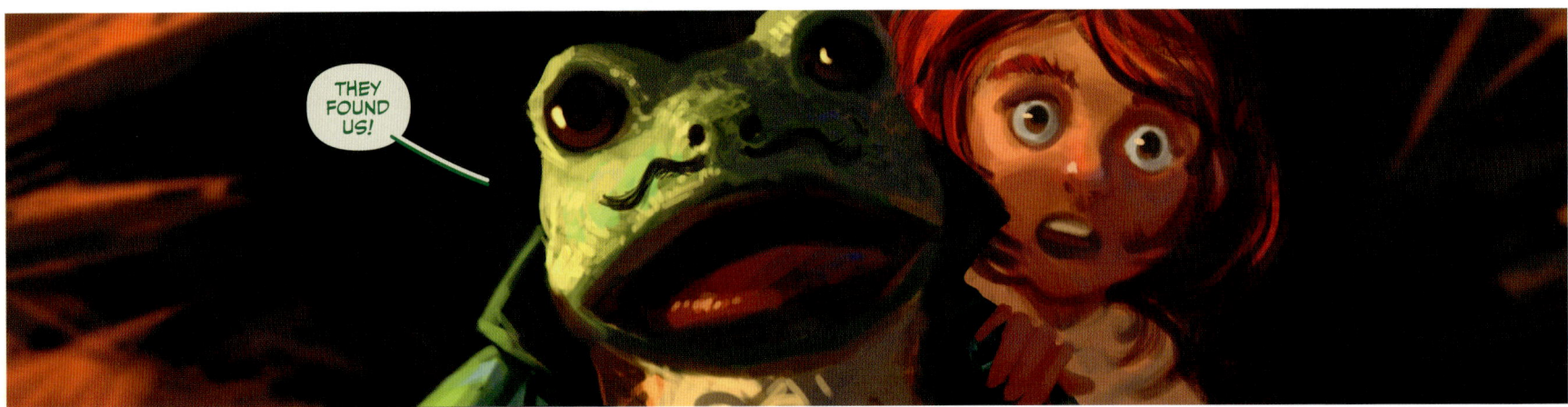

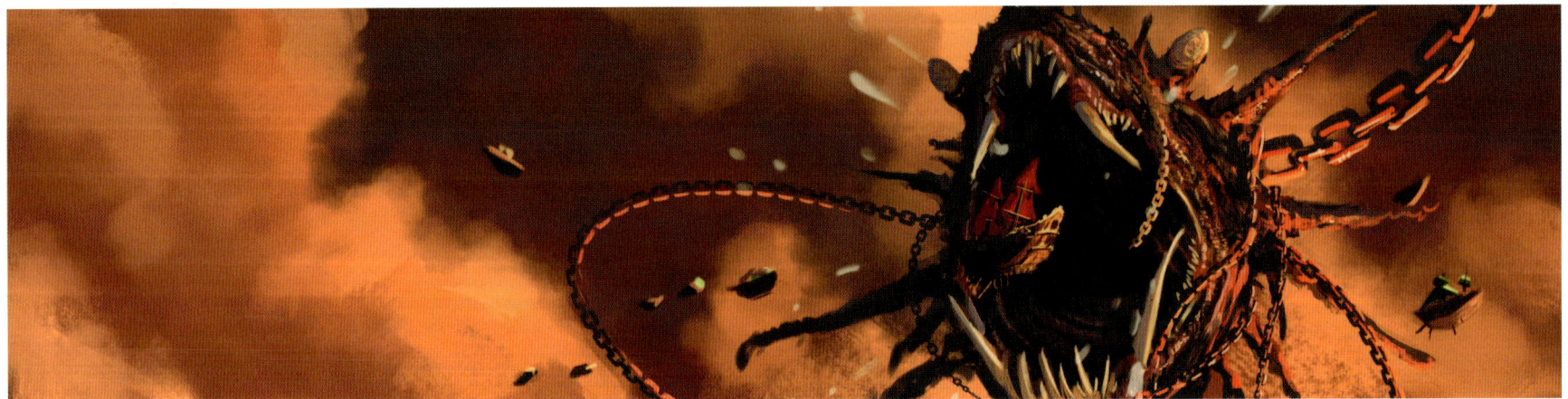

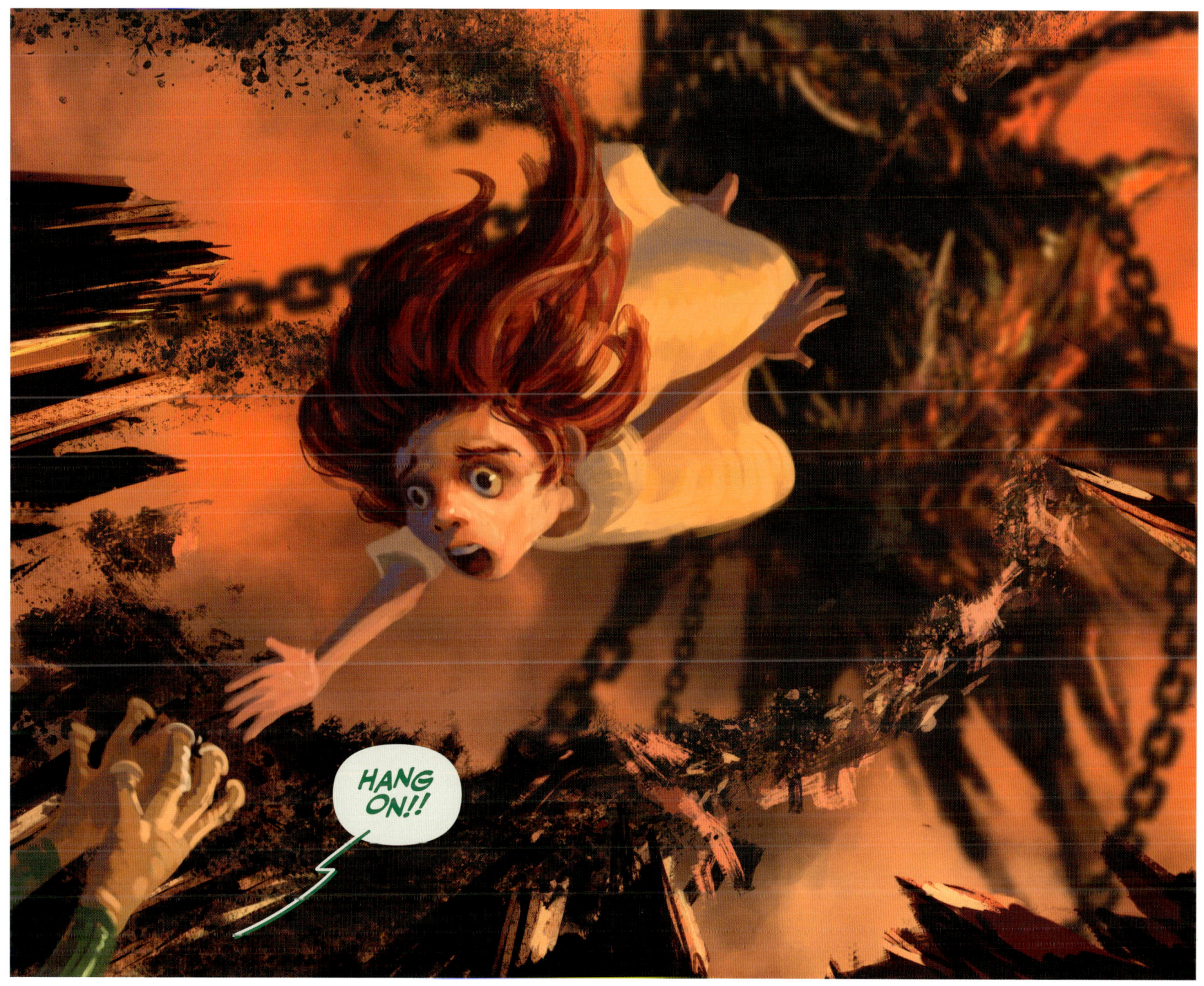

With six spreads of content to cover, I decided to try my hand at telling a story sequentially. "Ayala and the Dreamcatchers" is a story I have kicked around in my head for a while now. You may have seen a few pieces of Ayala-related artwork posted on my blog years ago. The story draws inspiration from Miyazaki movies, *Little Nemo: Adventures in Slumberland*, and many other stories I grew up with. Here, I am trying to tell a snippet of Ayala's story, throwing the reader into the middle of her adventures...

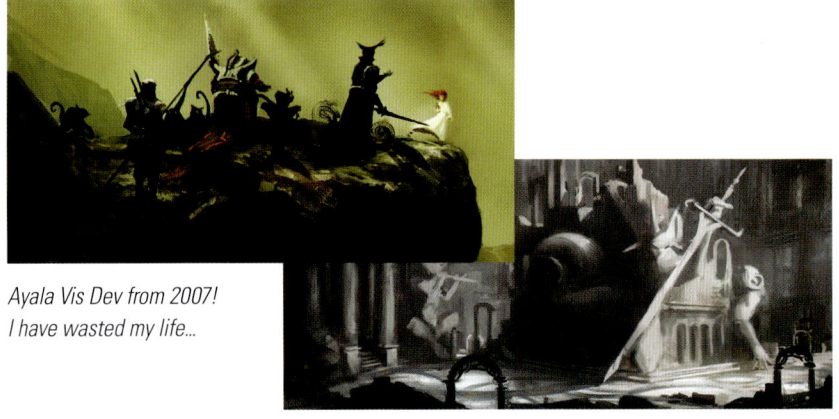

Ayala Vis Dev from 2007!
I have wasted my life...

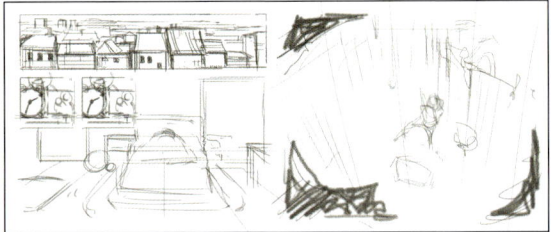
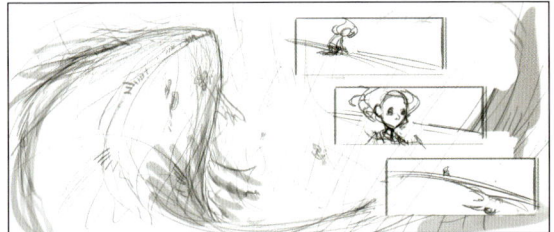
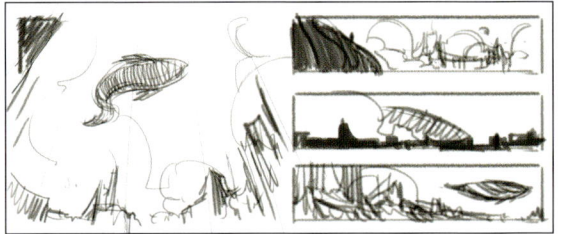
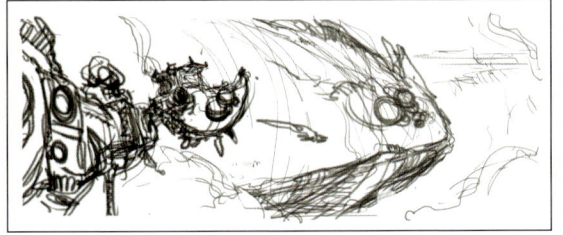
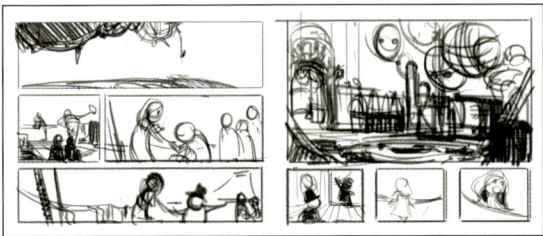
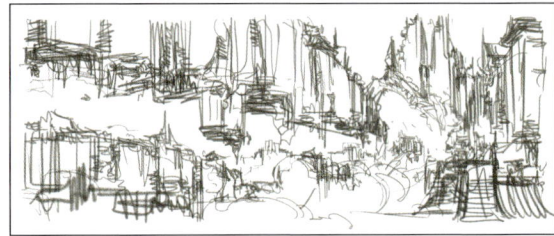

These are my initial sketches. I found it useful to think about the story while I sketched out the spreads. I had to make sure this section of Ayala's adventures could fit into six spreads. The entire section needed a simple beginning, middle, and end. The beginning establishes the real world, and Ayala entering Dreamworld. The middle is her journey, aided by Khonsu and Octavio. And the end is when she reaches her destination, the Dream City.

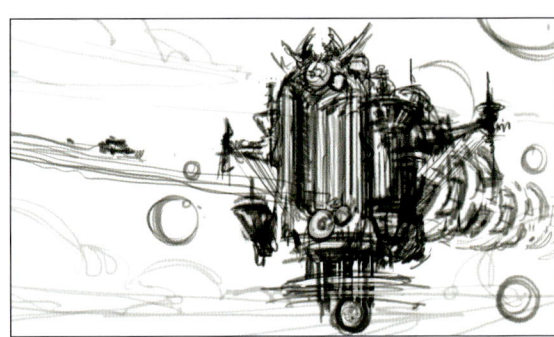

Early Ayala Concept for Battle Milk Volume 3.

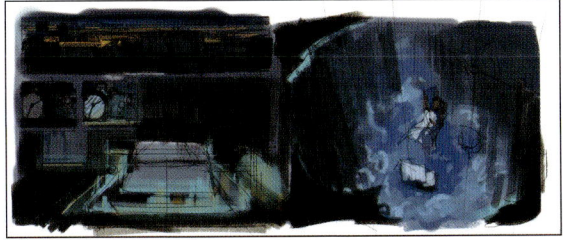
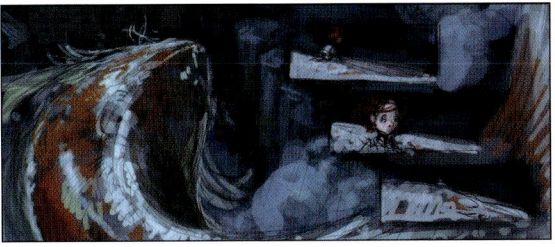
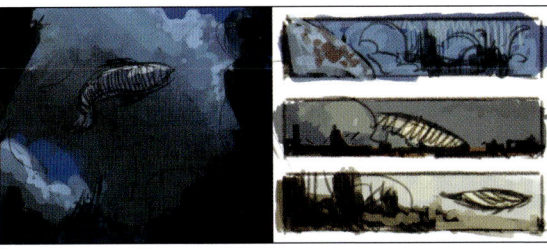
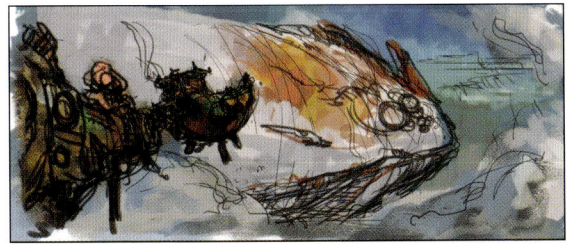
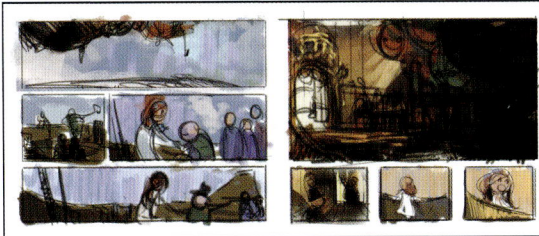
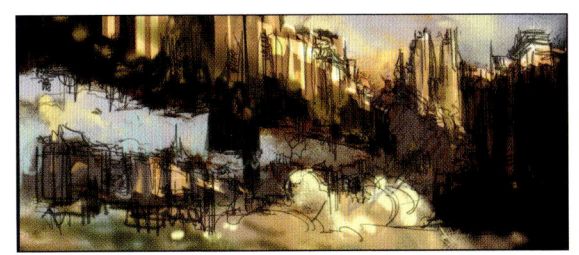

The color script came next. There isn't much space to establish an intricate color script that reflects the emotional beats of the story. I could, however, use time of day to my advantage and start with cooler colors to reflect the desolation of the Dreamscape, and bring in warms as Ayala and her friends reach their destination. Finally, the last spread was supposed to be an establishing shot of the Dream City, still standing strong, with millions of citizens, bathed in sunset light to sell its scale and majesty.

Upon reflecting on the story, however, I found it to be kind of ho-hum. I had Ayala going from point A to B to C to D. There was no conflict, so there was no interest. Visuals alone were driving the story. So instead, I had Ayala's journey interrupted by the Dreamcatchers (hey, they are in the title!). Hopefully this will lend the story a better sense of drama and action—with a cliff-hanger to boot! The color script, if you can call it that, still works from cools to warms. I look forward to fully realizing this story in the near future!

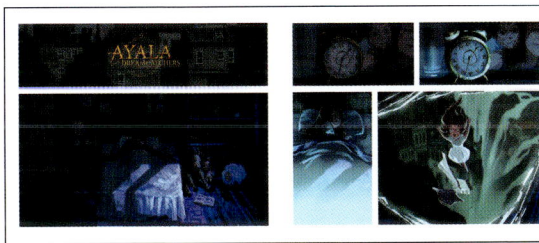
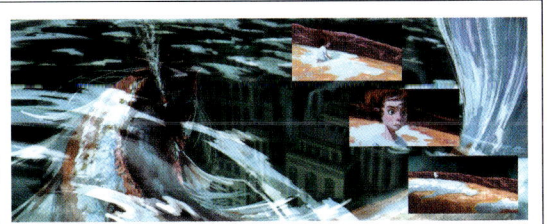
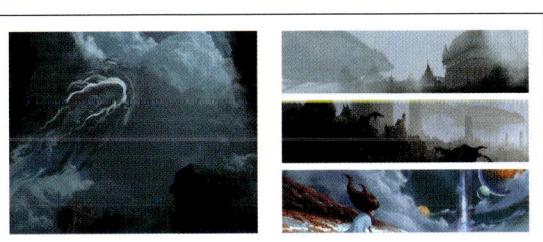
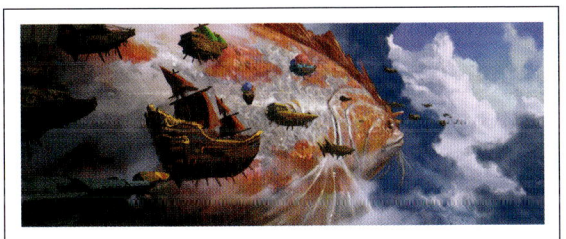
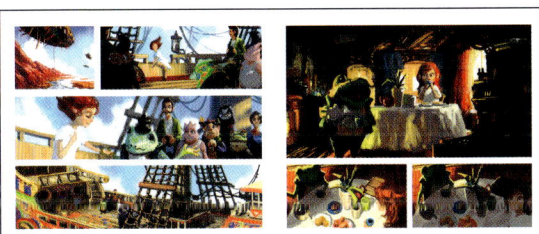
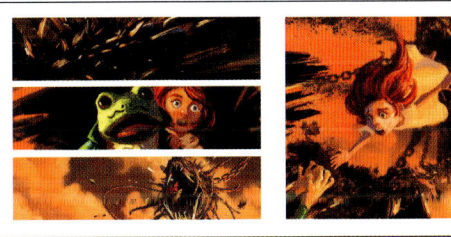

JUSTIN RIDGE

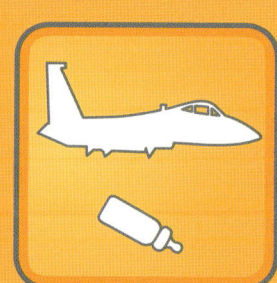

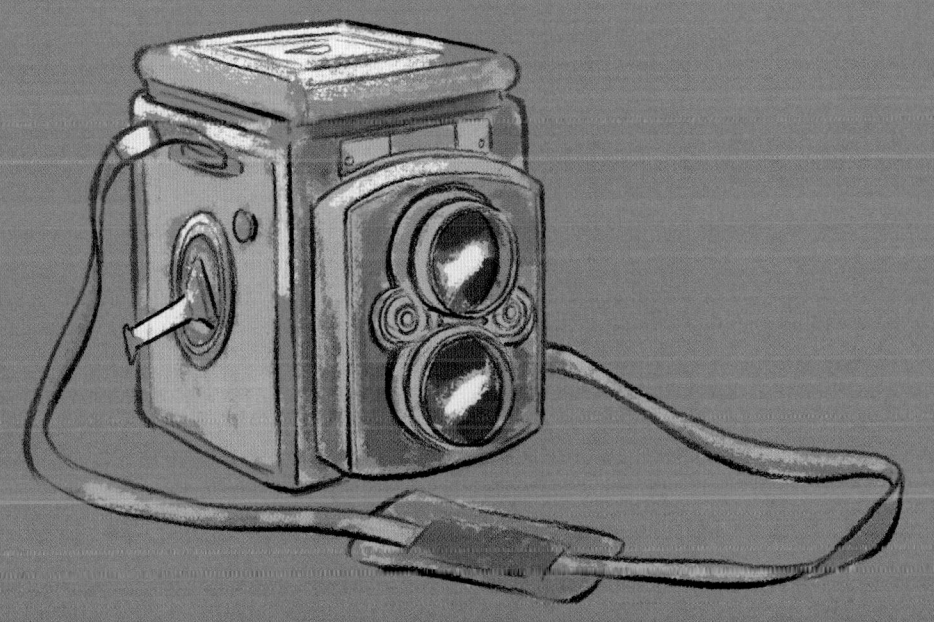

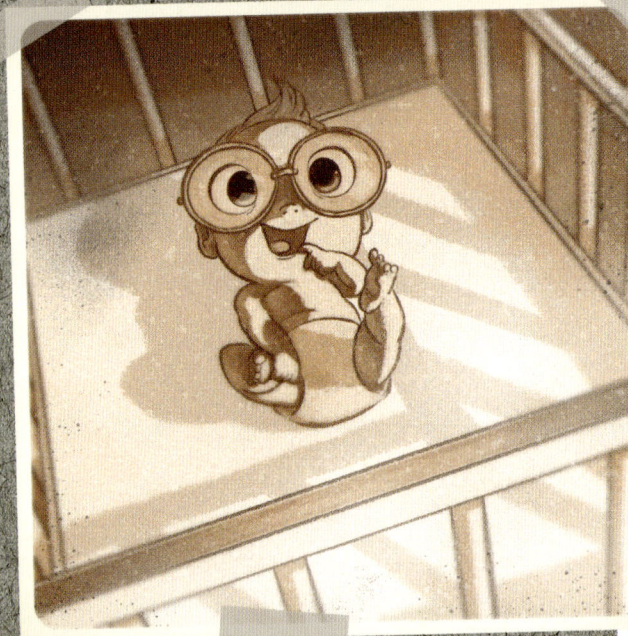

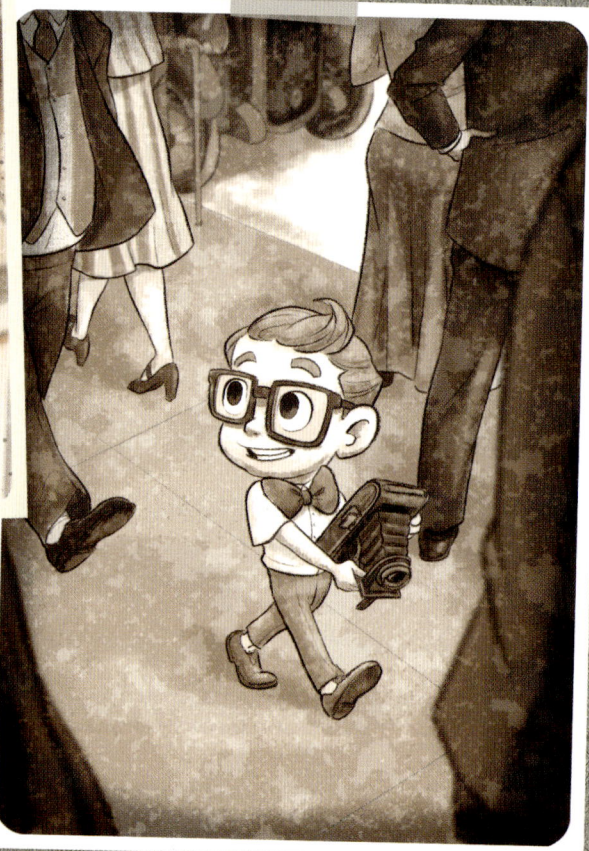

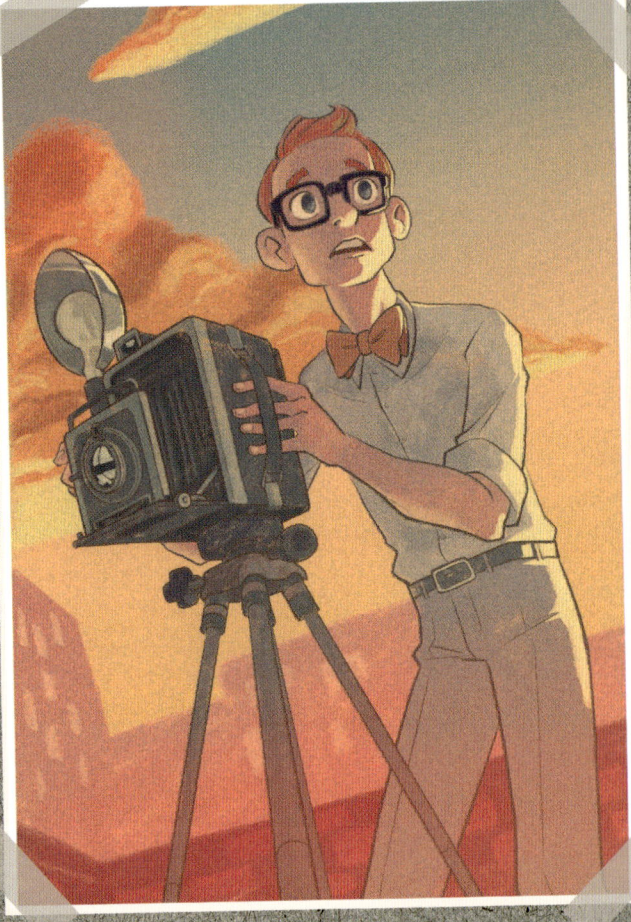

On April 31st, 1922, a prodigy was born.

Arthur B. Murkell, nicknamed the "Little Shutter Boy," became the world's greatest photographer at age five.

But during his travels, he witnessed some things so bizarre and baffling, he hid the photos away in his secret vault, never to be seen by anyone.

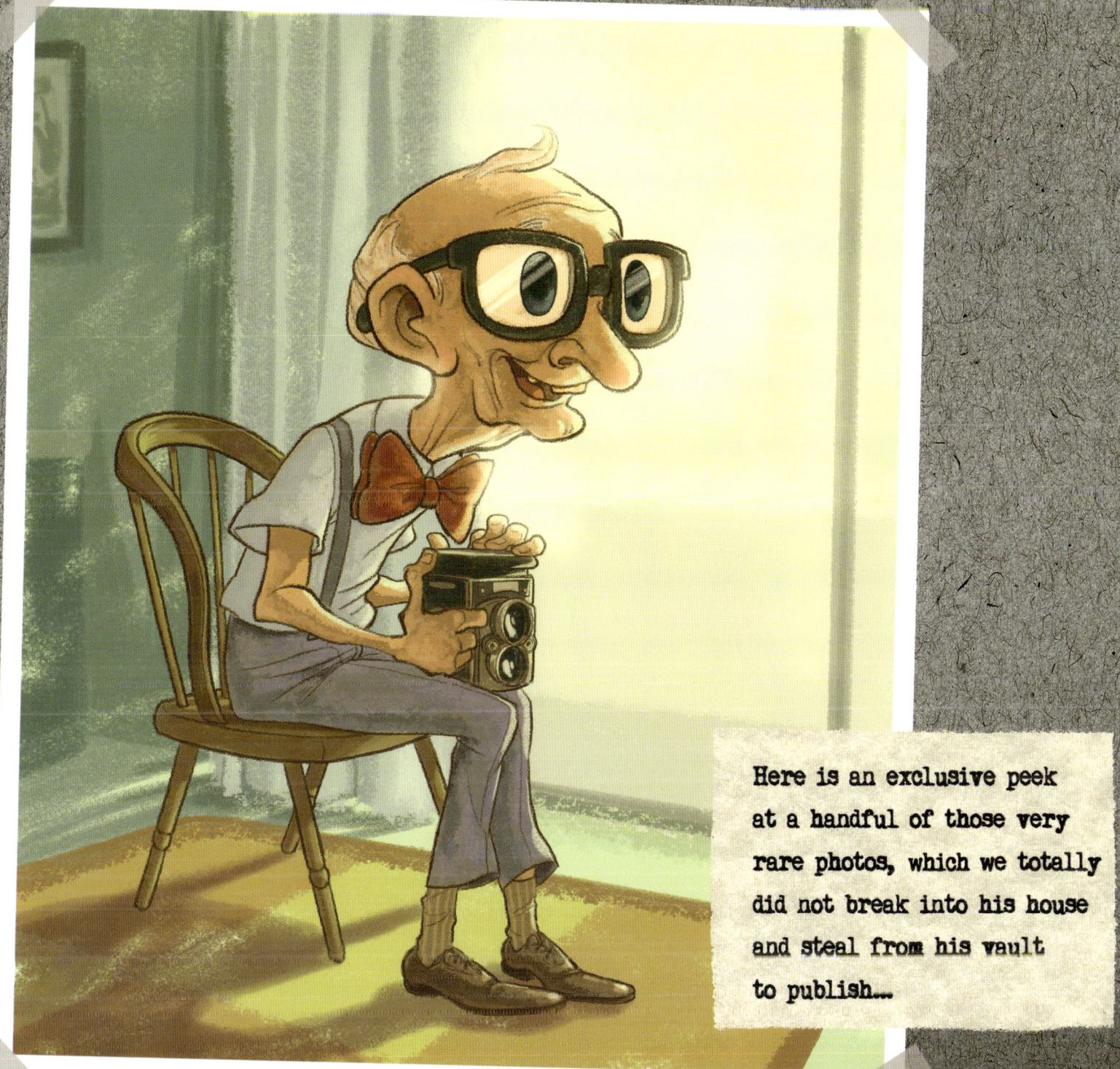

Here is an exclusive peek at a handful of those very rare photos, which we totally did not break into his house and steal from his vault to publish...

Justin Ridge

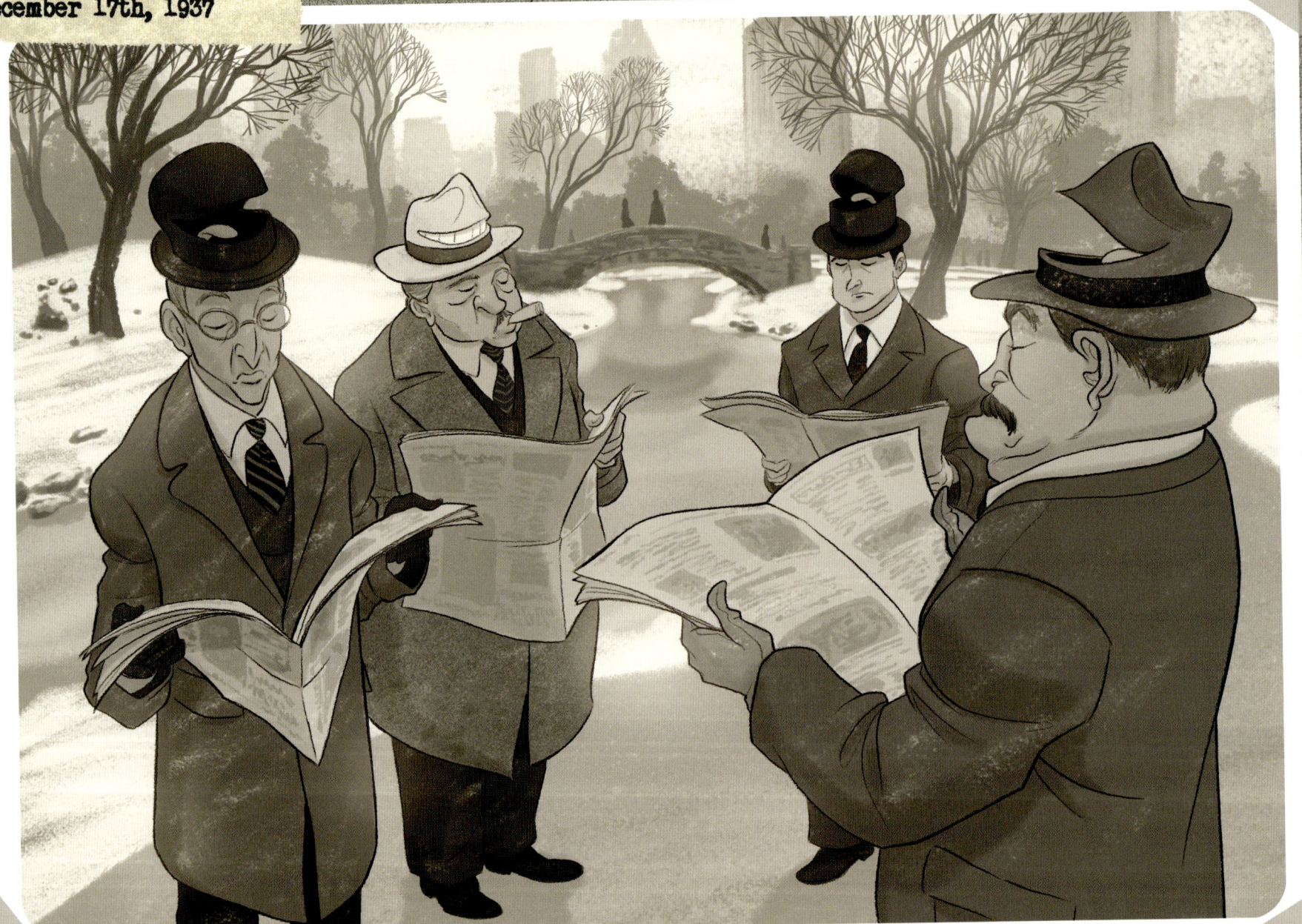

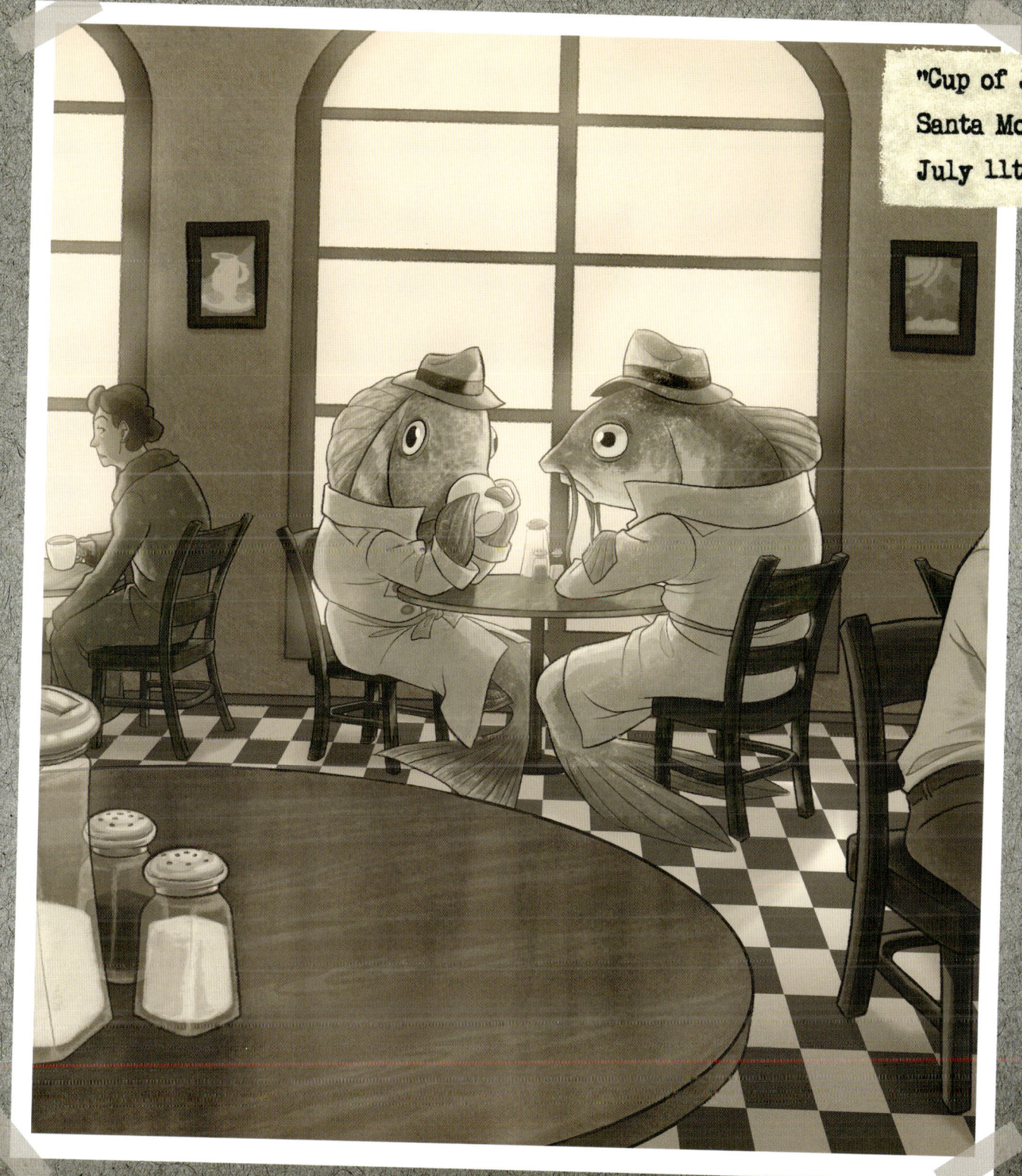

"Cup of Joe"
Santa Monica, CA
July 11th, 1942

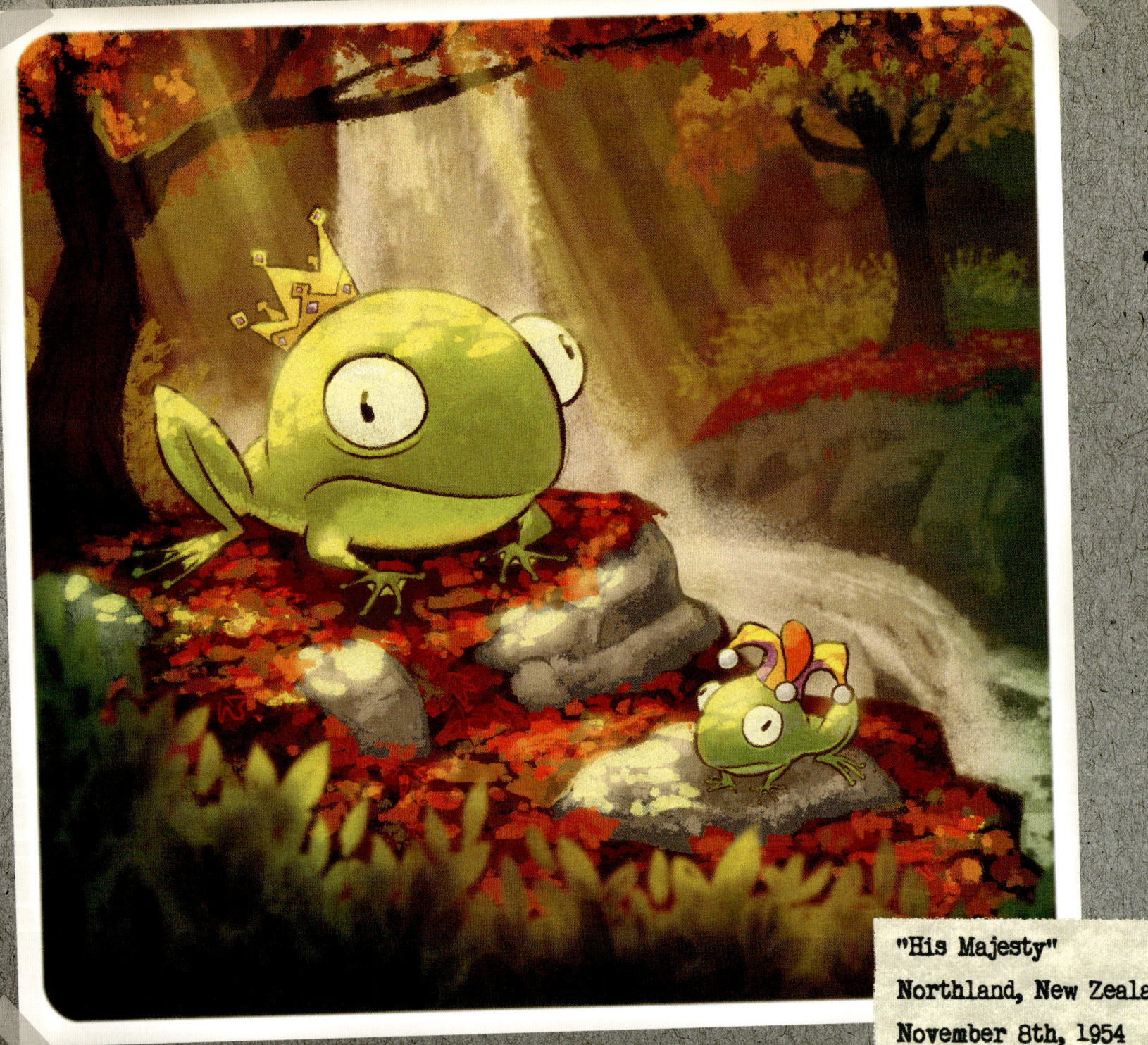

"His Majesty"
Northland, New Zealand
November 8th, 1954

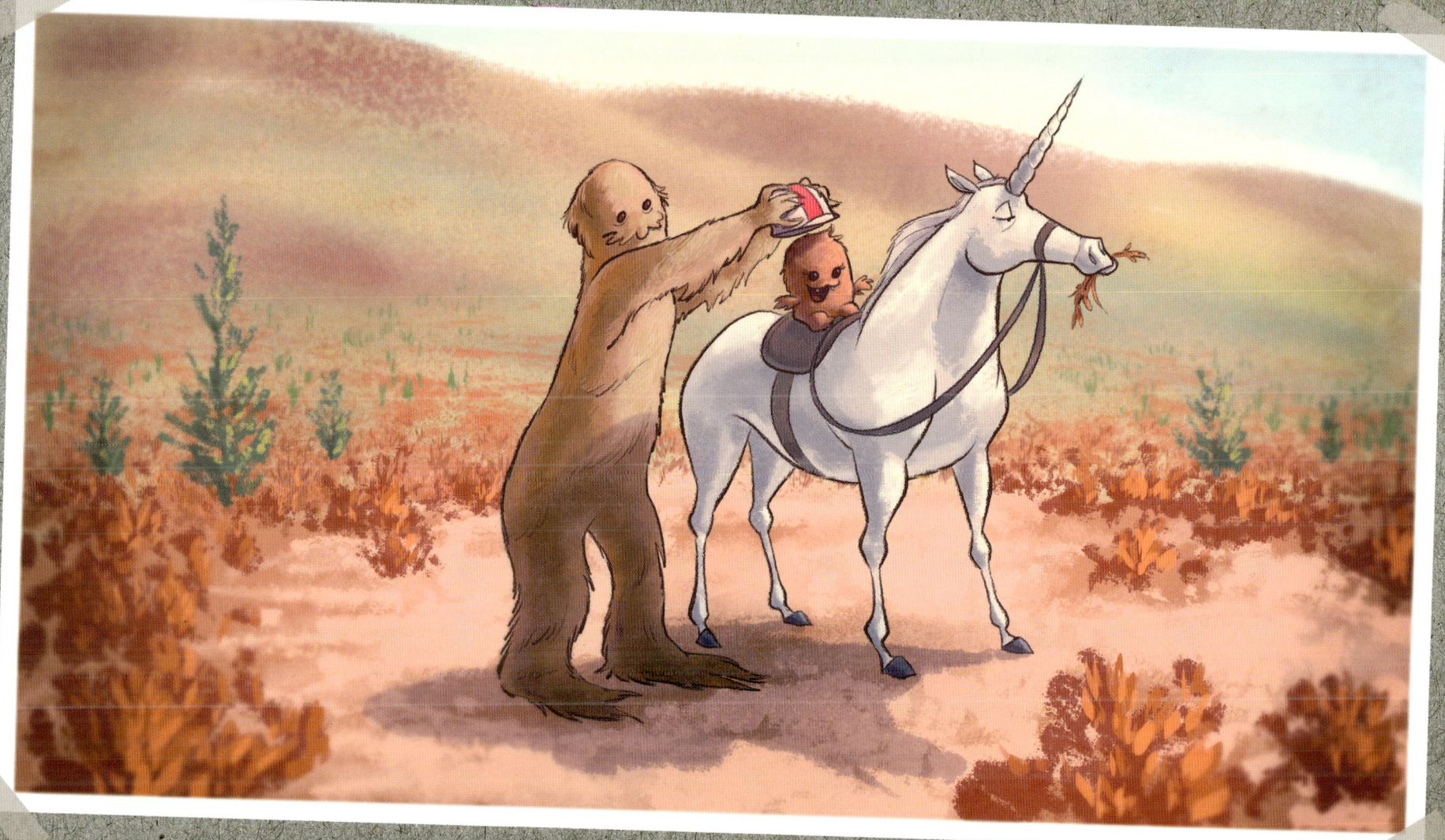

"Ready to Ride"
High Plains, Wyoming
September 24th, 1958

Justin Ridge

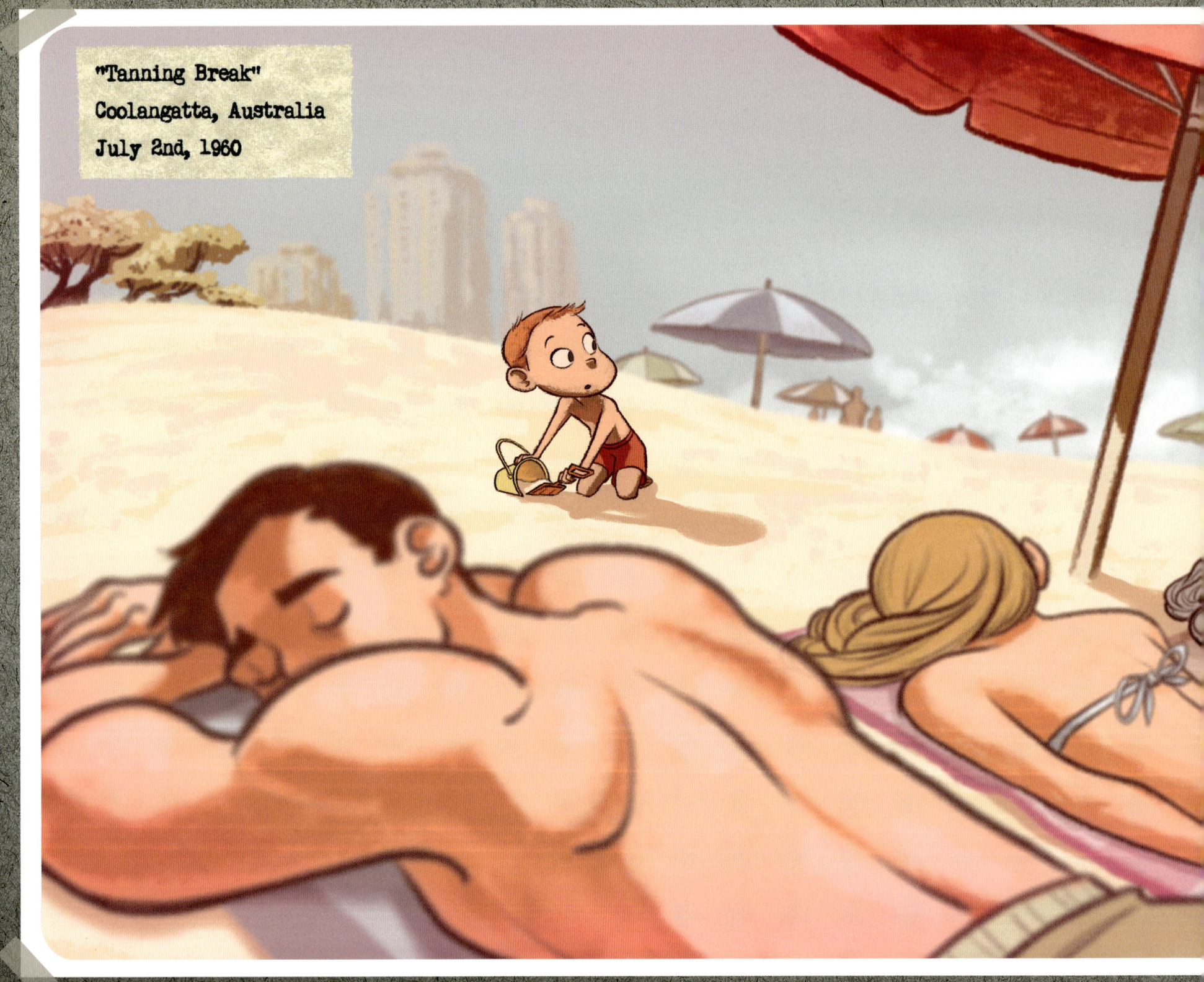

"Tanning Break"
Coolangatta, Australia
July 2nd, 1960

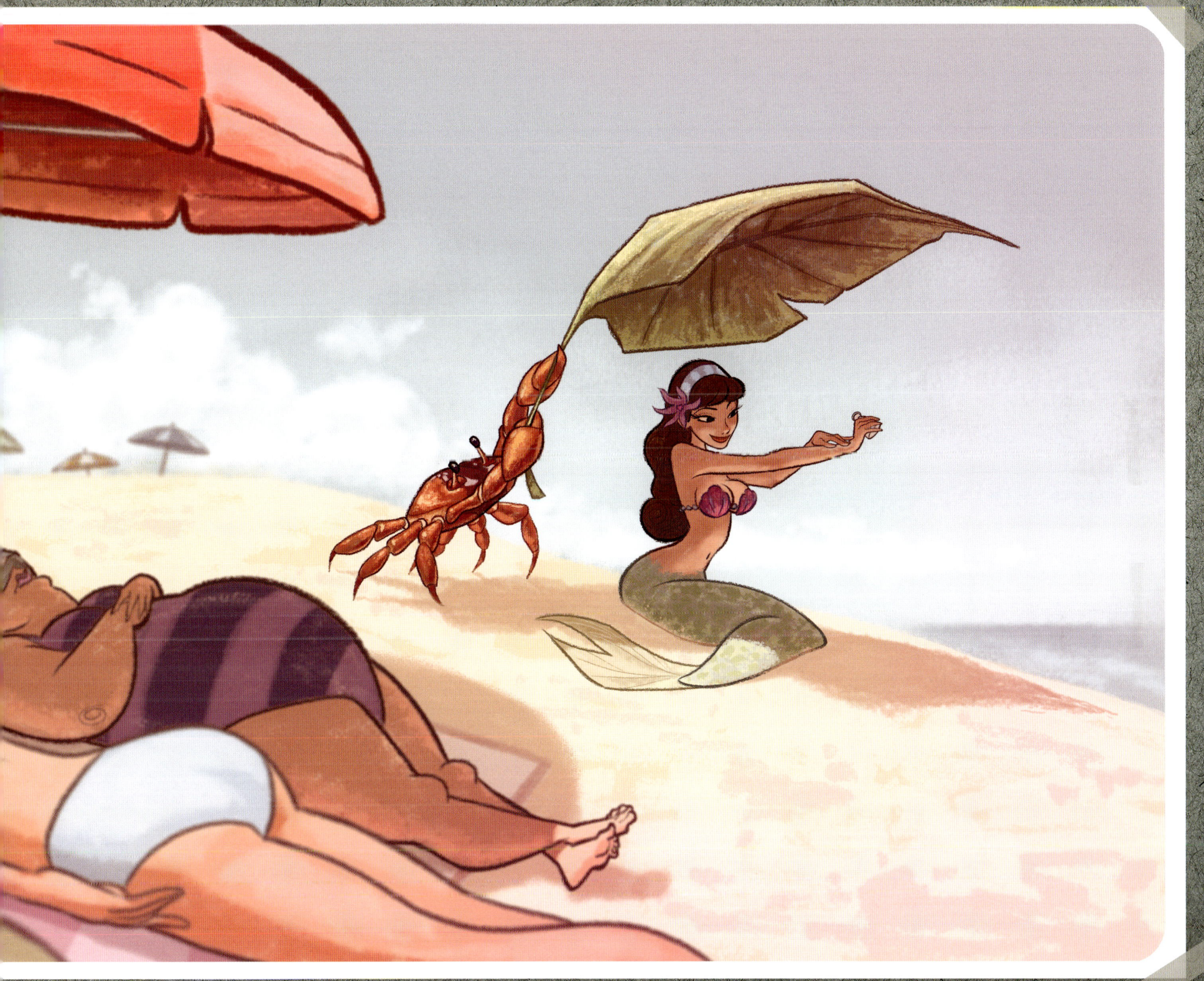

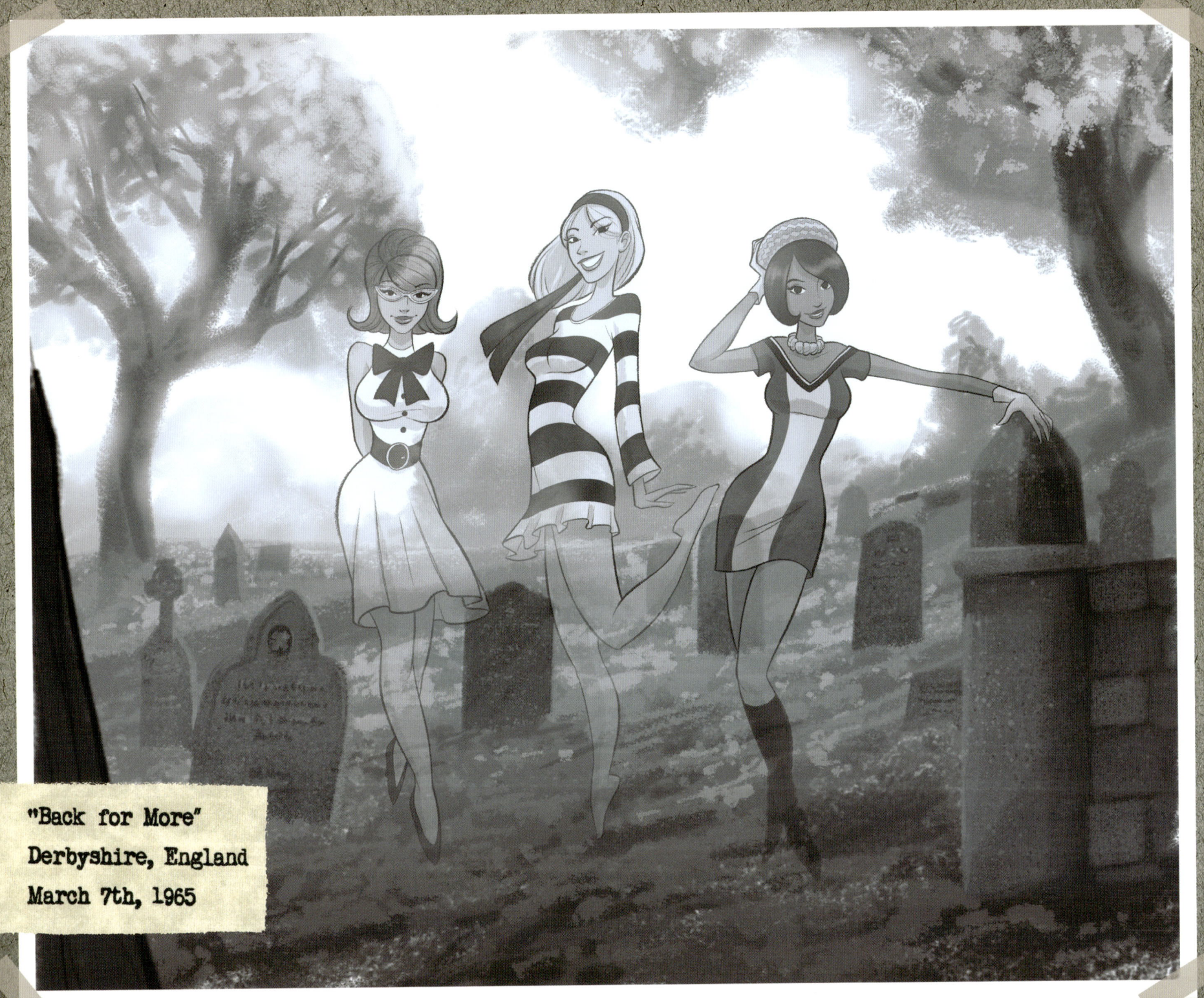

"Back for More"
Derbyshire, England
March 7th, 1965

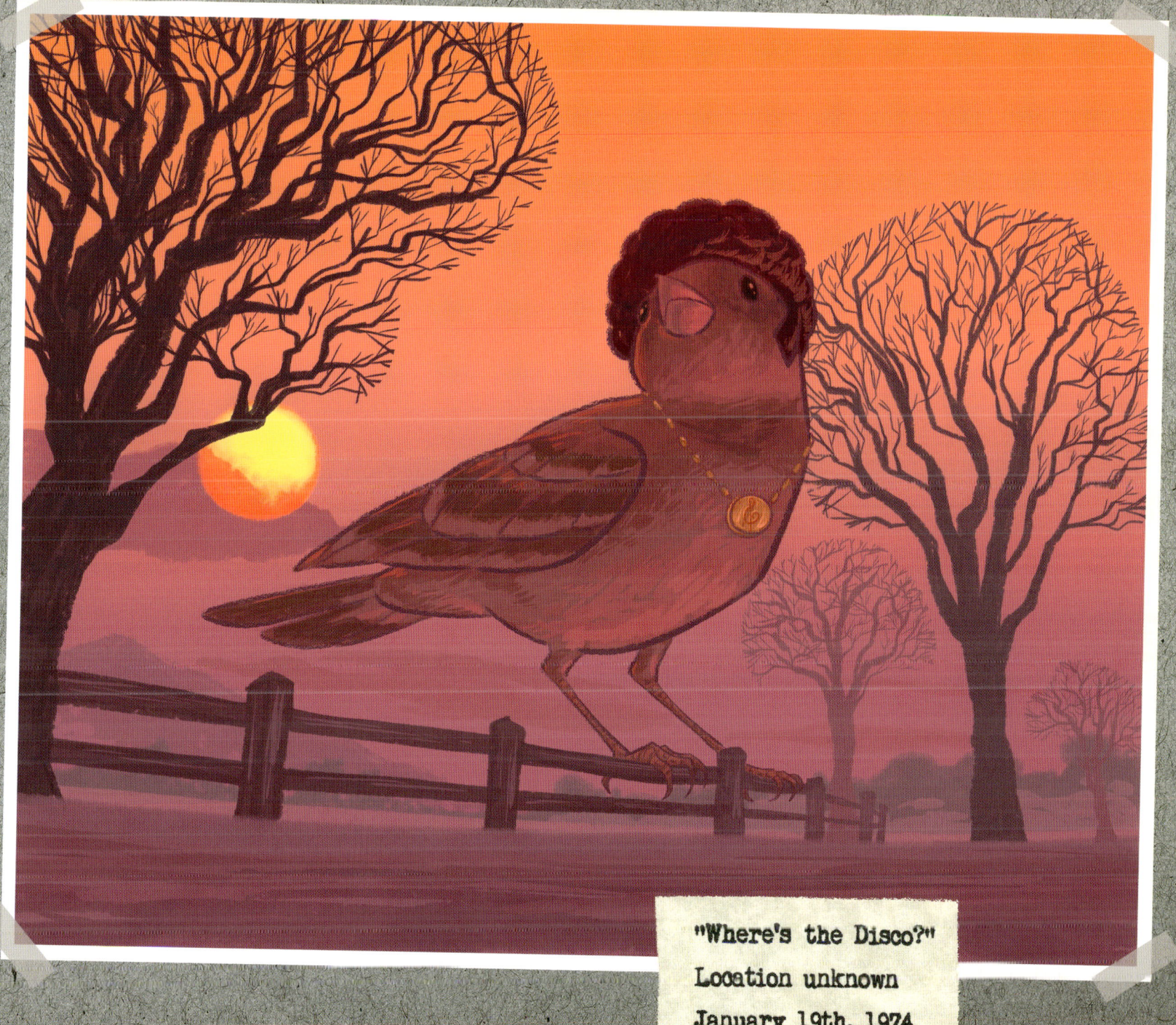

"Where's the Disco?"
Location unknown
January 19th, 1974

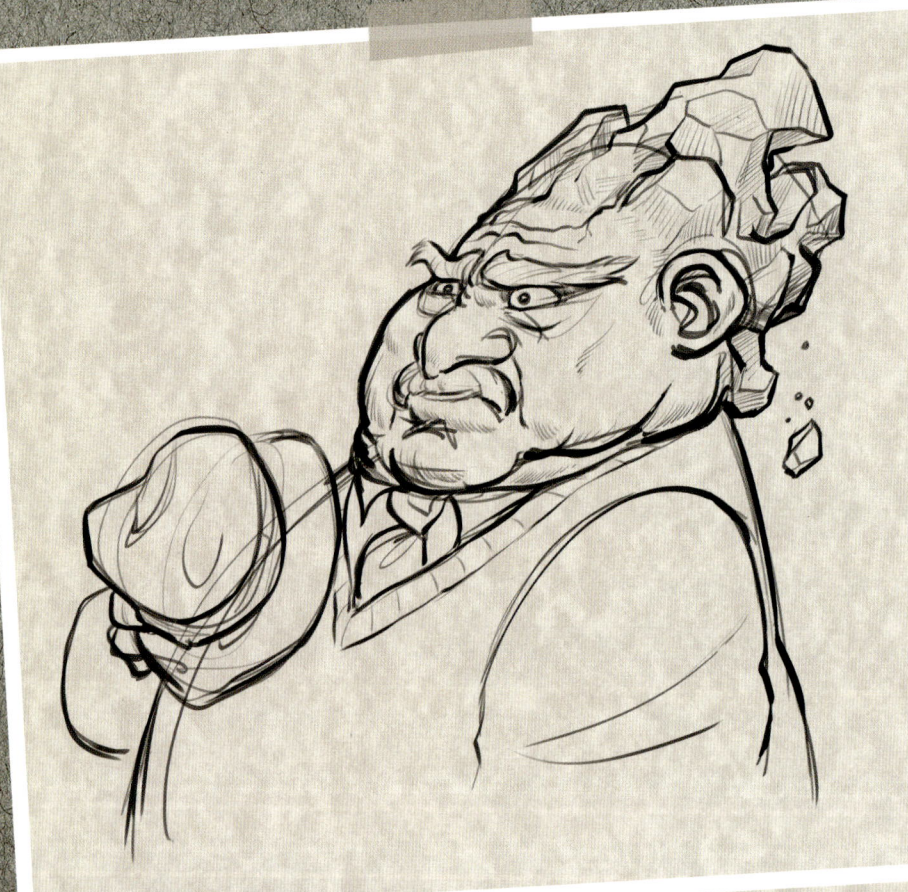

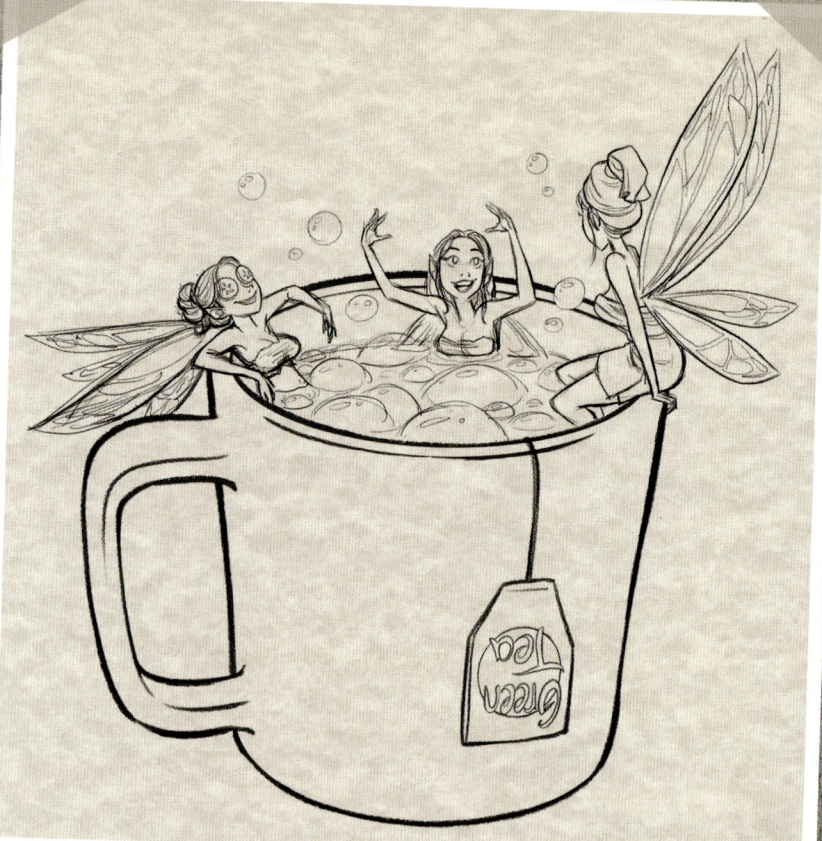

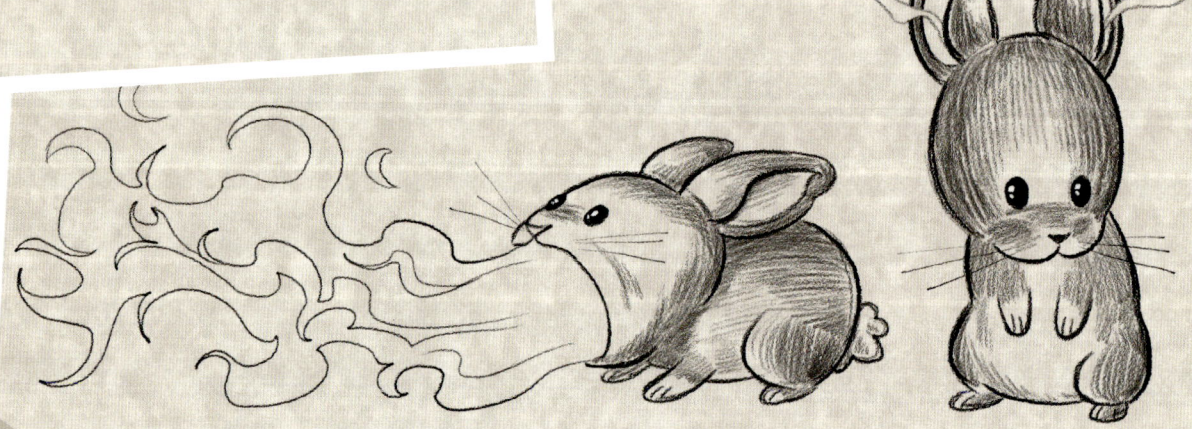

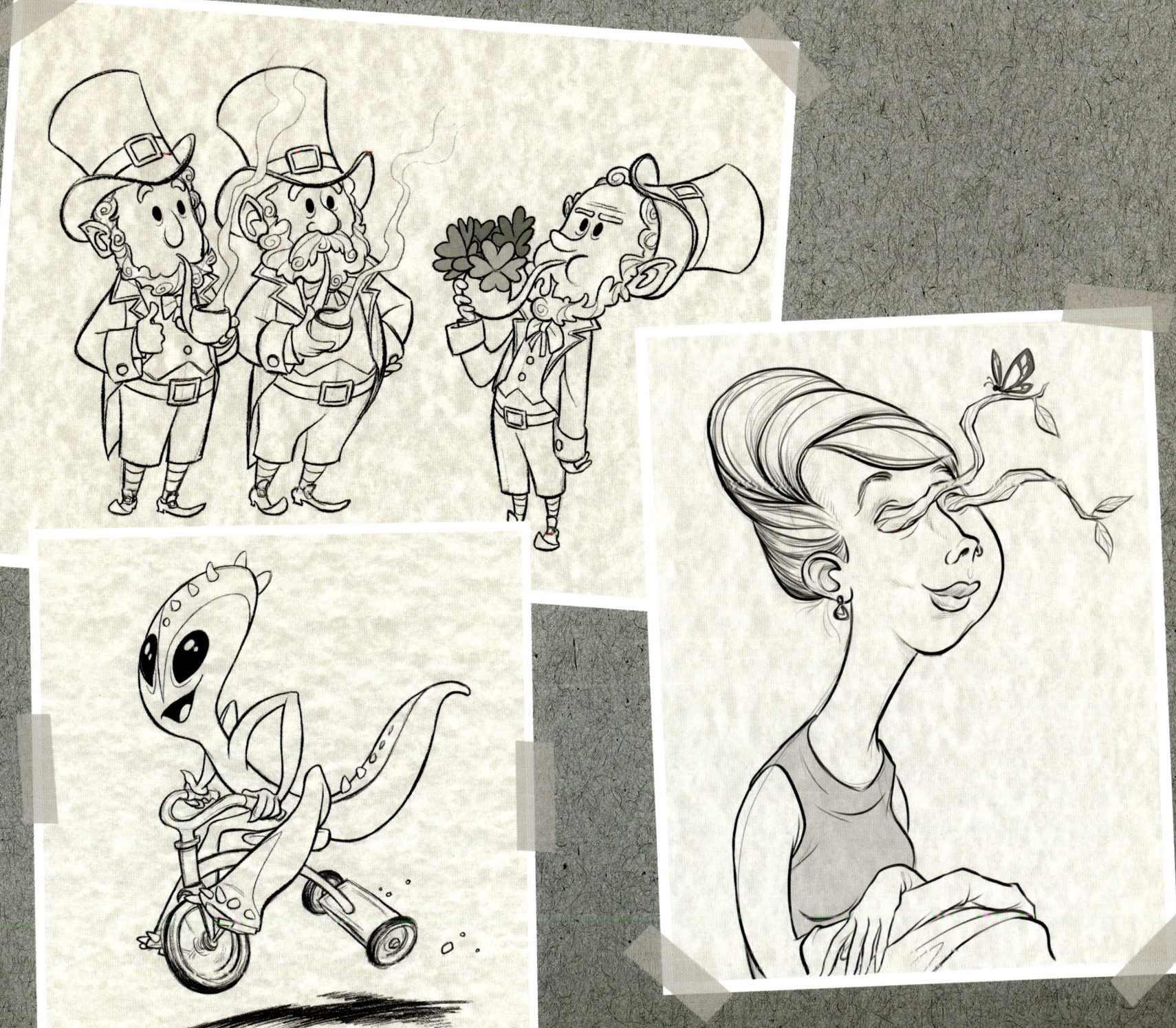

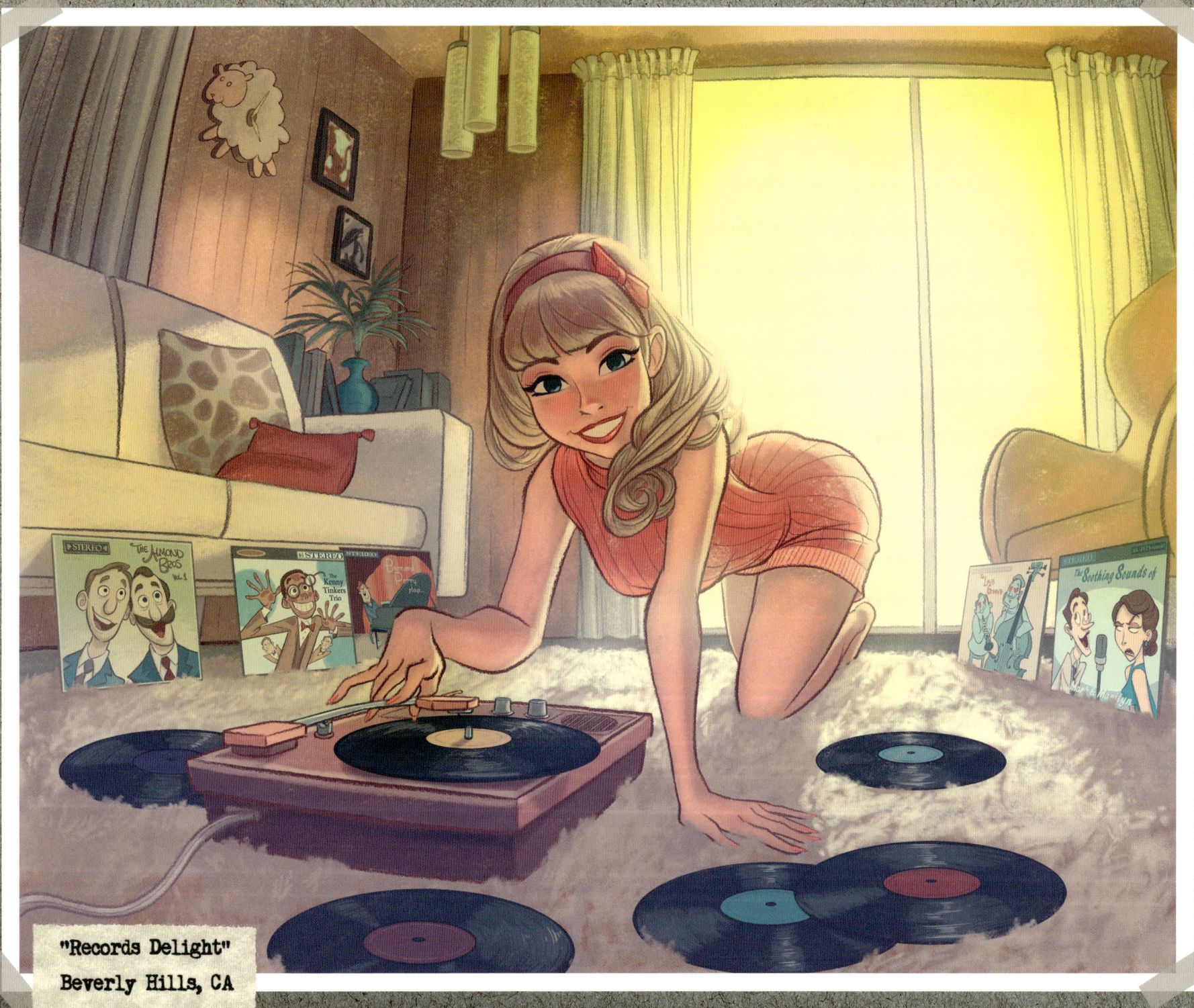

"Records Delight"
Beverly Hills, CA
July 23rd, 1963

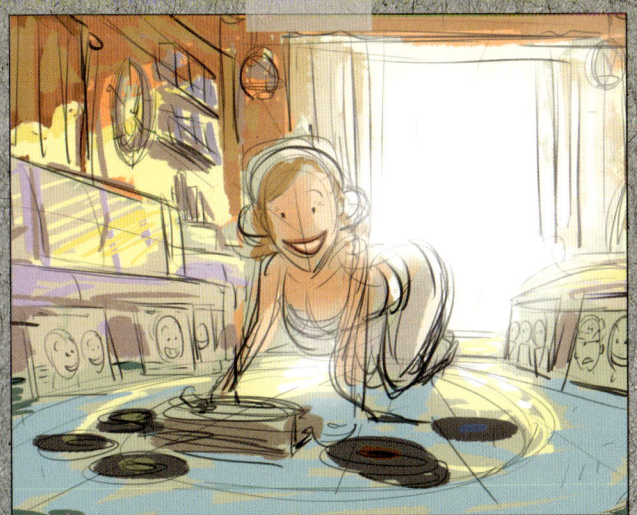

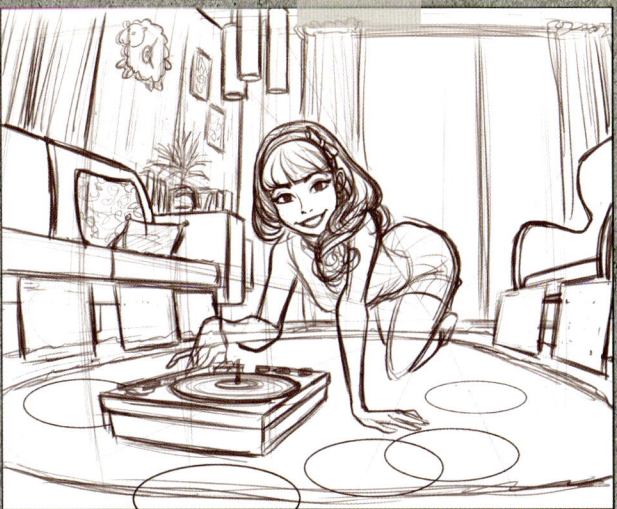

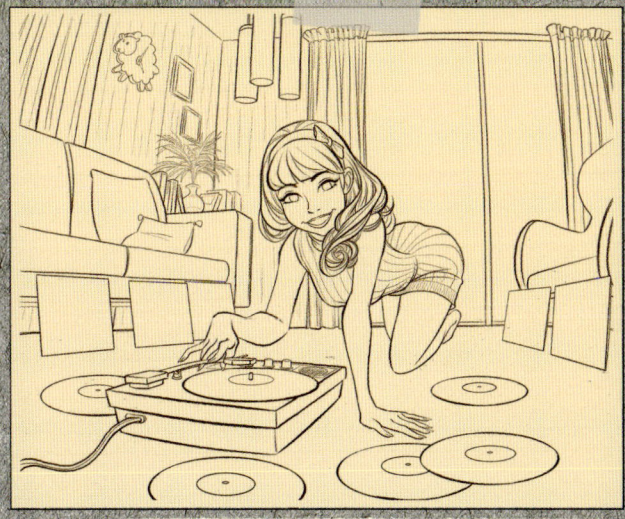

The first step is to quickly rough in the composition in Photoshop, and throw in a rough color comp underneath to get a sense of mood.

Next, I tie down the rough, making sure the forms are solid and work in space. This is where a lot of problems need to be solved, as any bad decisions can really snowball from here on out.

Using a textured brush to simulate a pencil, I clean up all of the lines, trying to keep the energy of the rough and not feel stiff or clunky.

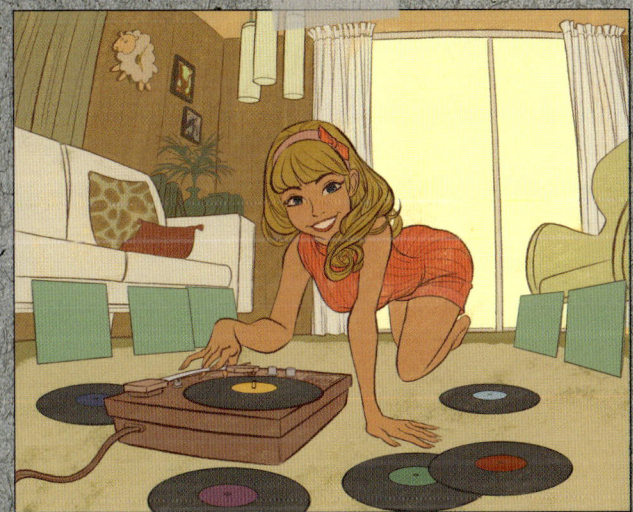

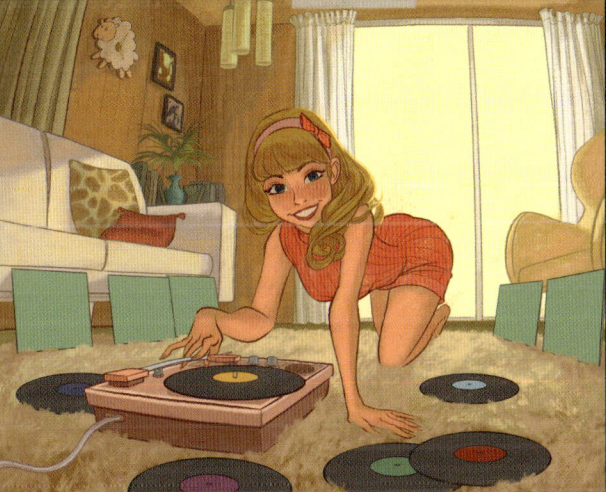

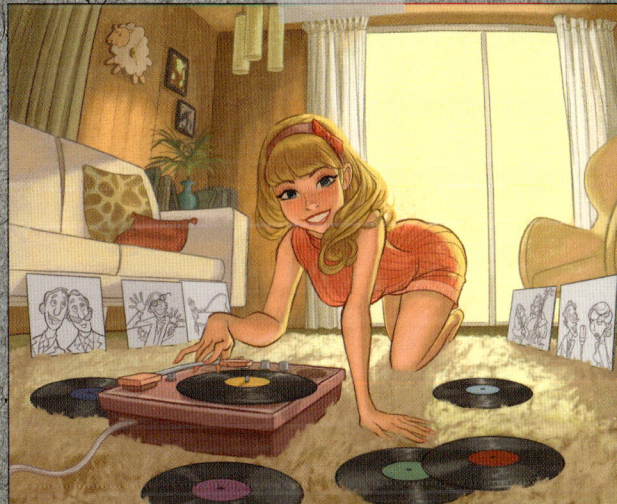

On separate levels, I block in the flat colors using another textured brush. Doing this reveals bits of the underlying colors, and helps the piece to maintain more of a handmade feeling.

I now start putting in the darks and lights and some textures, and coloring the lines to give a softer feeling. The woman is the focus here, so I want to make sure she'll have the most contrast.

Darks and lights are enhanced more, with the brightest light on the woman. More texture and detail is painted in, and I will lastly add some adjustment layers for levels and color balancing.

KILIAN PLUNKETT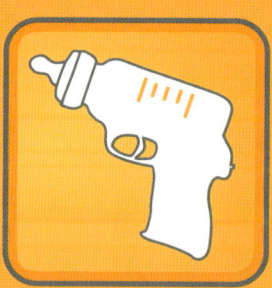

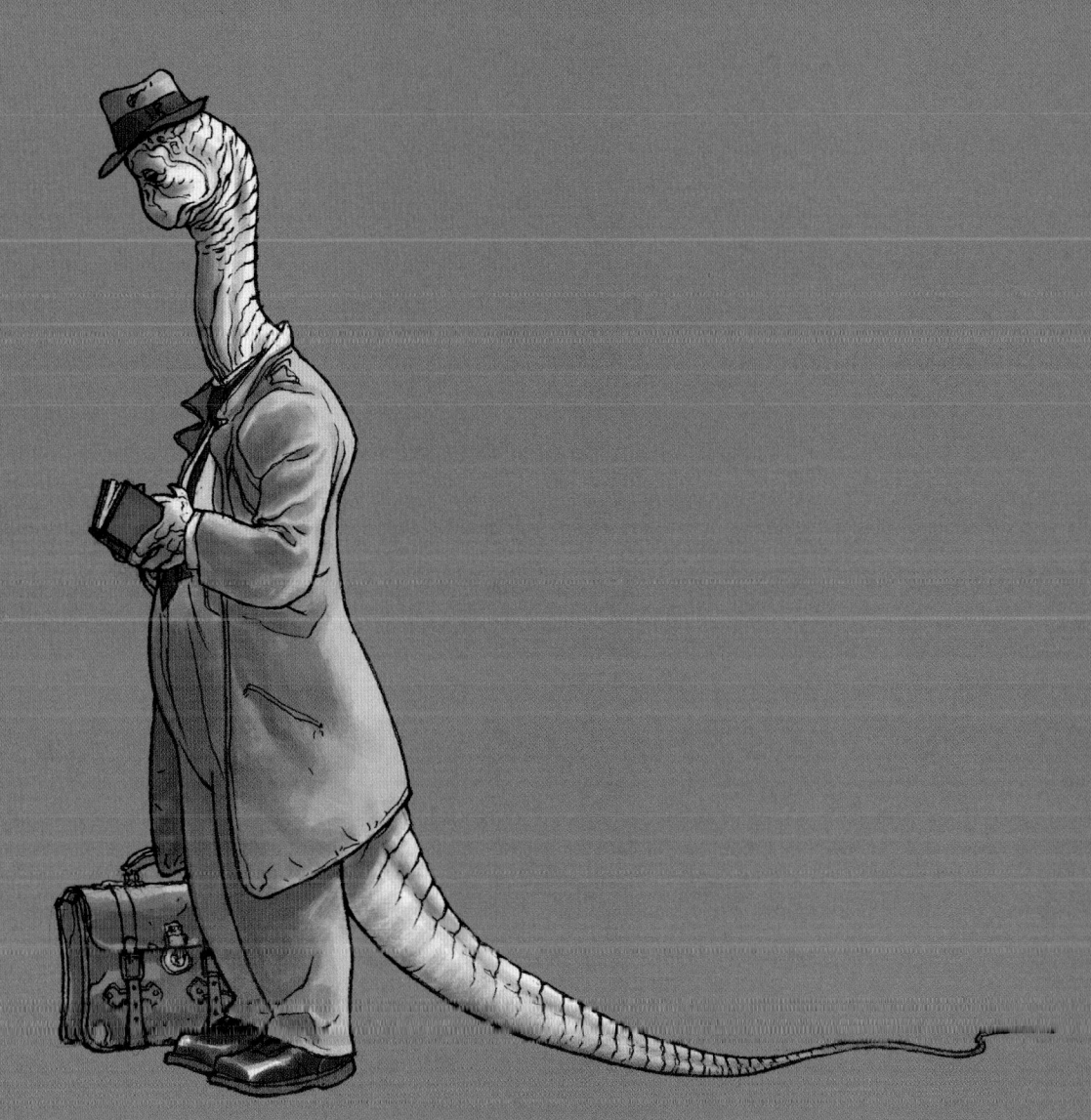

THE WINGED GOD'S WHISPER

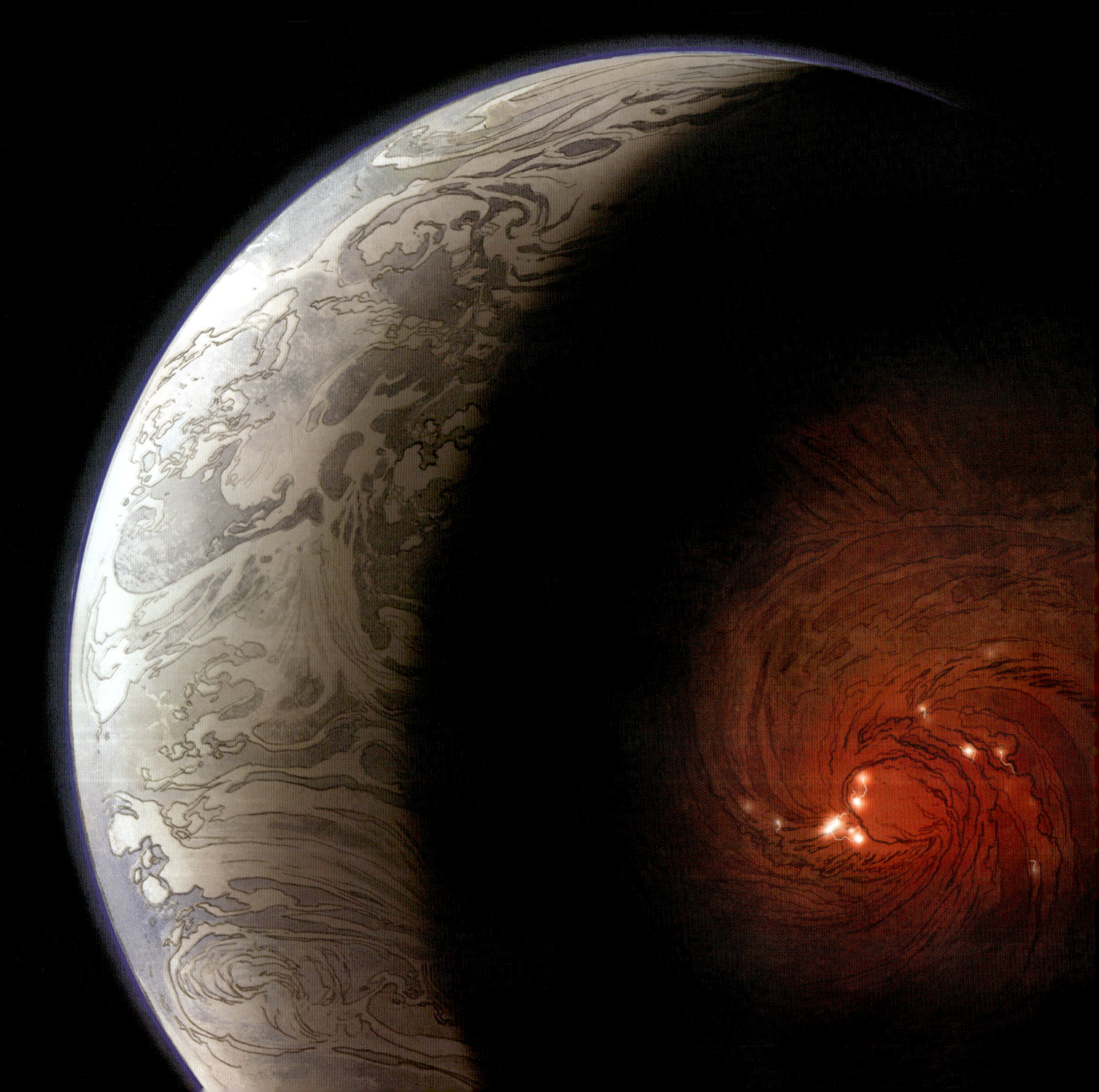

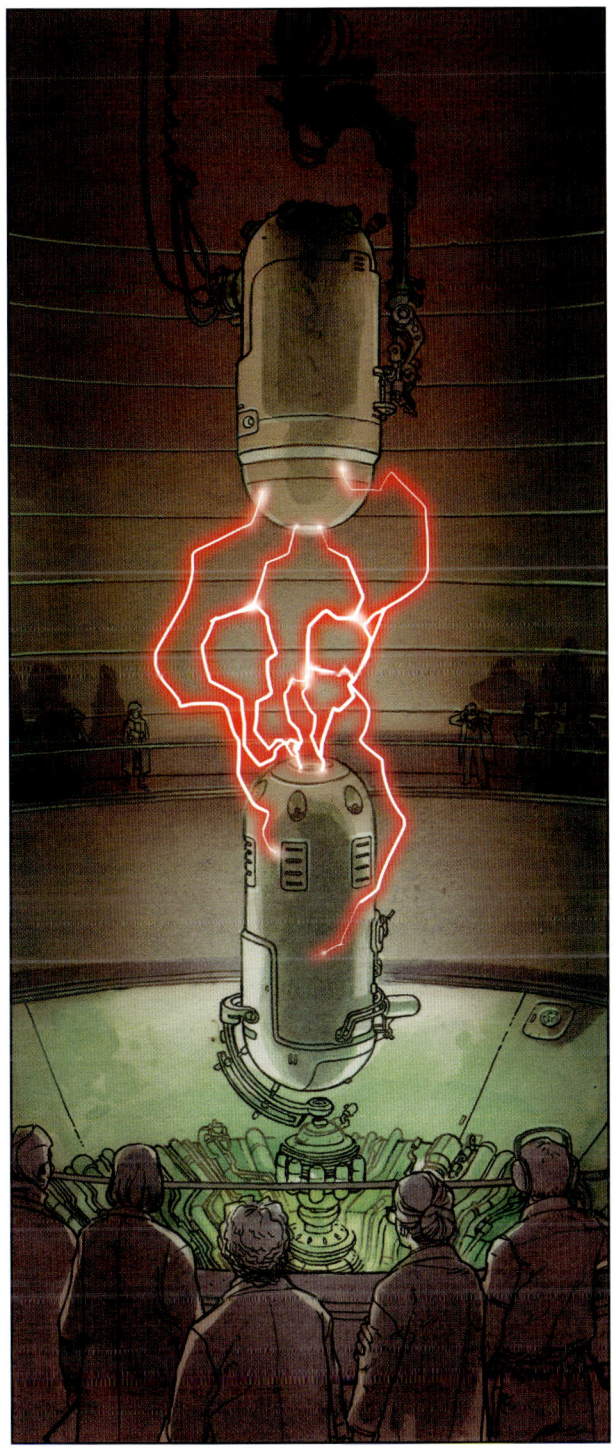

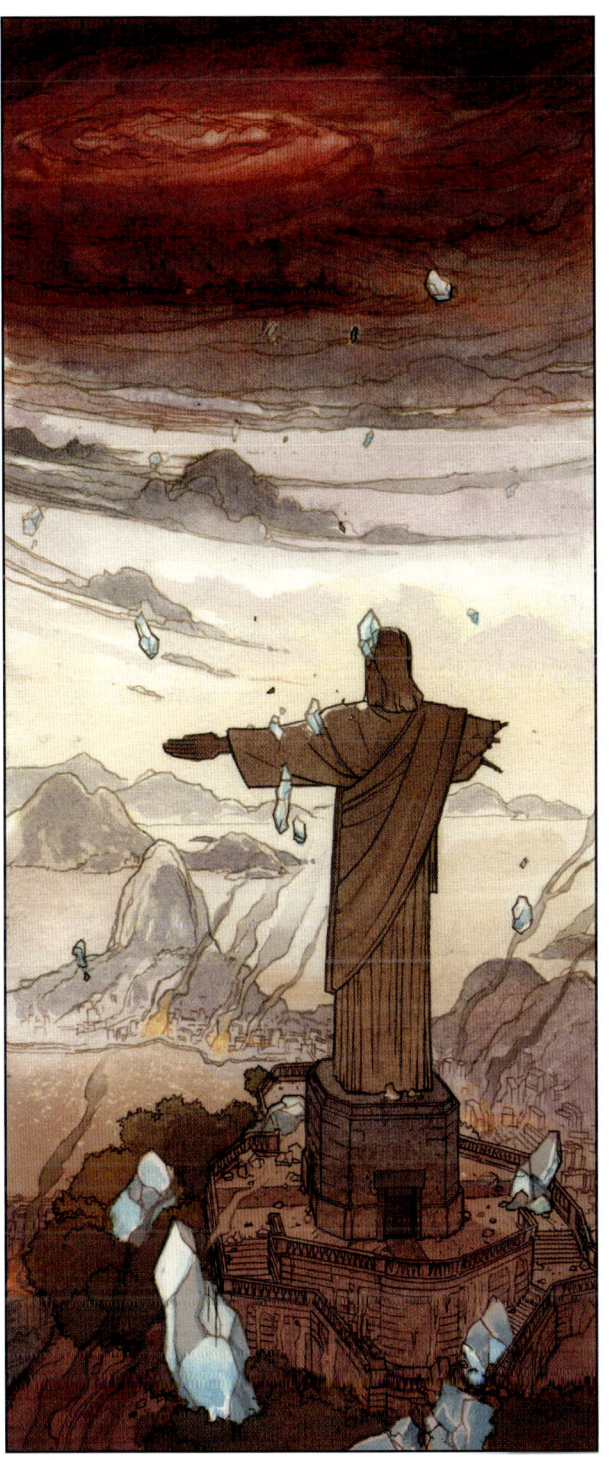

This is a planet called Earth, one in a continuum of near-infinite variations. If an Alpha-State Earth ever existed, it has been lost in the constantly shifting timelines of what is estimated to be the mid-twentieth century AD.

At some point earlier in this period, it appears a powerful nation conducted a program of experimental tests. Their purpose was to generate and sustain a contained quantum lens, through which alternate realities could briefly manifest and coexist with the original, "real" world.

The zone of potentiality created was evidently unstable. A chain reaction ensued, resulting in the Quantum Storm, visible from outer space, that now drifts across the sky.

Within this maelstrom, portals to other worlds flicker in and out of existence. Life forms and artifacts can pass through these rifts intact. An early instance of this phenomenon was the hail of "Philosopher's Stones" over Central and South America. These crystals possess many bizarre qualities, among them levitation. What makes the stones so highly prized, however, is their innate ability to dampen the effects of the quantum field.

In spite of its fearsome appearance, the storm of chaos is eerily quiet as it approaches; only the hissing of wind precedes it. When the storm first coalesced over South America it was dubbed the "whisper of Quetzalcoatl." This ancient Mesoamerican deity, creator and destroyer of worlds, usually took the form of a feathered serpent.

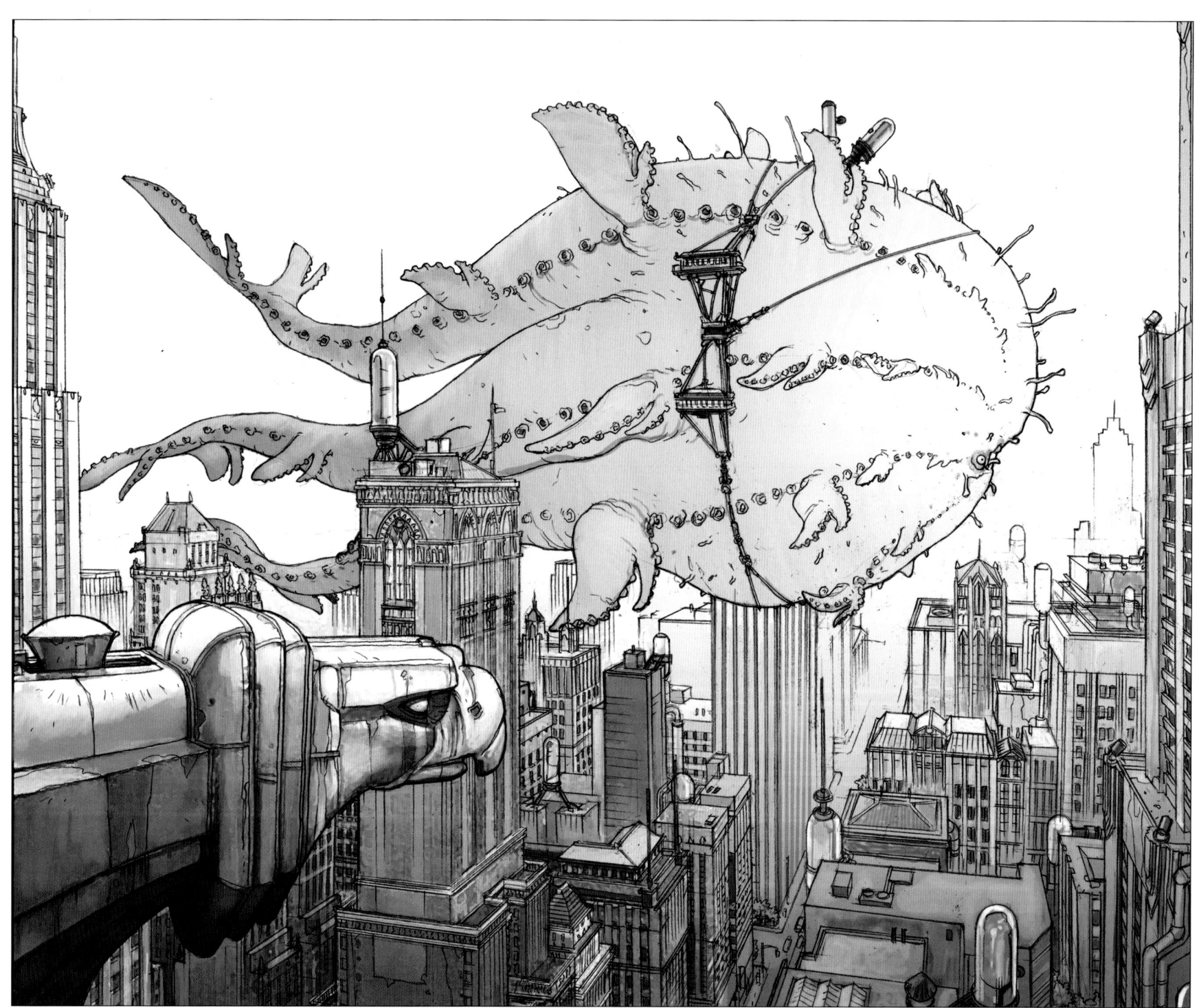

Impossible Ecosphere (opposite)

The range of life forms from other Earths that can survive across realities is staggering. This Impossipod gliding through midtown Manhattan generates its own improbability field, making it seemingly indestructible.

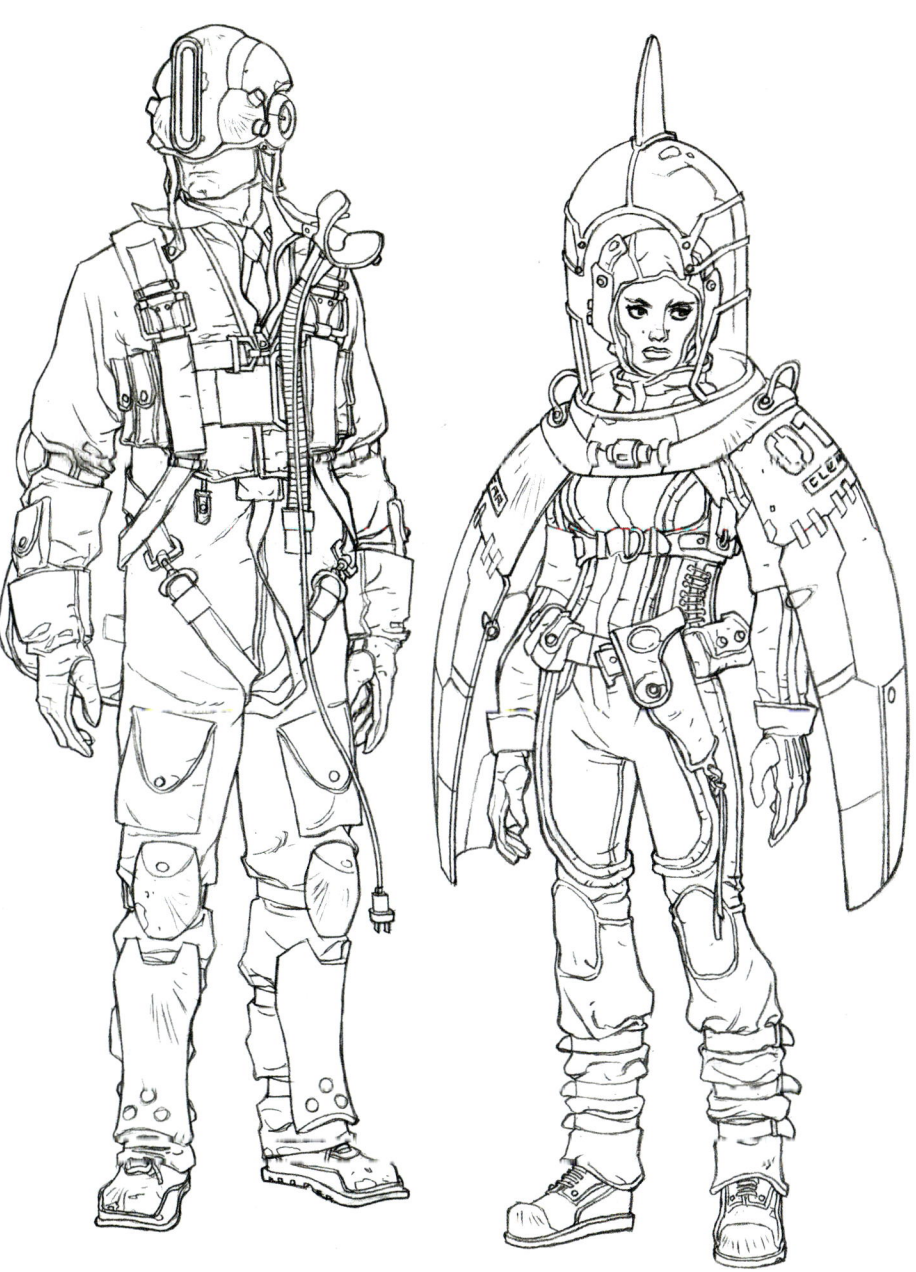

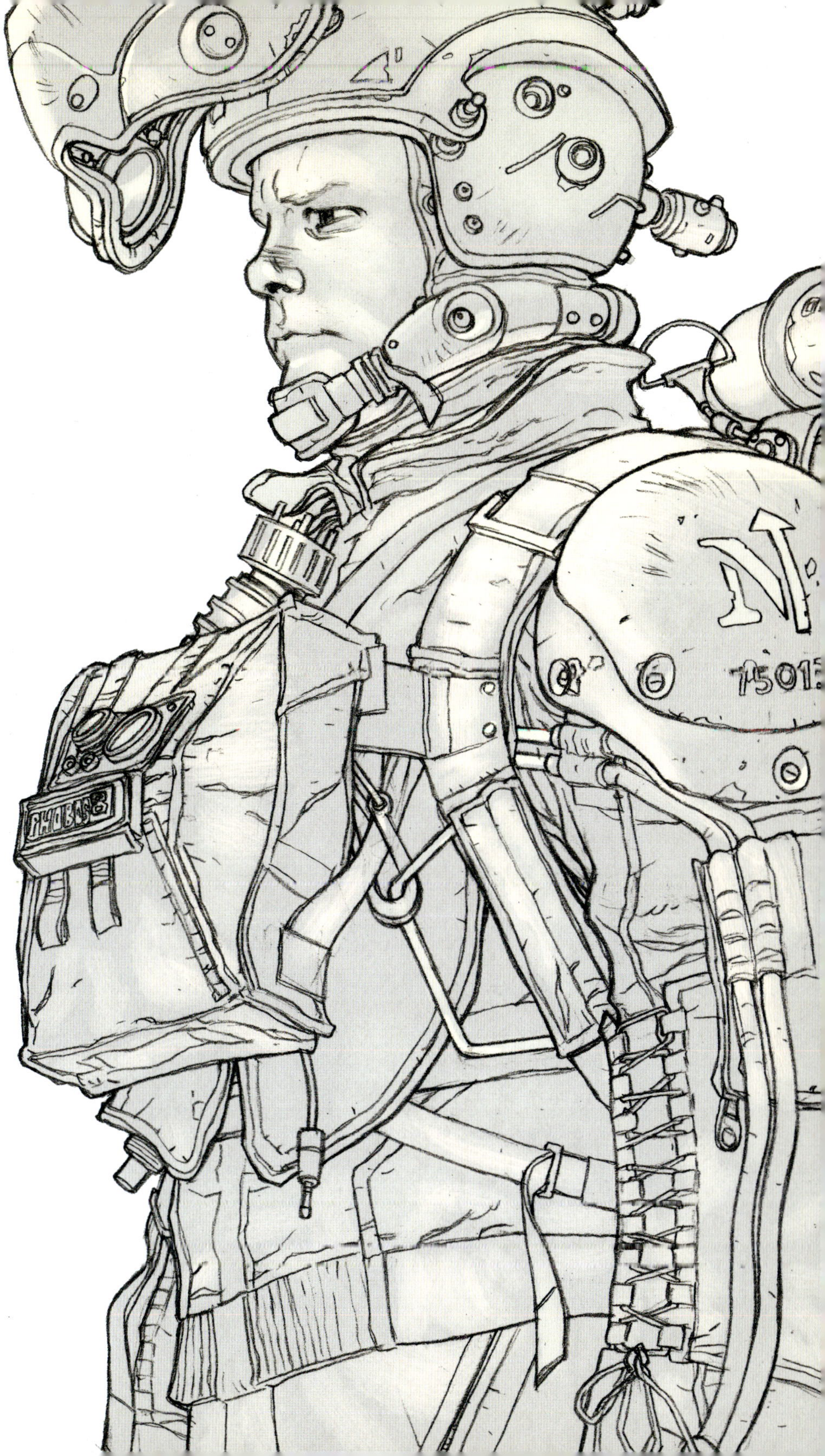

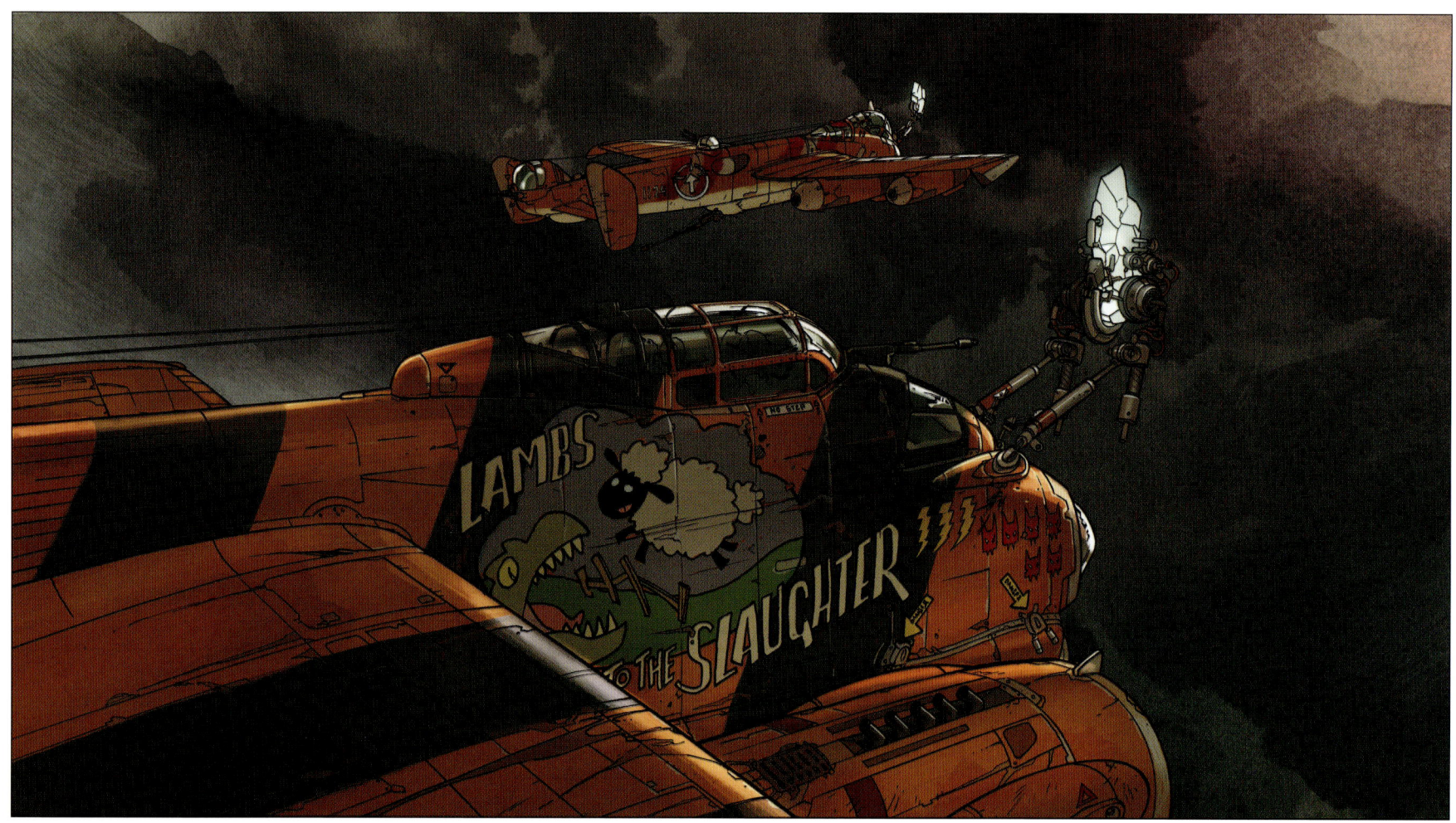

Cryptopilgrims (previous page)

The destruction of civilization in the Southern Hemisphere led to the formation of the Northern Hemispheric Actuality Alliance, most often called North Hem by its citizens. Volunteers sign up for dangerous exploratory missions, flying into the storm, hoping to discover a means to dissipate it and return their world to stability. Mission patches and dog tags are regulation; all other rigs and apparatuses are at the individual Cryptopilgrim's discretion.

Lambs to the Slaughter (above)

The tone of the Noseart found on many North Hem Aircraft tends toward the mordant, as so many flights into the whispering storm end in disappearance, death, or worse.

Goddess of Chance (opposite)

Another recurring motif seen throughout the exploratory forces of North Hem is Eris, goddess of chance, usually depicted wielding a crystal-powered chaos-containment device of one type or another. Variations on this concept have adorned structures, crew gear, vehicles, and weaponry for decades. The enormous risk each mission poses is offset by the potential rewards a successful flight can offer. Vast fortunes and great discoveries have been made by those brave or unbalanced enough to enter the vortex and return alive and sane.

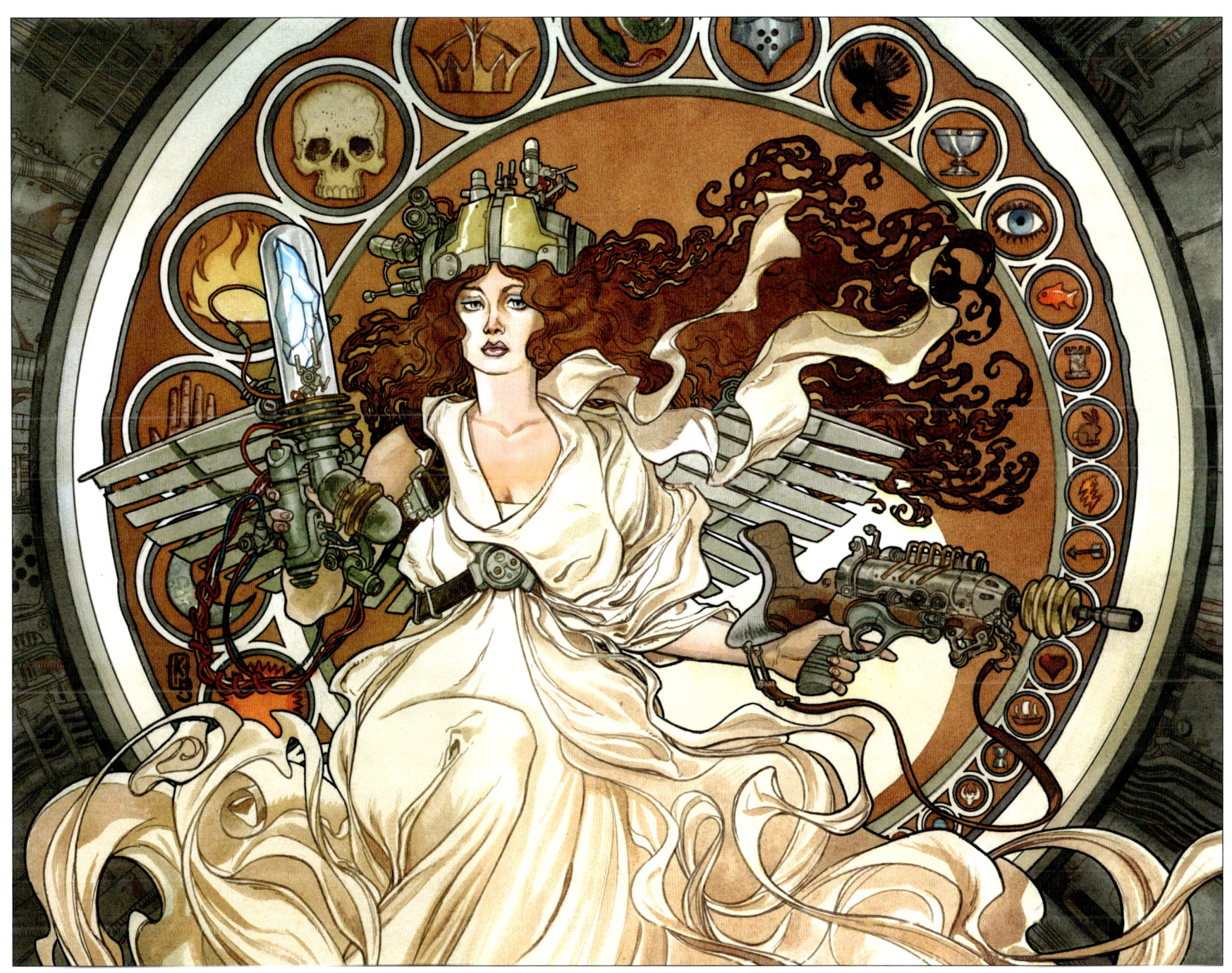

Kilian Plunkett

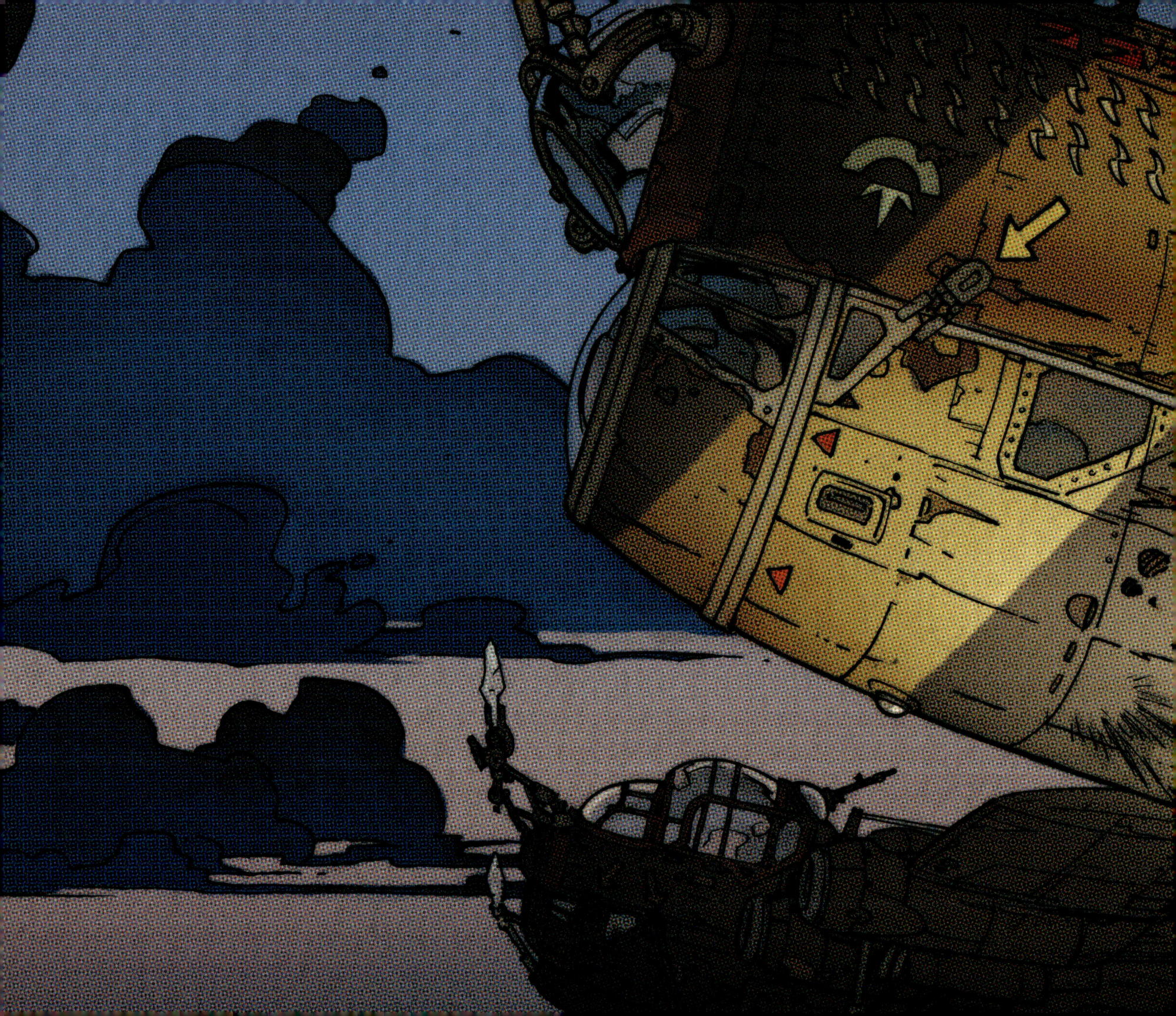

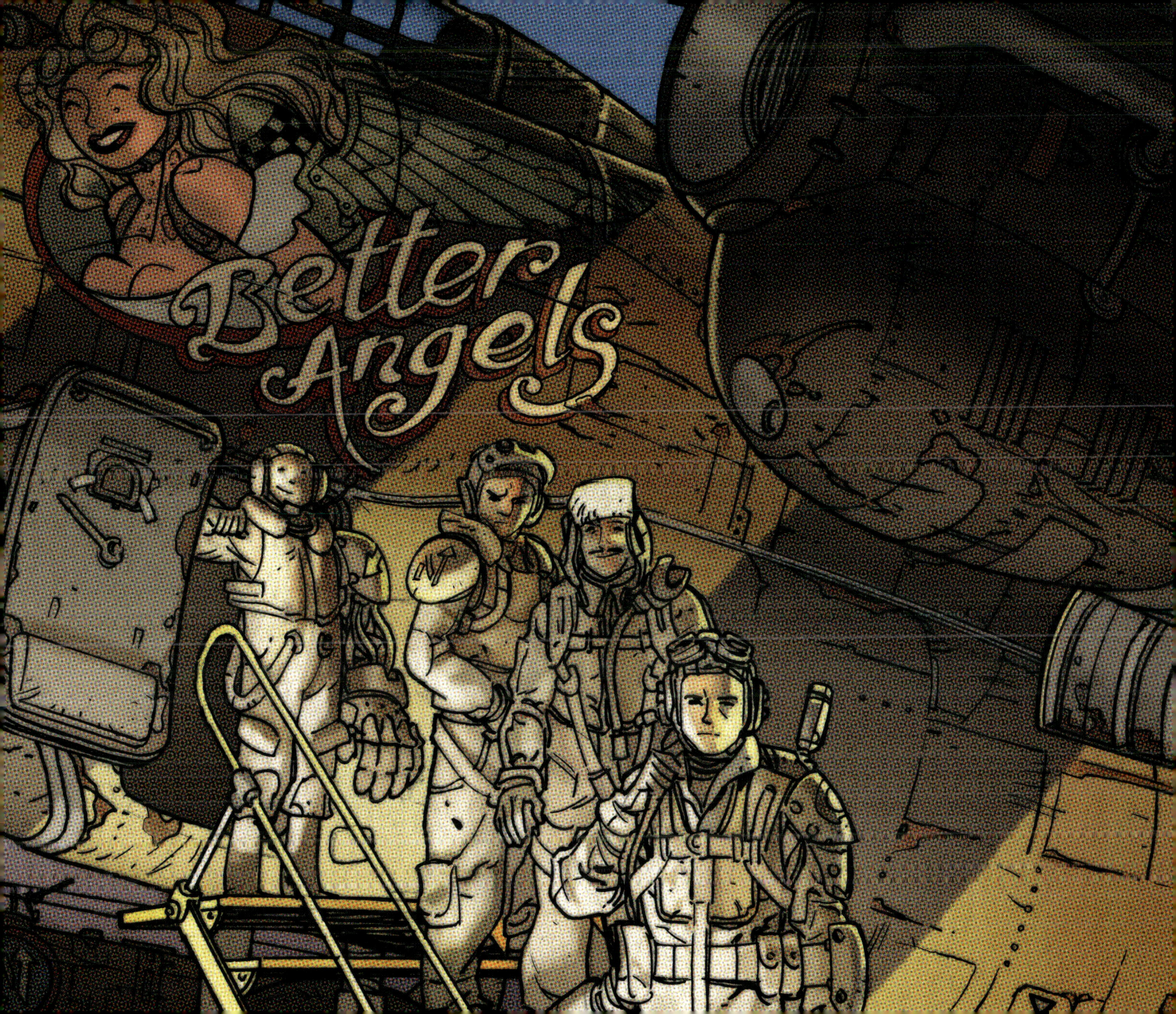

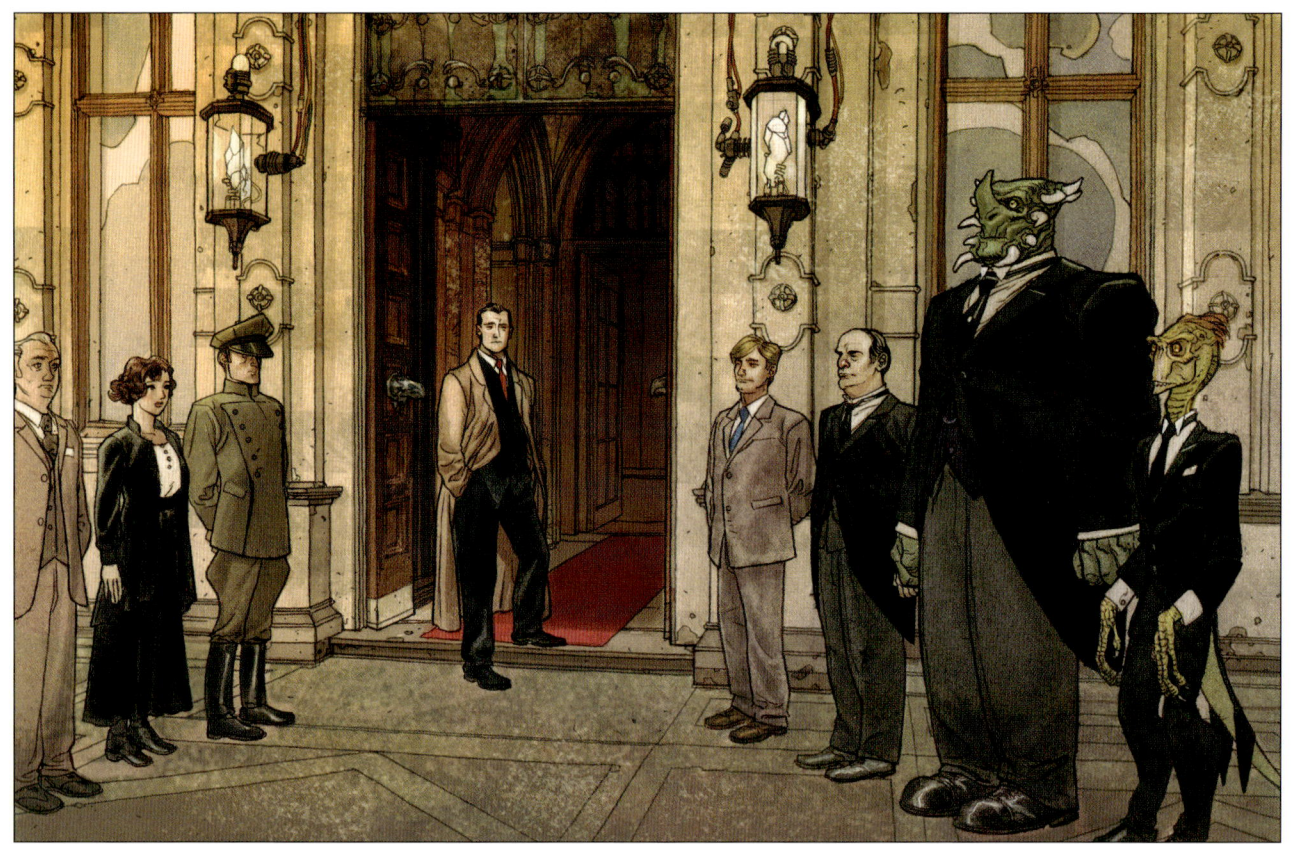

Falling Star Hall

A self-made adventurer, Chester August would likely have found his fortune and glory in any eventuality. The lone survivor of the ill-fated Serendipity Squadron, his five sorties into the maelstrom have made him the most famous North Hem Pilgrim in the world. His coterie includes several of the homosauri species that appeared en masse after the largest landfall the cloud made in the northern hemisphere, in the badlands of South Dakota in the year 38 PS (Post Storm).

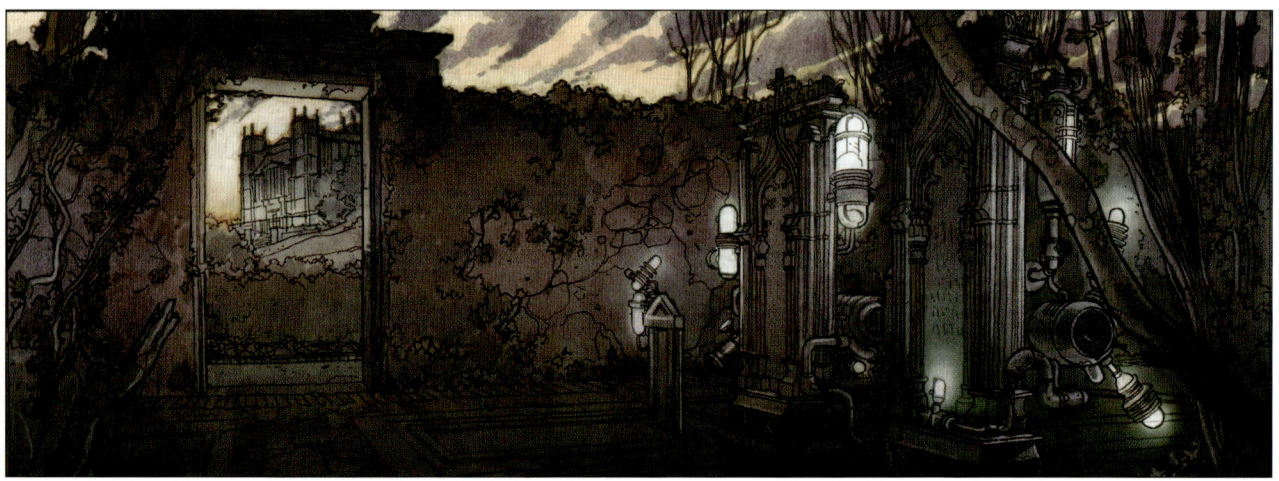

Money offers no protection from the chaos cloud. The family graveyard on the grounds of Falling Star Hall had these reanimation suppressors attached to every headstone after an unfortunate bit of business with great uncle Snidely.

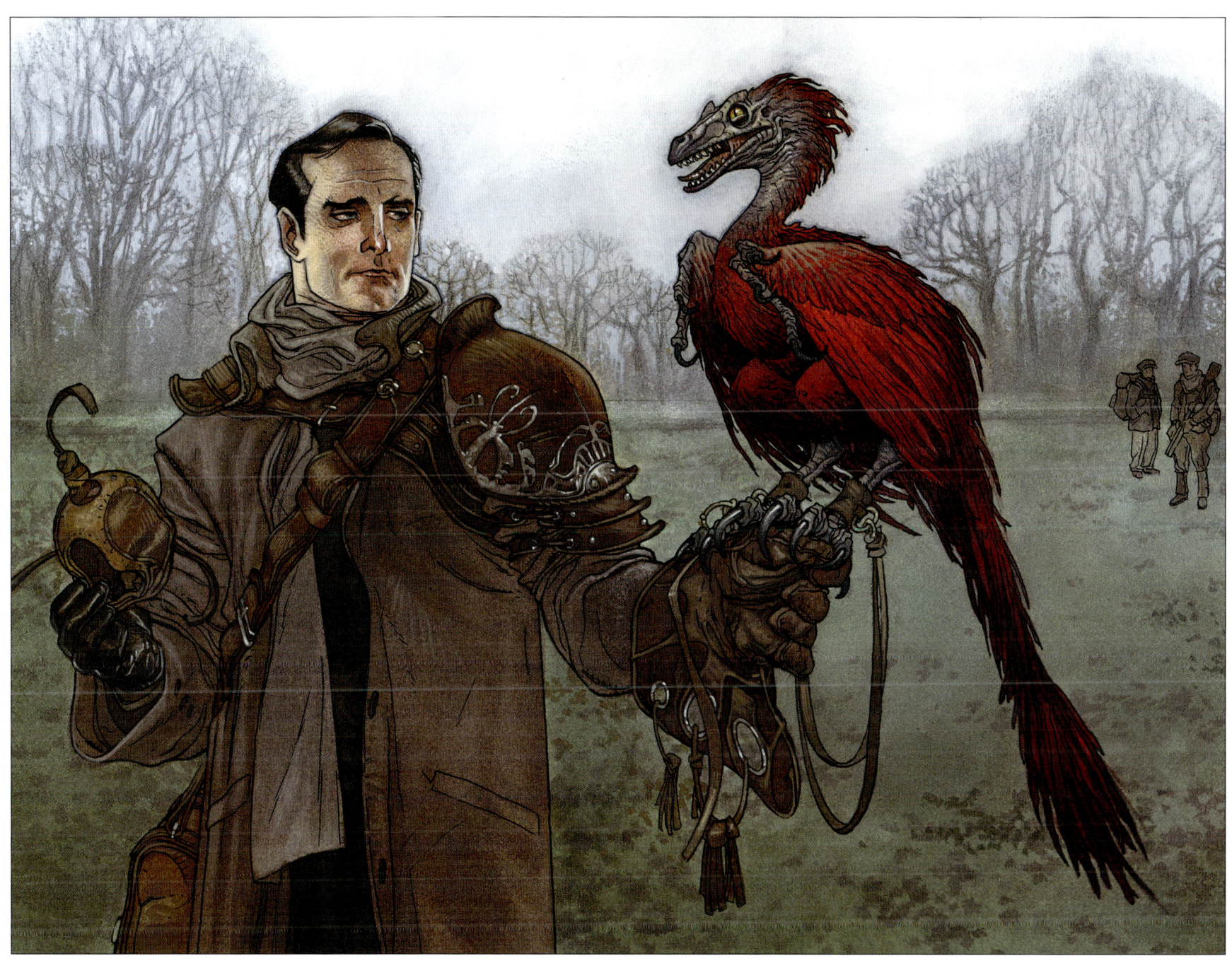

Raptor. Captain August out with his archaeopteryx, one of the very rare pure dinosaur species to drop from the cloud in what seems to be a straight line from the old history.

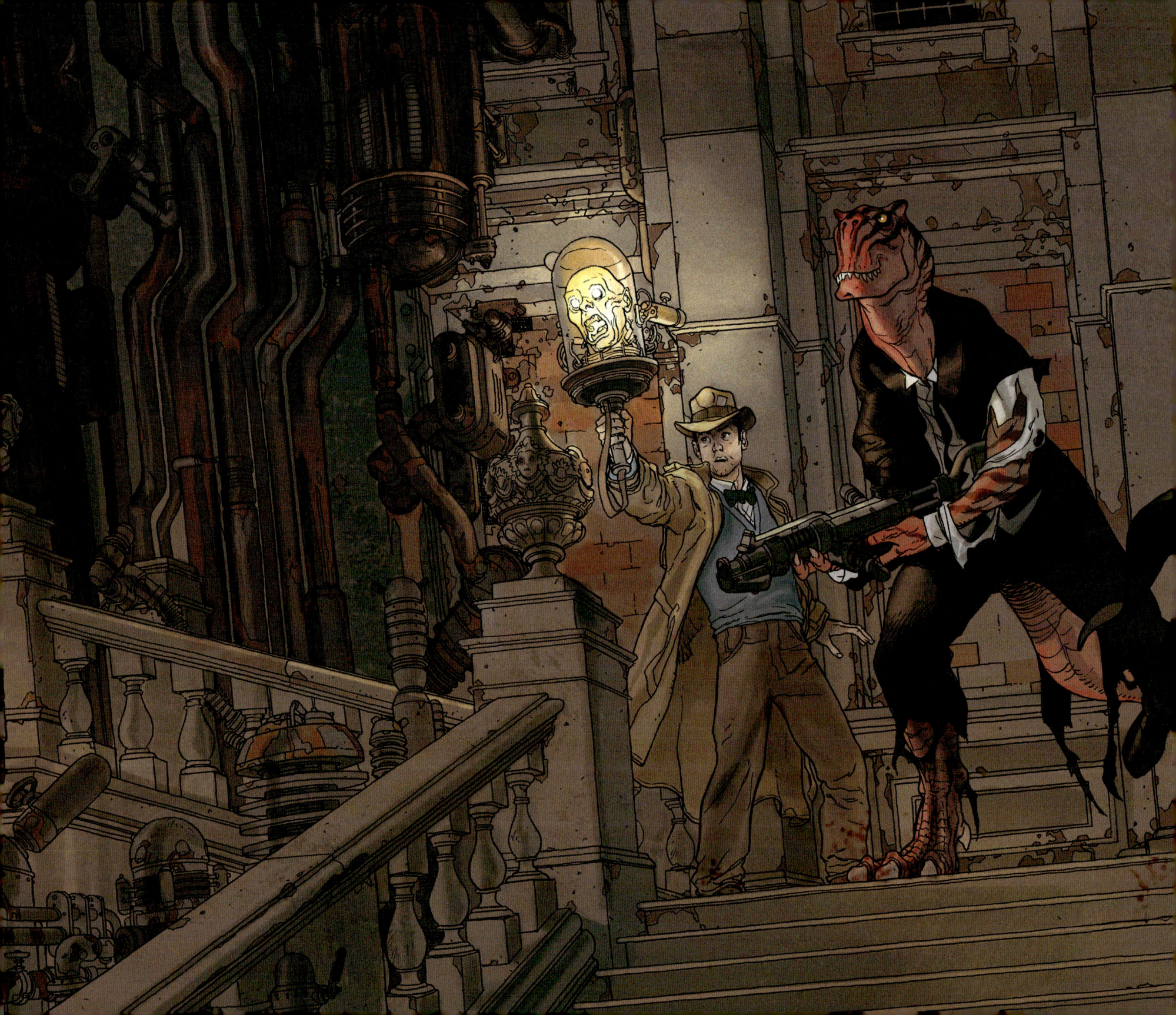

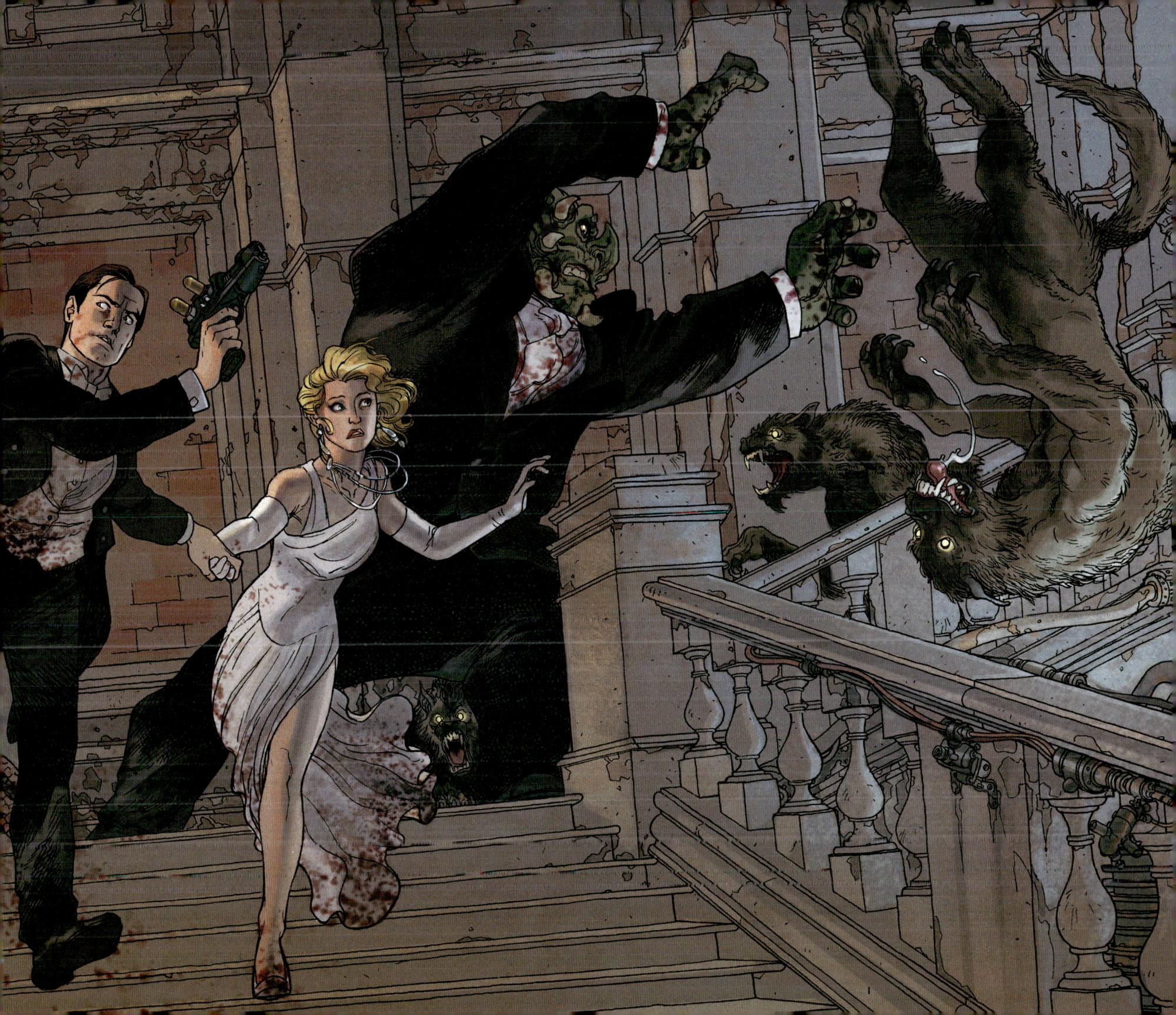

New Year's End (previous spread)

At a climactic point in the story, the encroaching chaos can no longer be avoided. While the doomed Falling Star Hall begins its slide into several other realities at once, a group of New Year's Eve revelers makes a desperate bid for escape. Pan-dimensional werewolves are only one obstacle in our heroes' path.

Step 1. The thumbnail marker sketch, printed here at actual size, was my starting point. The basic placement of characters was working, but the angle of the ground plane made the werewolves to the right of the image too cramped in the corner.

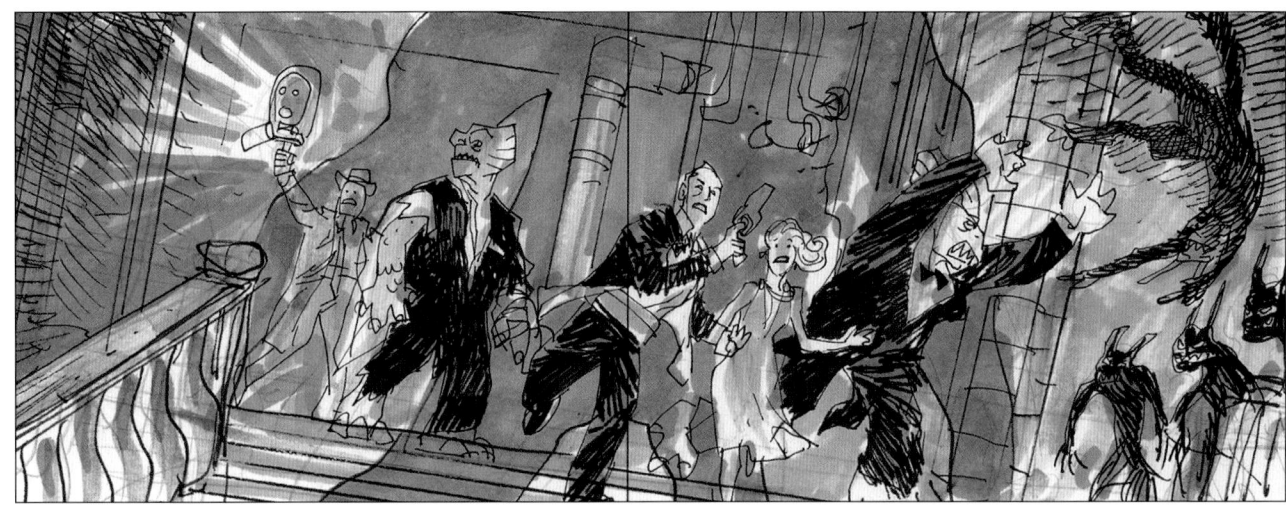

Step 2. In the tighter pencil drawing, I flipped this angle to allow myself some more room. I also refined the details of the costumes and added some variety to the dinosaur footmen.

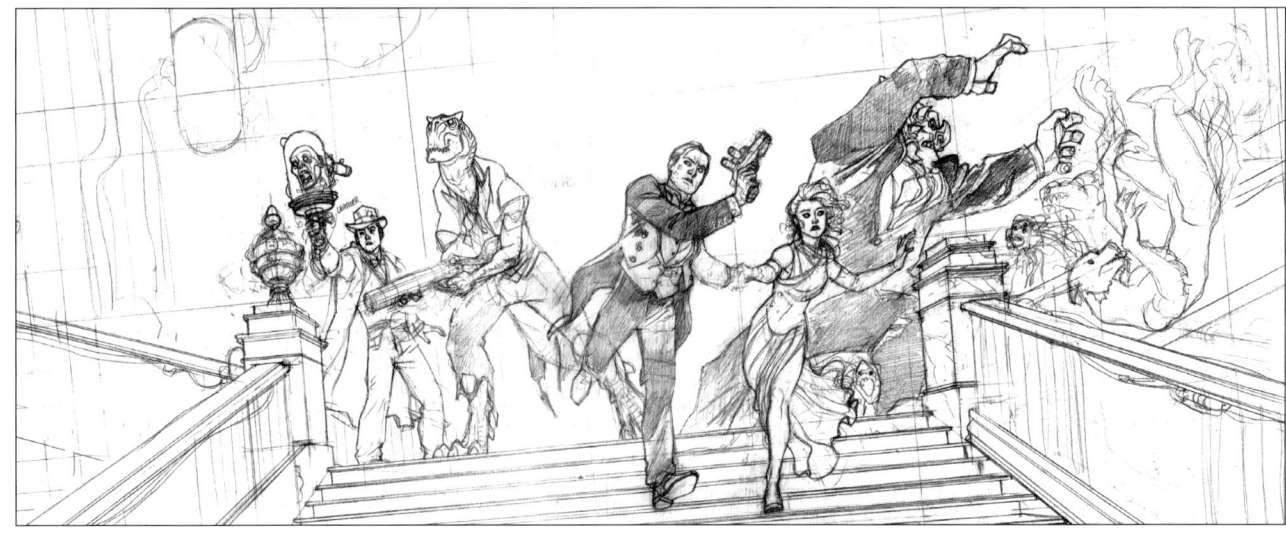

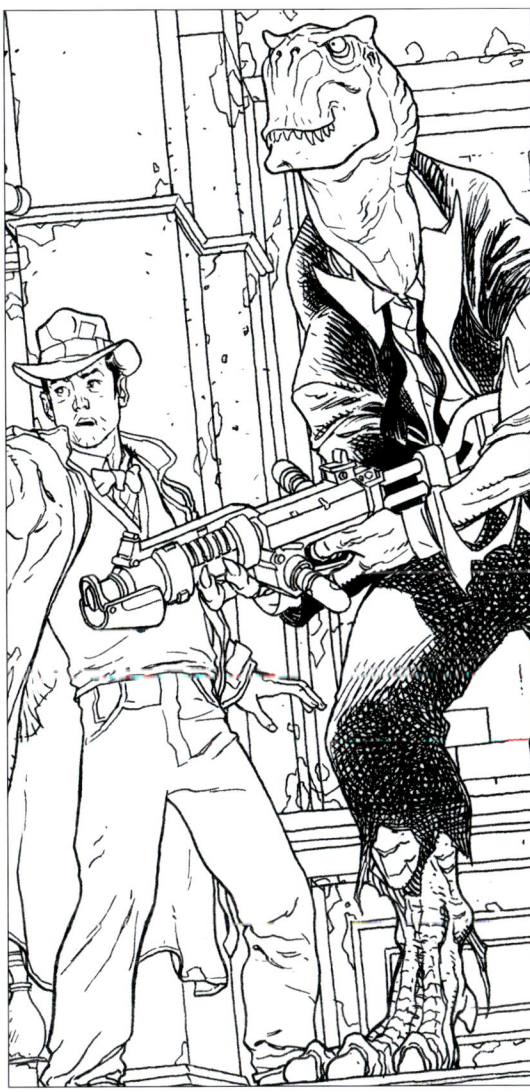

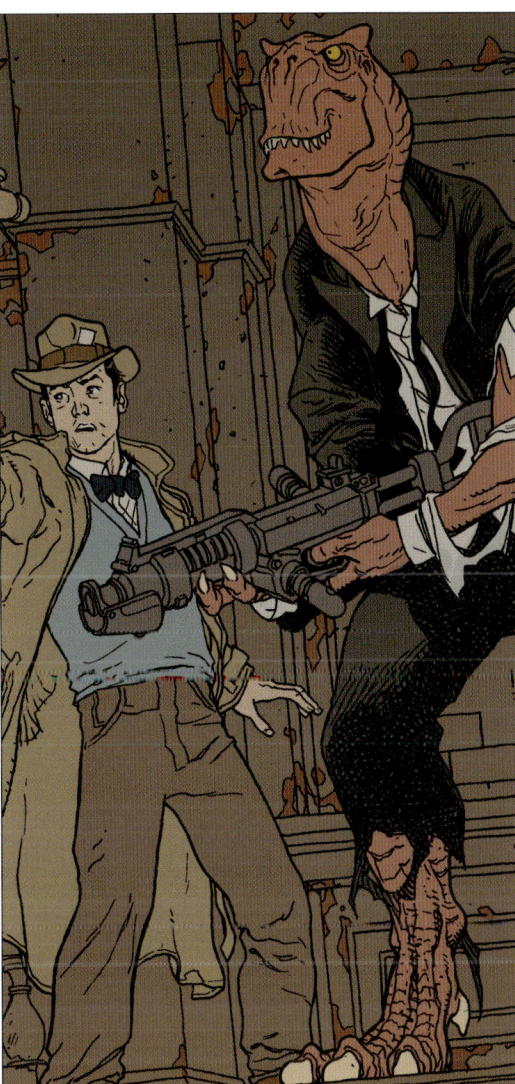

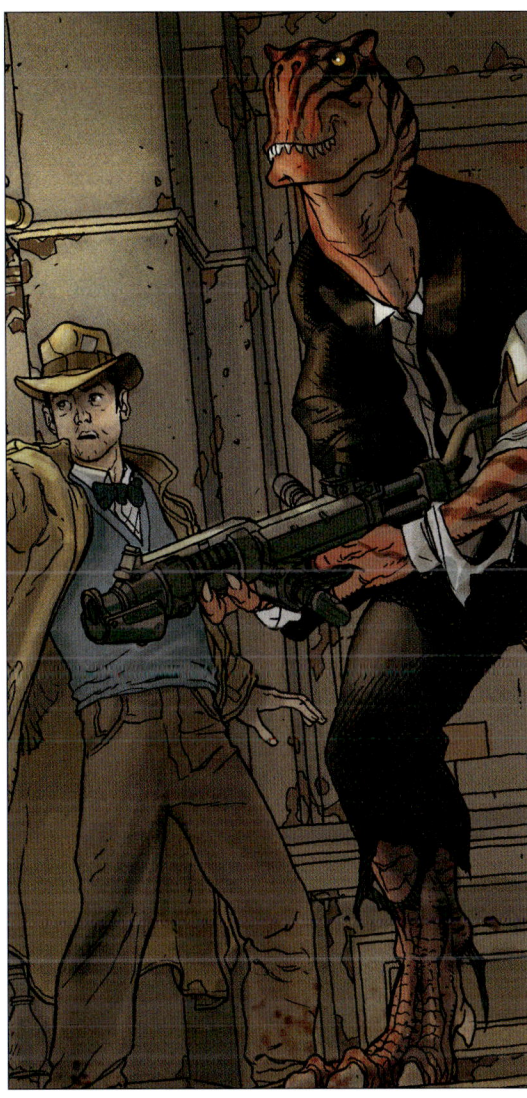

Step 3. I used a mapping pen and black india ink to refine the line work further. The hatching on the tuxedos seemed to fit the retro feel of the world, but I used a more "open line" approach to the other areas of the drawing for contrast. Small details such as the rifle seen here would be tightened using a 2B pencil before I inked them.

Step 4. I laid in my flat colors digitally after roughing out a few options in Photoshop. It was important to find a balance between the line work and the color values underneath it. The goal was to add to the drama of the image without it getting too muddy from the digital color becoming over-rendered. Ideally the line and colors work together and enhance each other. The best comic colorists have mastered this challenging skill. I'm doing my best here to avoid catastrophe.

Step 5. This step is the modeling and final touches. Highlights, shadows, and reflections all add interest. The hardest and most valuable lesson to learn, however, is when to stop working on an image. While it's tempting to add texture and detail to the stonework and the dinosaur hide, this would result in a final image that was very busy. Just as an overall composition needs areas of rest, this is true of characters and any other successful design.

LE TANG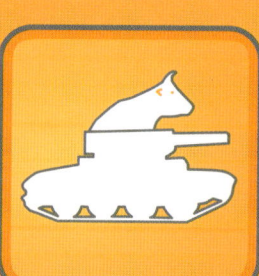

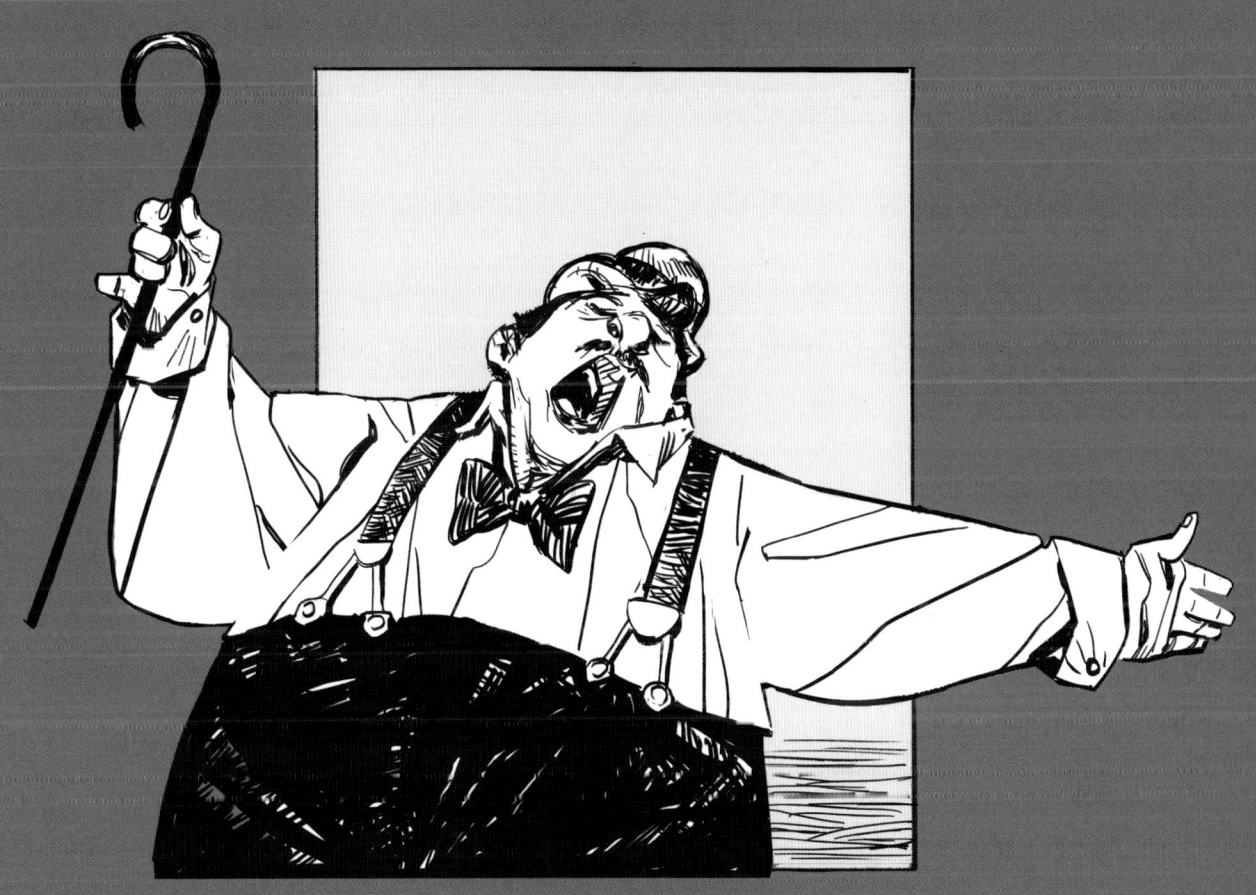

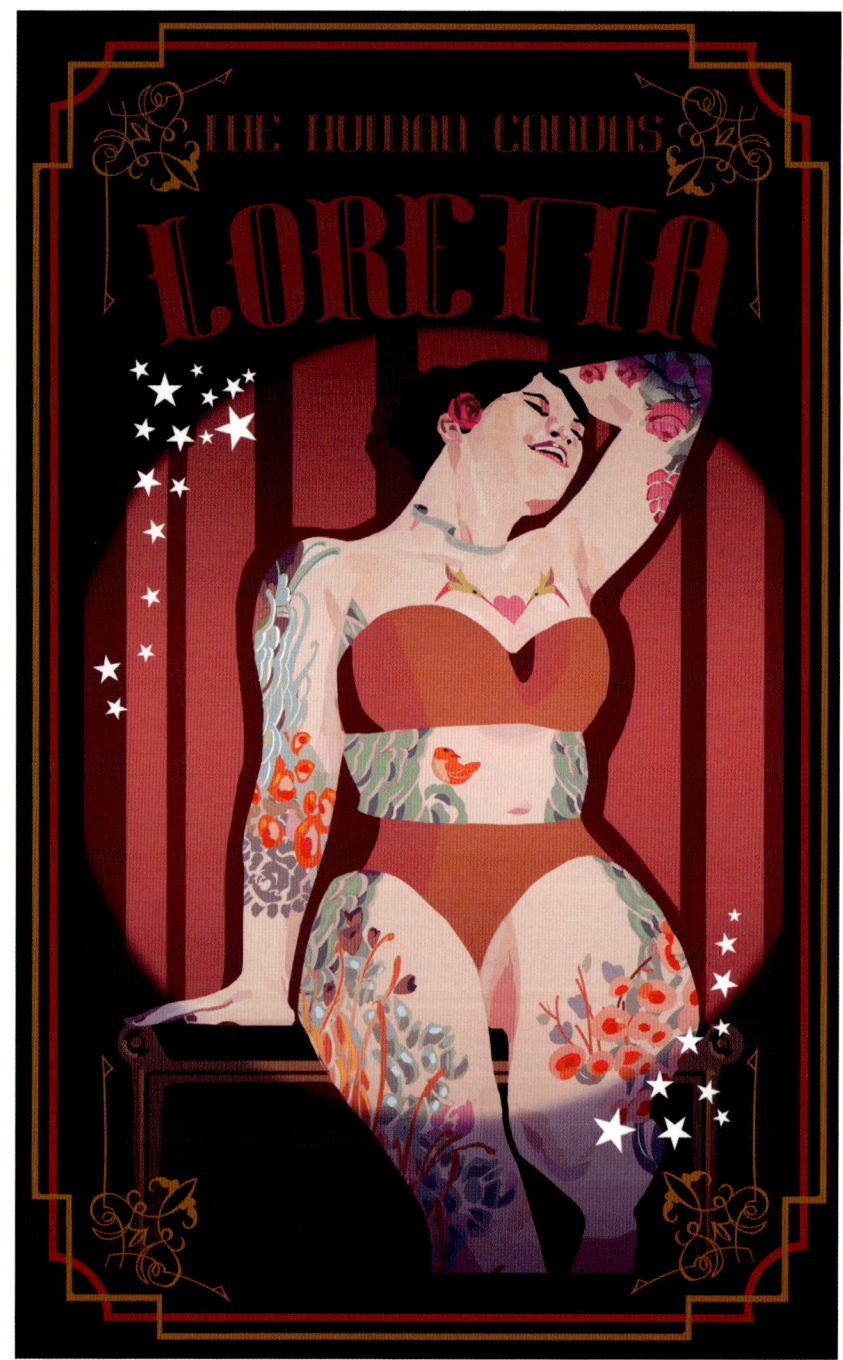

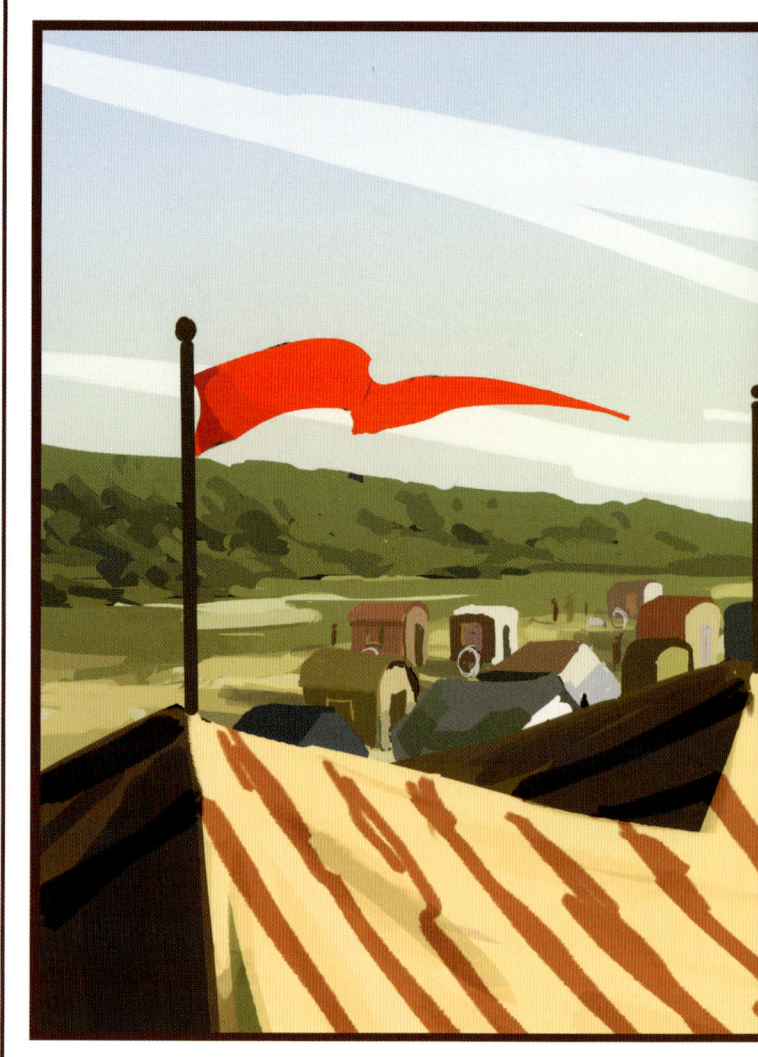

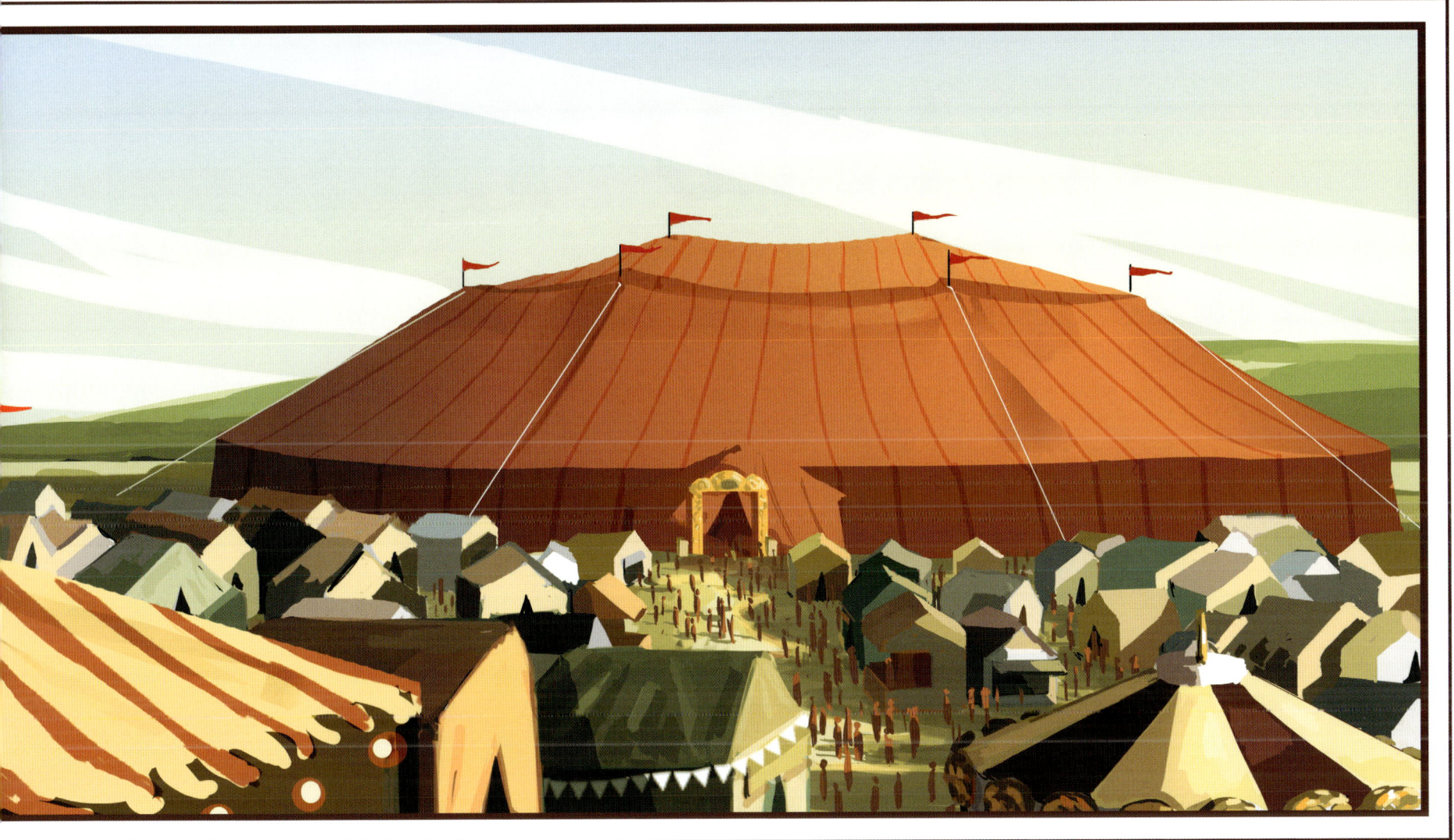

The masses flow through the landscape of booths and tents. Behind cloth walls and atop rickety stages they find the unfamiliar and exotic. Music, laughter, and gasps take up residence in this usually silent field.

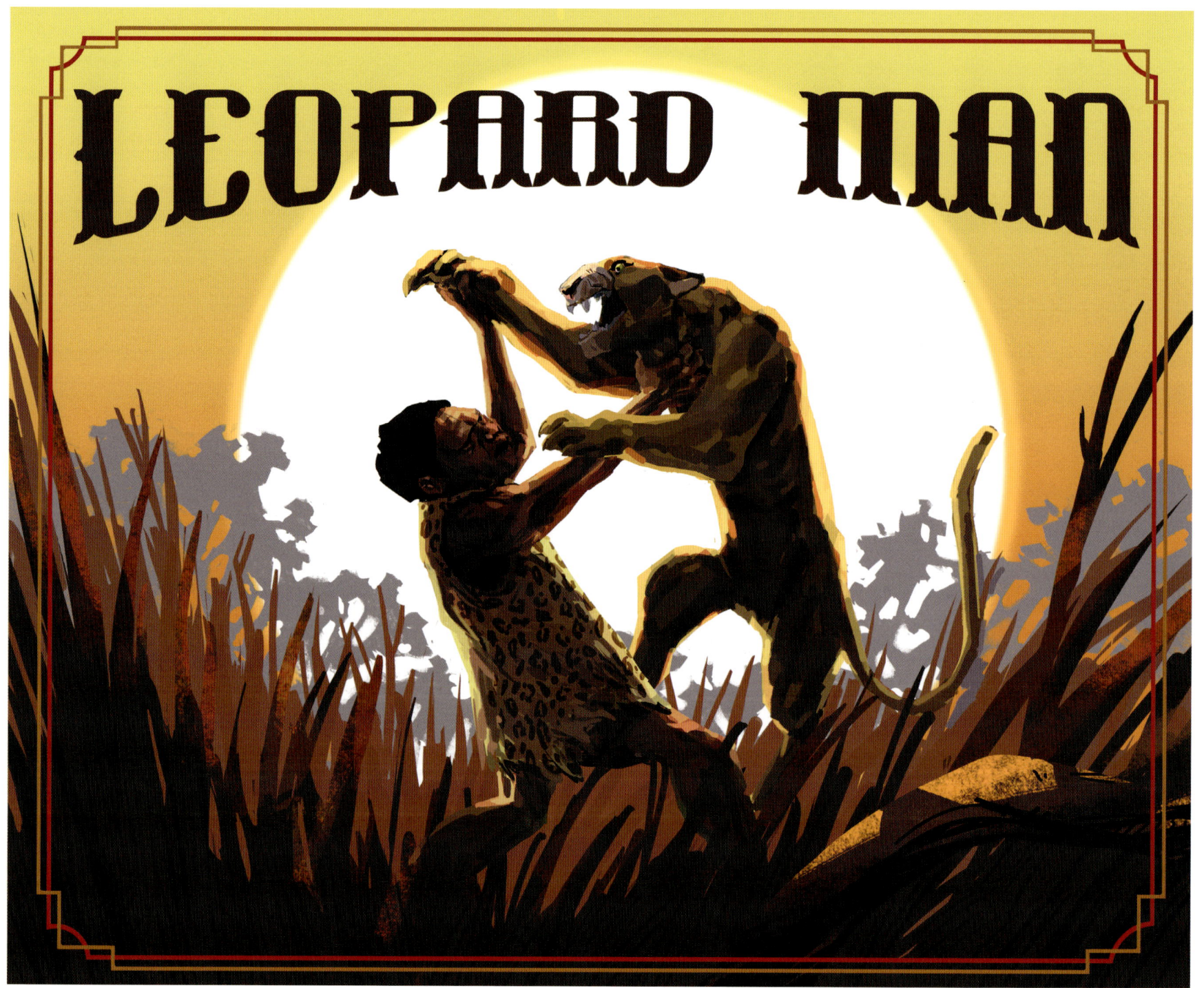

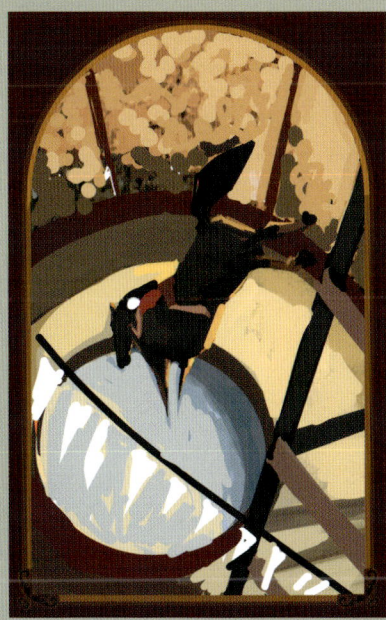

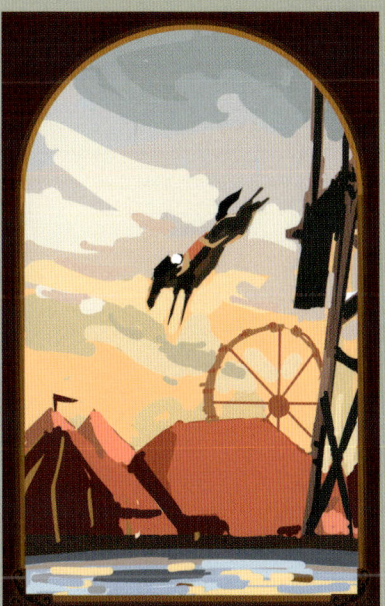

I played around with different ideas for the Ulysses poster; some were more dynamic, some more straight-on. I made my decision on the final version because I liked the flatter, more graphic visual and how simply the horse and rider are showcased.

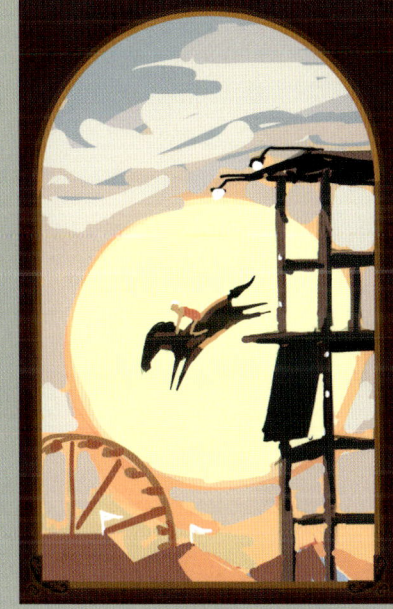

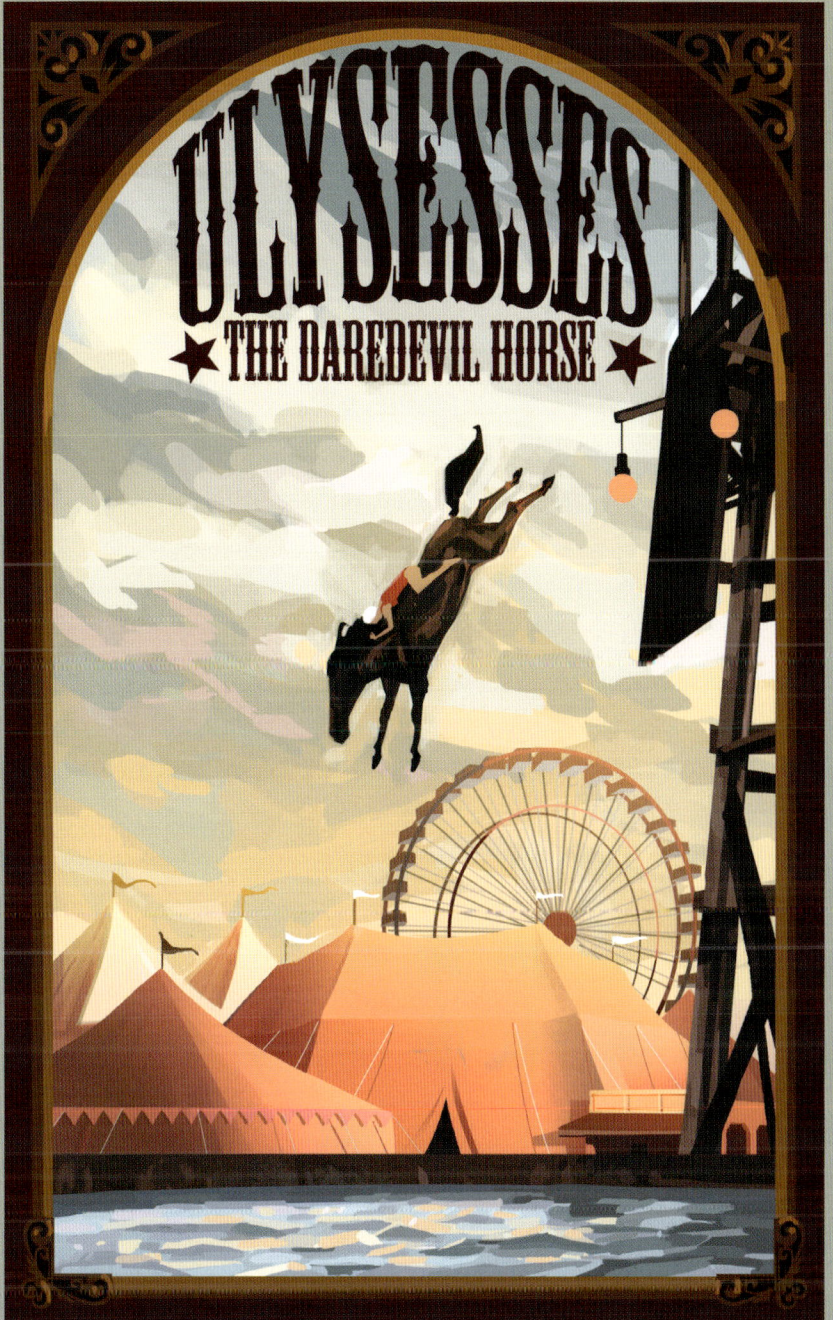

ULYSESSES
★ THE DAREDEVIL HORSE ★

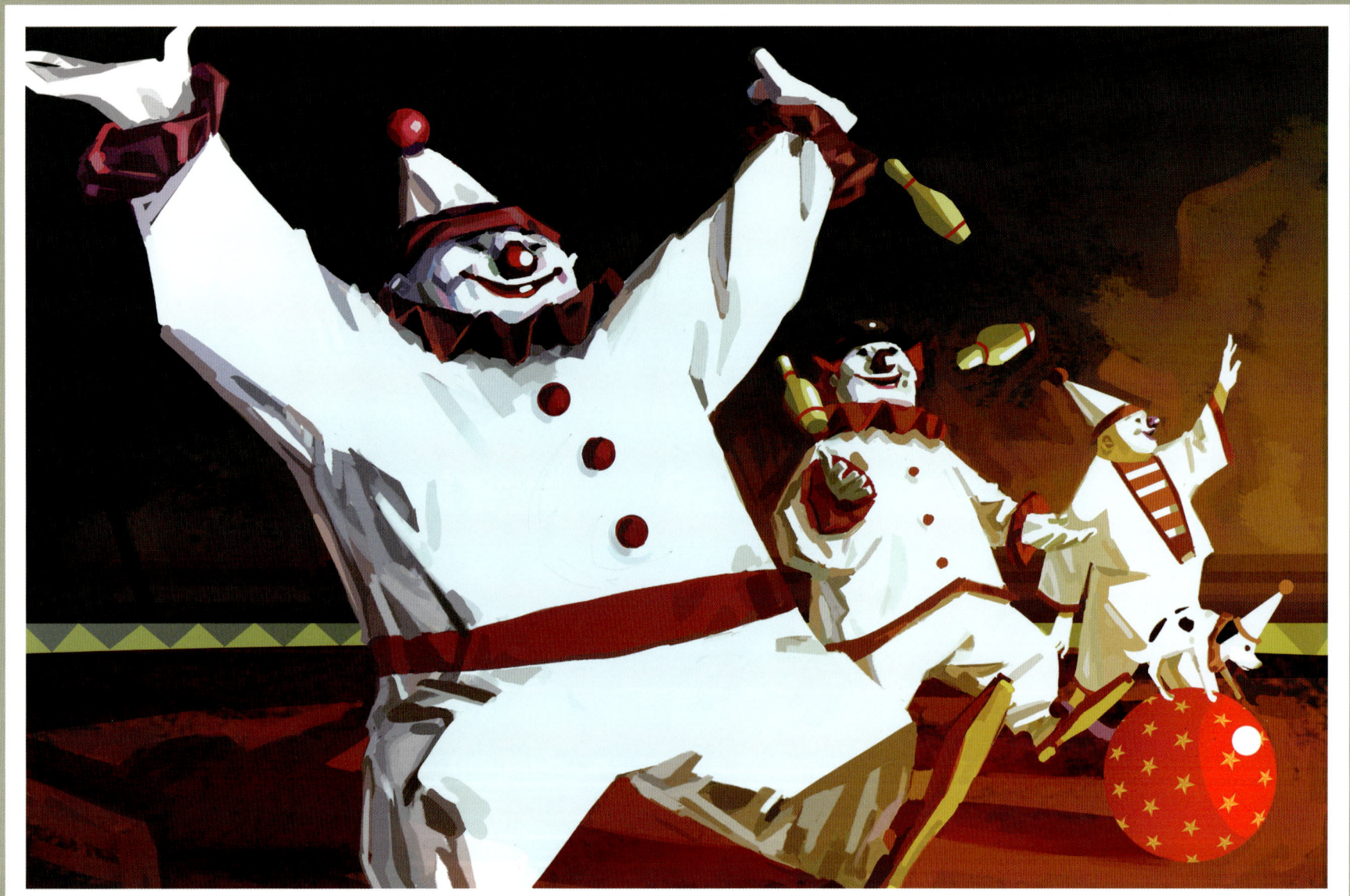

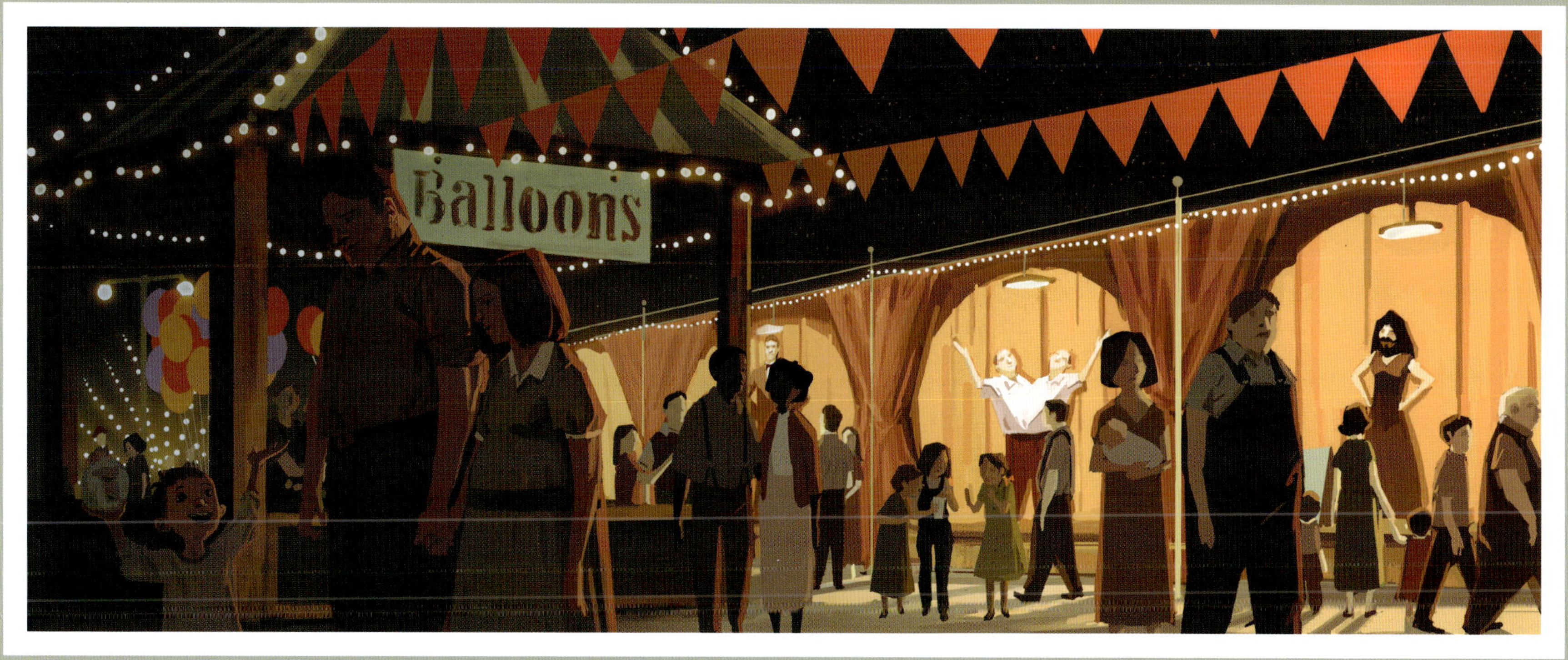

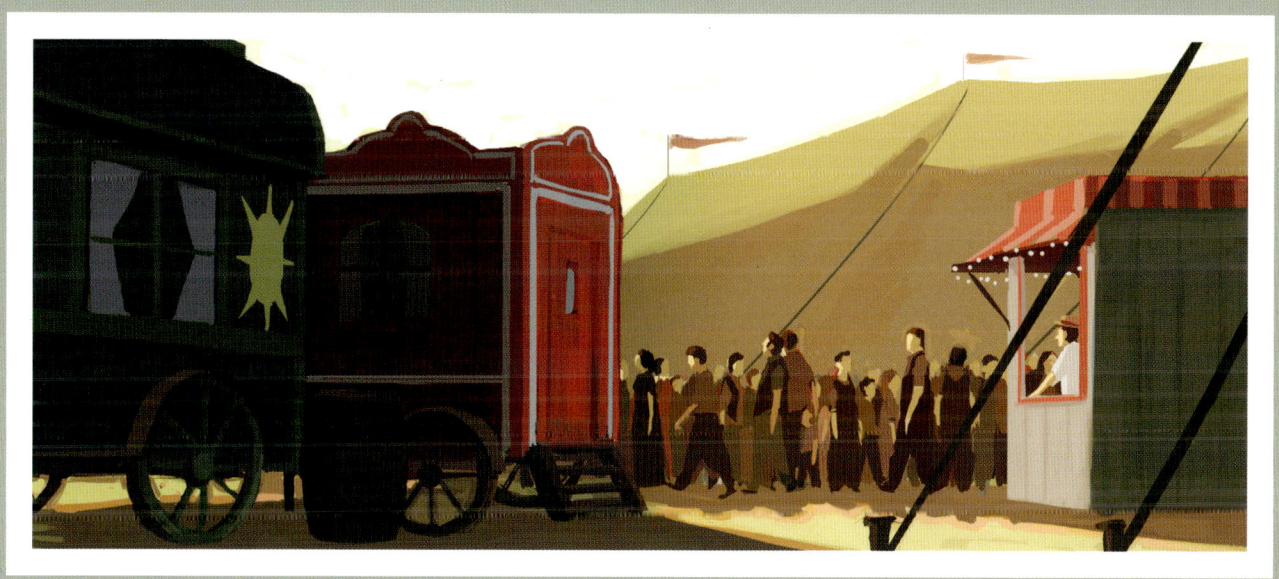

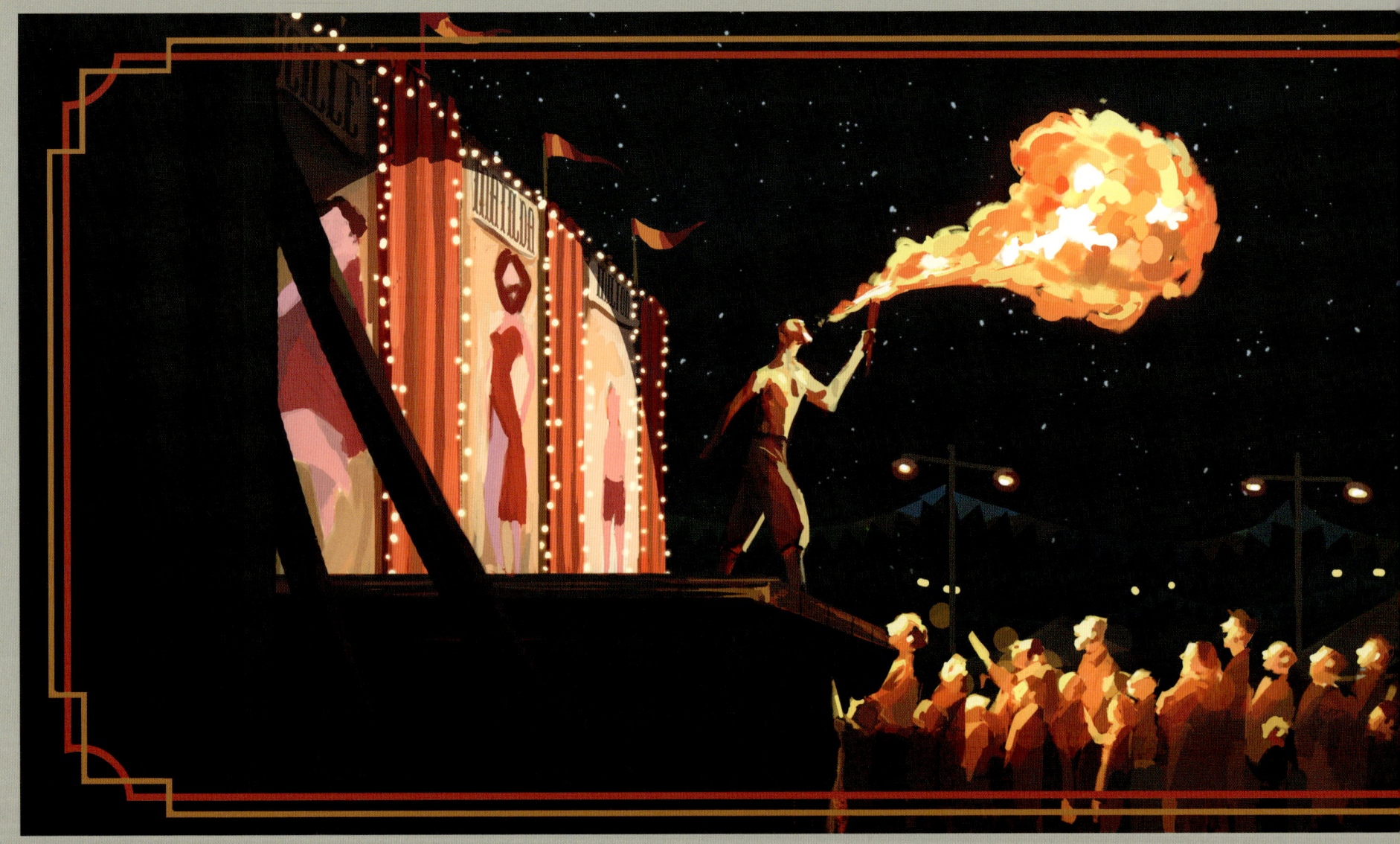

The crowd gathers around the stage, anxiously chattering as they huddle together to escape the crisp evening air. As the performance builds, stillness takes over them until suddenly an eruption of fire and heat dances above their heads, momentarily overpowering the cold and darkness in a display of oranges and reds.

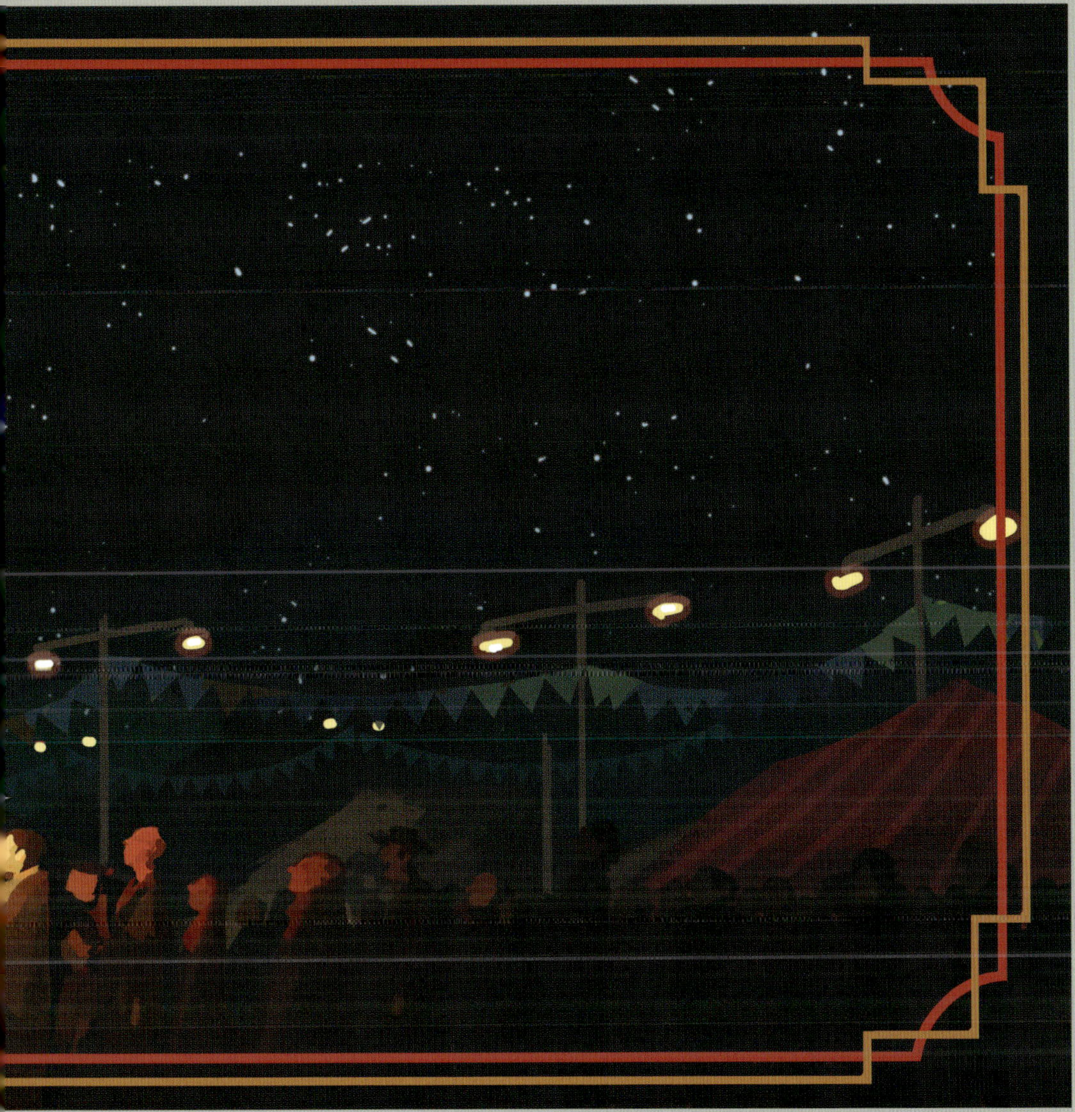

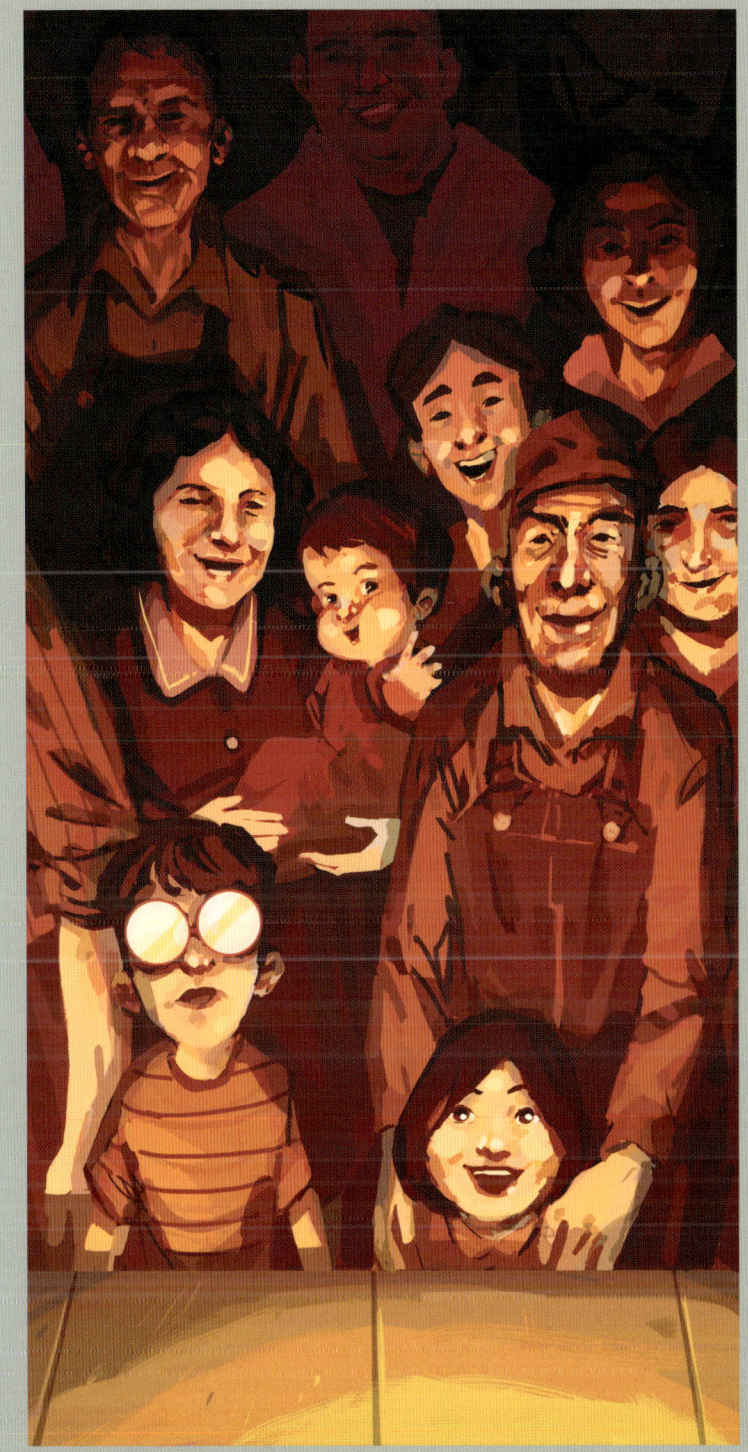

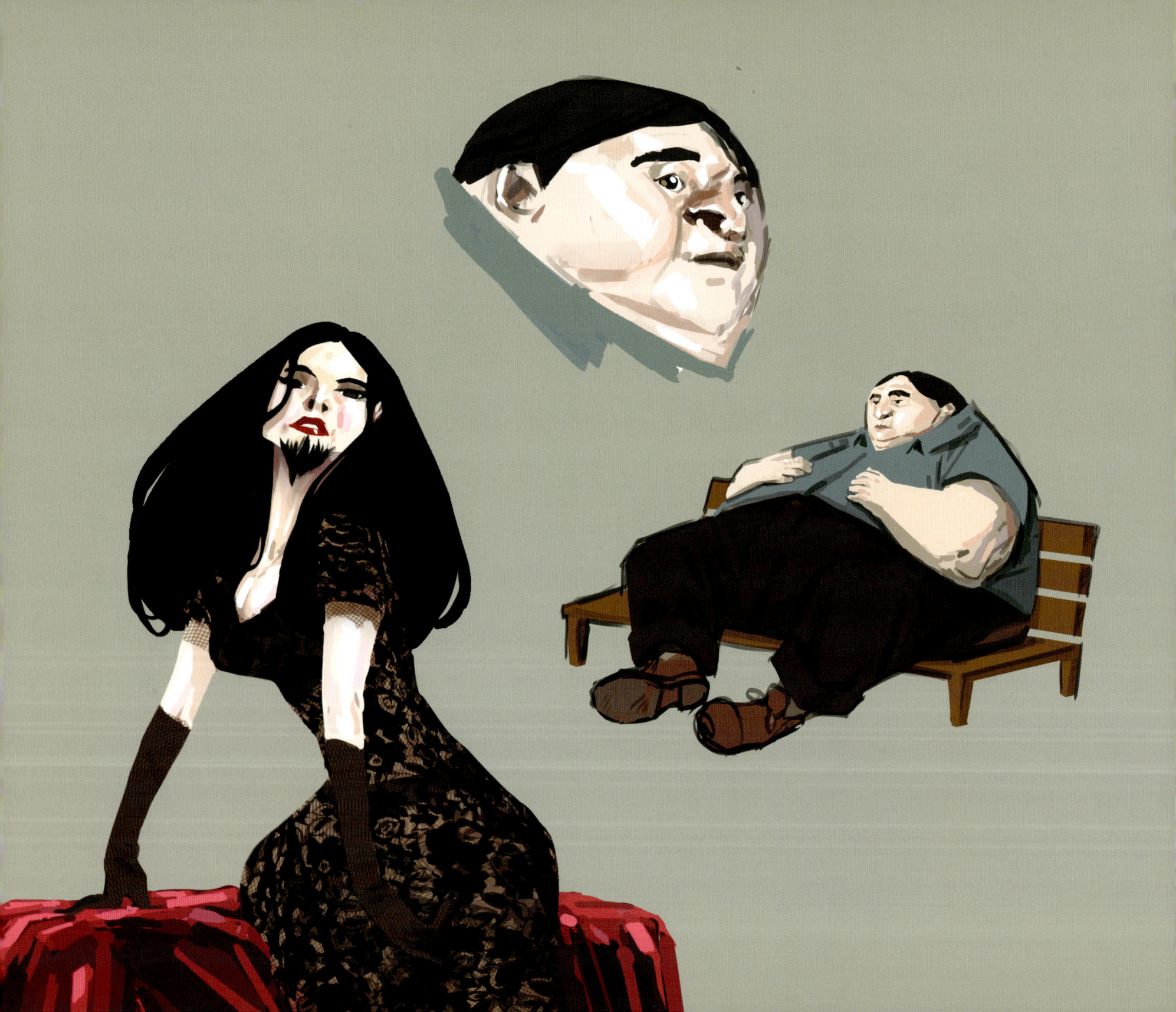

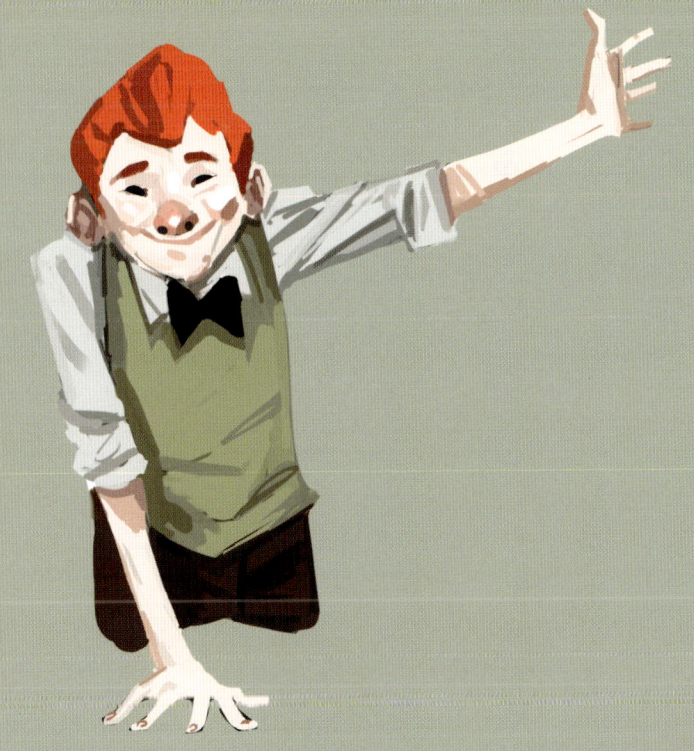
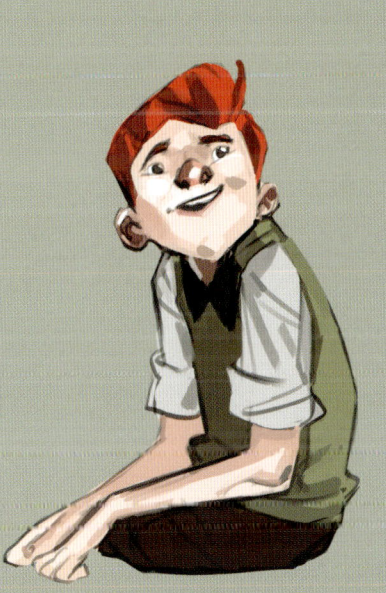
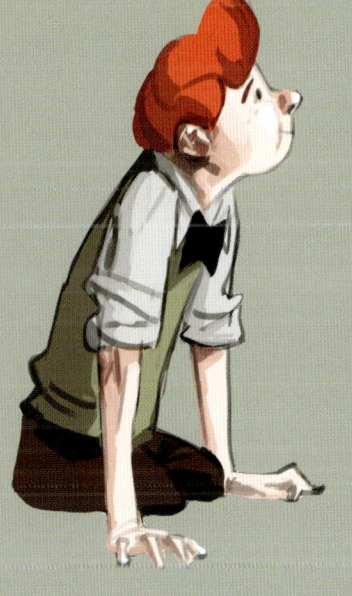
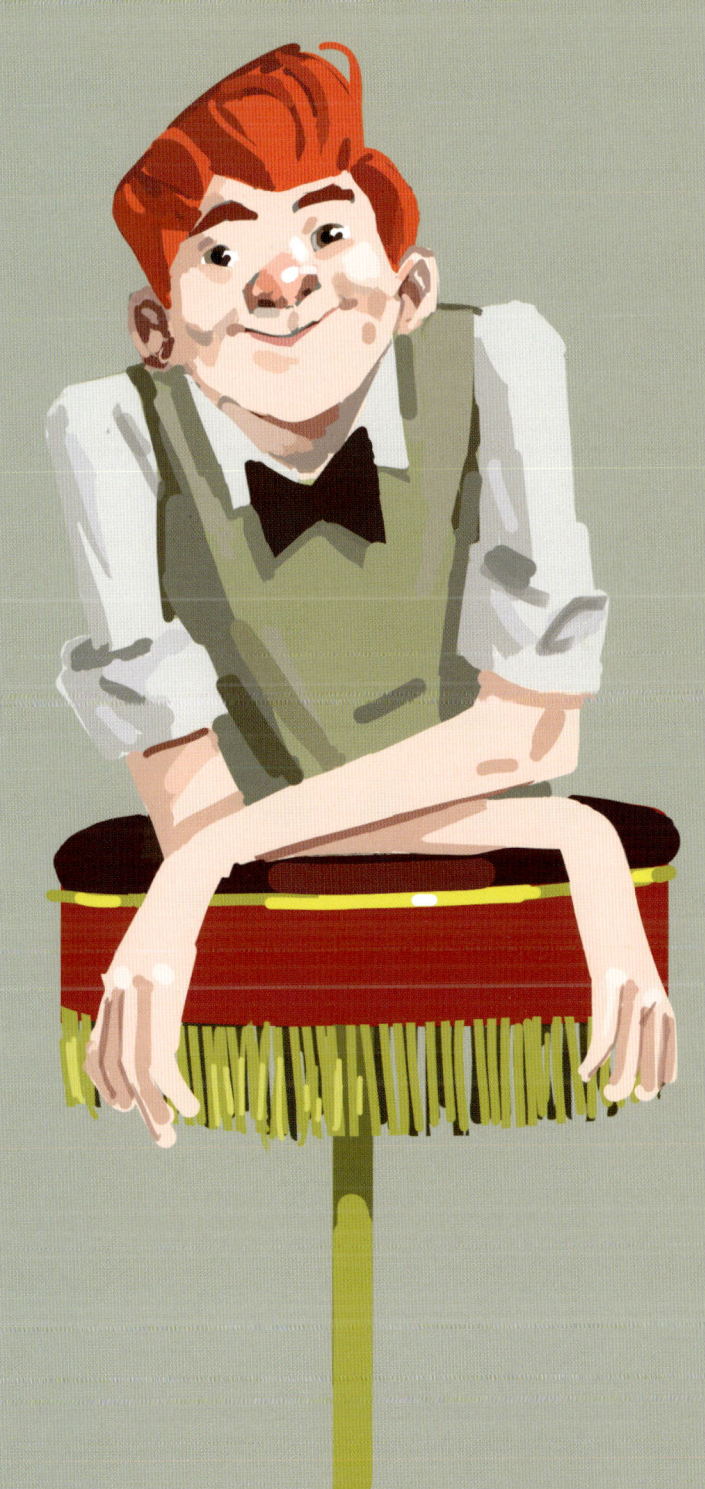

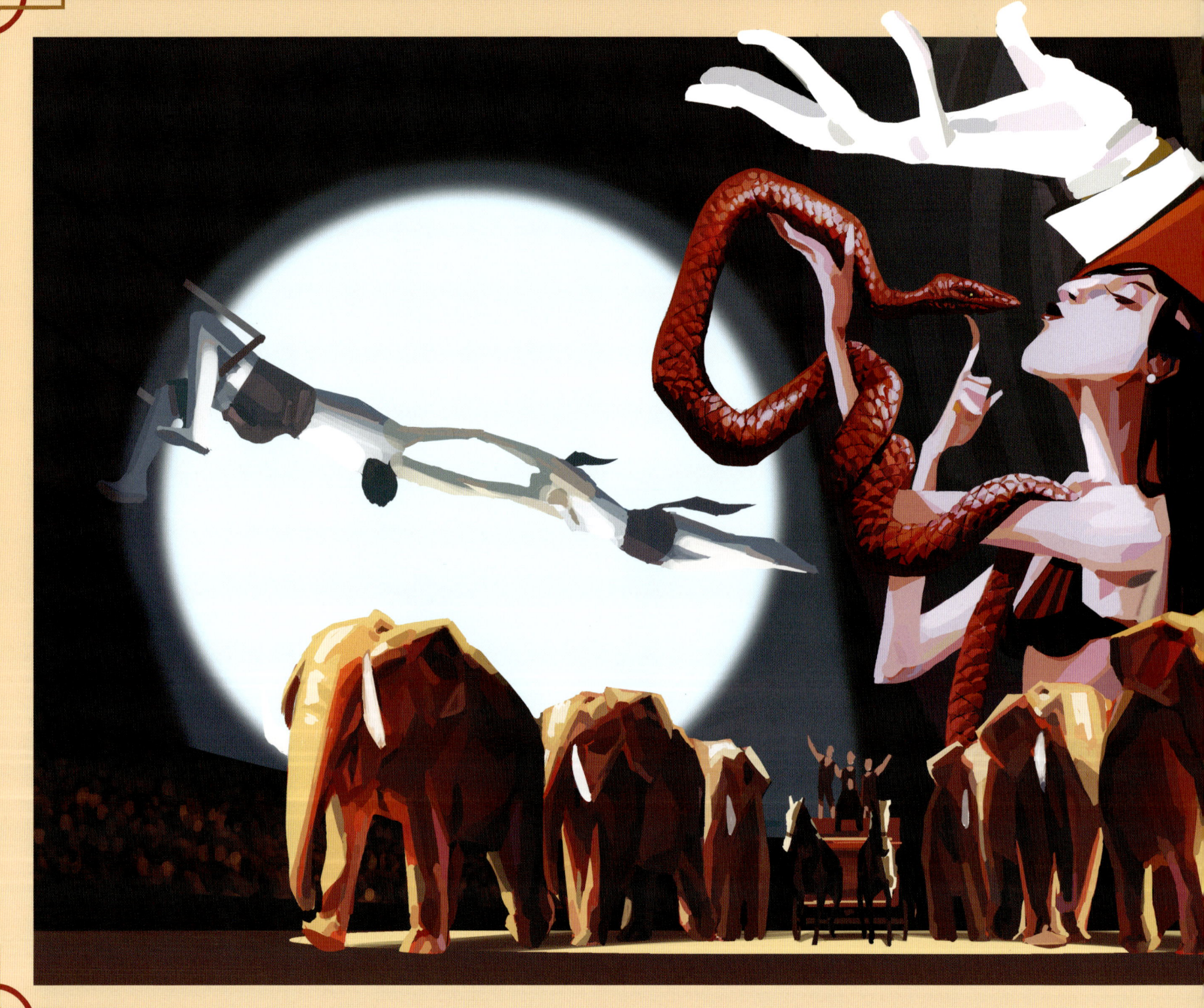

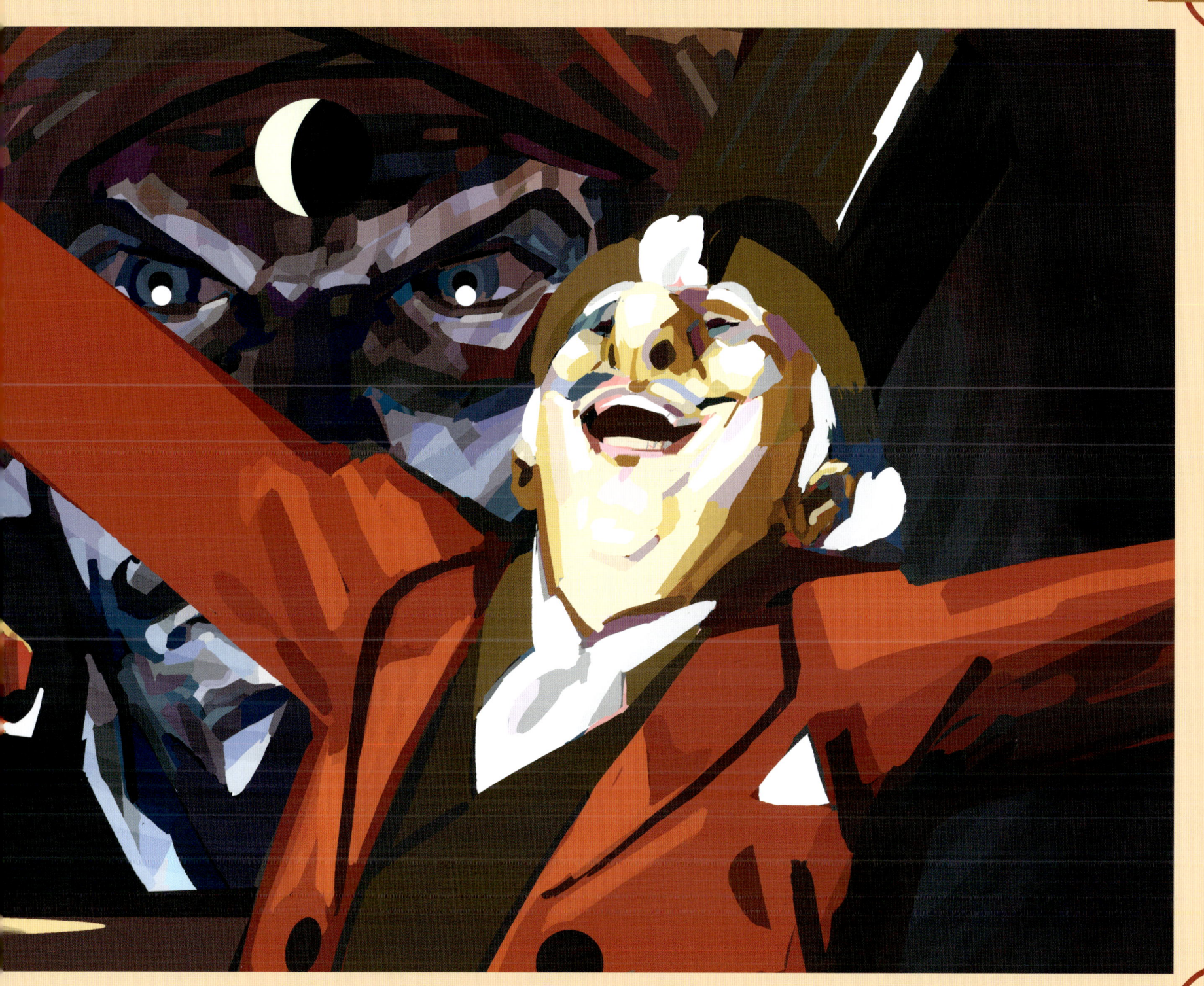

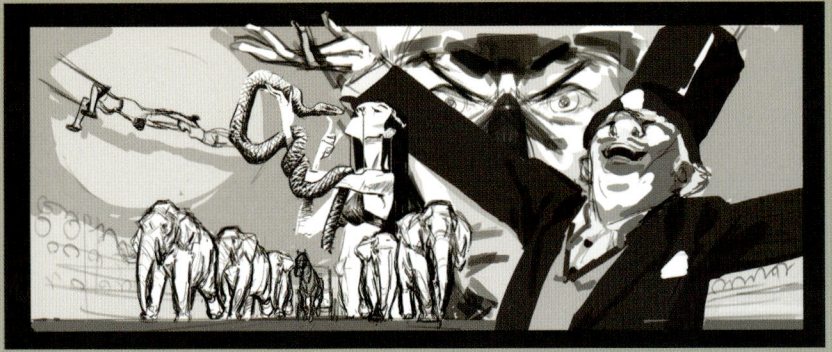

Step 1: Establishing Layout

Since I was intending on doing a collage of different subject matter, I had to spend a good amount of time figuring out the design of the piece. I used the ringleader as the "main attraction" of the piece; the placement of his arms would help the flow through the overall design.

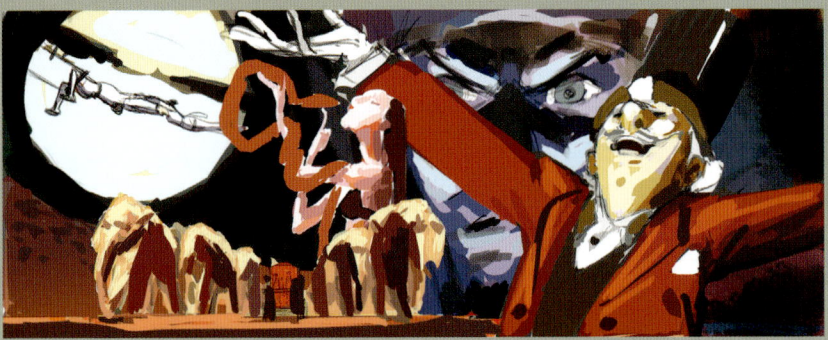

Step 2: Color & Lighting

I then laid down the general color and lighting scheme I wanted. I gave the magician's face a strong blue light to create a sense of mystery and drama, especially in comparison to the other, warmer elements. During this stage I usually study a lot of reference materials (e.g., advertisements, photographs, and illustrations).

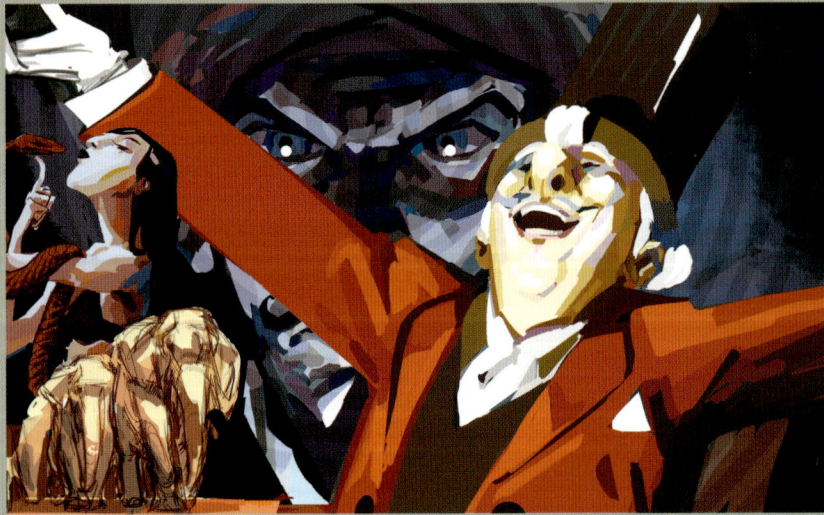

Step 3: Detailing Elements

As I started detailing each element I aimed to stay within the warmth/coolness that I established in Step 2. I added a serious of concentric circles emanating from the magician's mind, in order to create a hypnotic sense about him, and also to add some interest to the background.

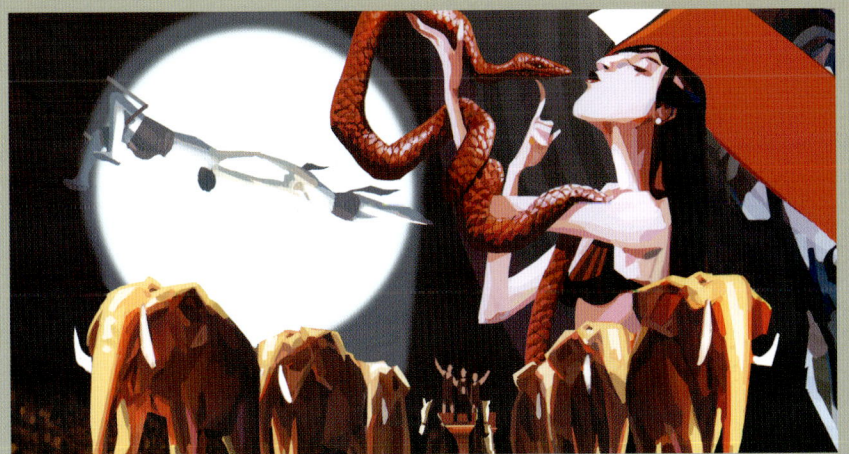

Step 4: Continuing to Detail & Adjust Colors

I continued to paint out the elements, paying attention to how the colors played off each other. I cooled down the snake charmer and trapeze artists a bit, and added more contrast to the elephant-scene elements. I also minimized the rendering details on these smaller elements so that they would be less busy.

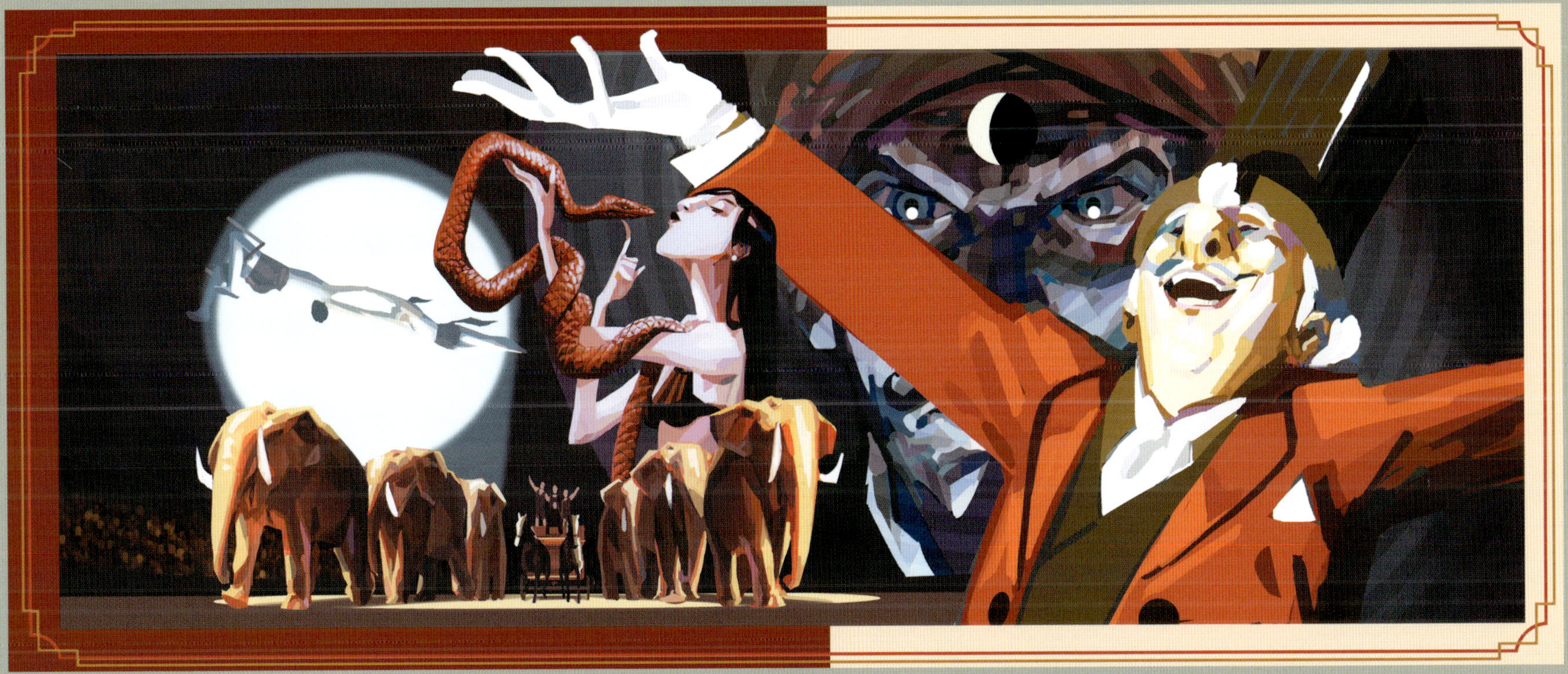

Step 5: Finalizing

I ended up nudging the elements a little here and there during the process (thank you, layers). Most drastically, I lowered the trapeze artists so the overall grouping of the elements would flow better. I was not sure what color to make the frame until the image was mostly done. I had it at a darker red, but it competed too much with the image instead of just accentuating it, so I lightened the frame color.

MATT GASER

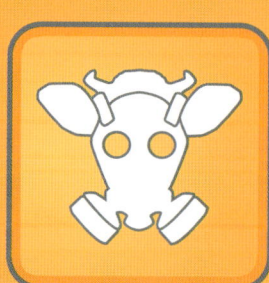

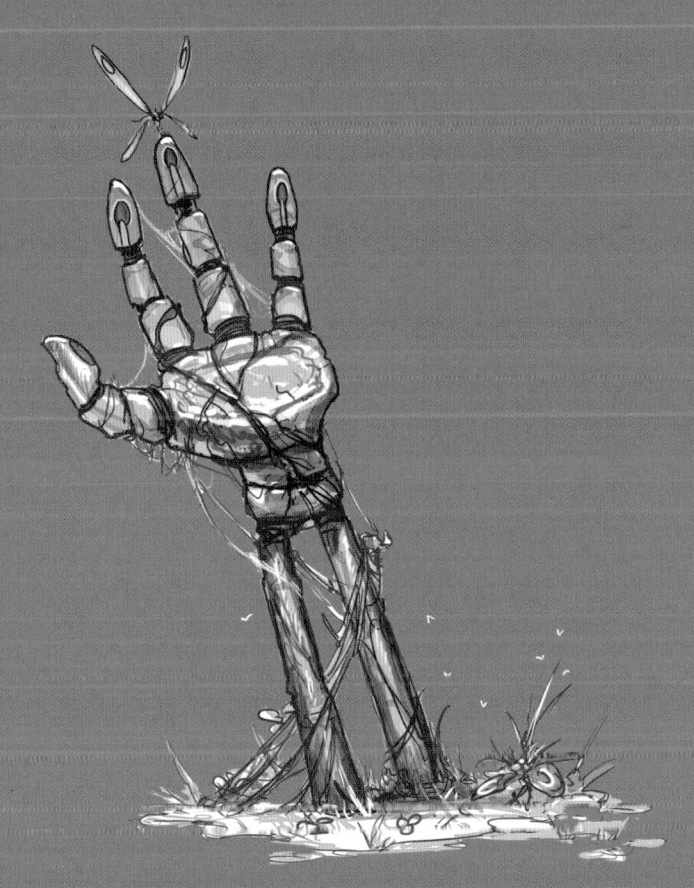

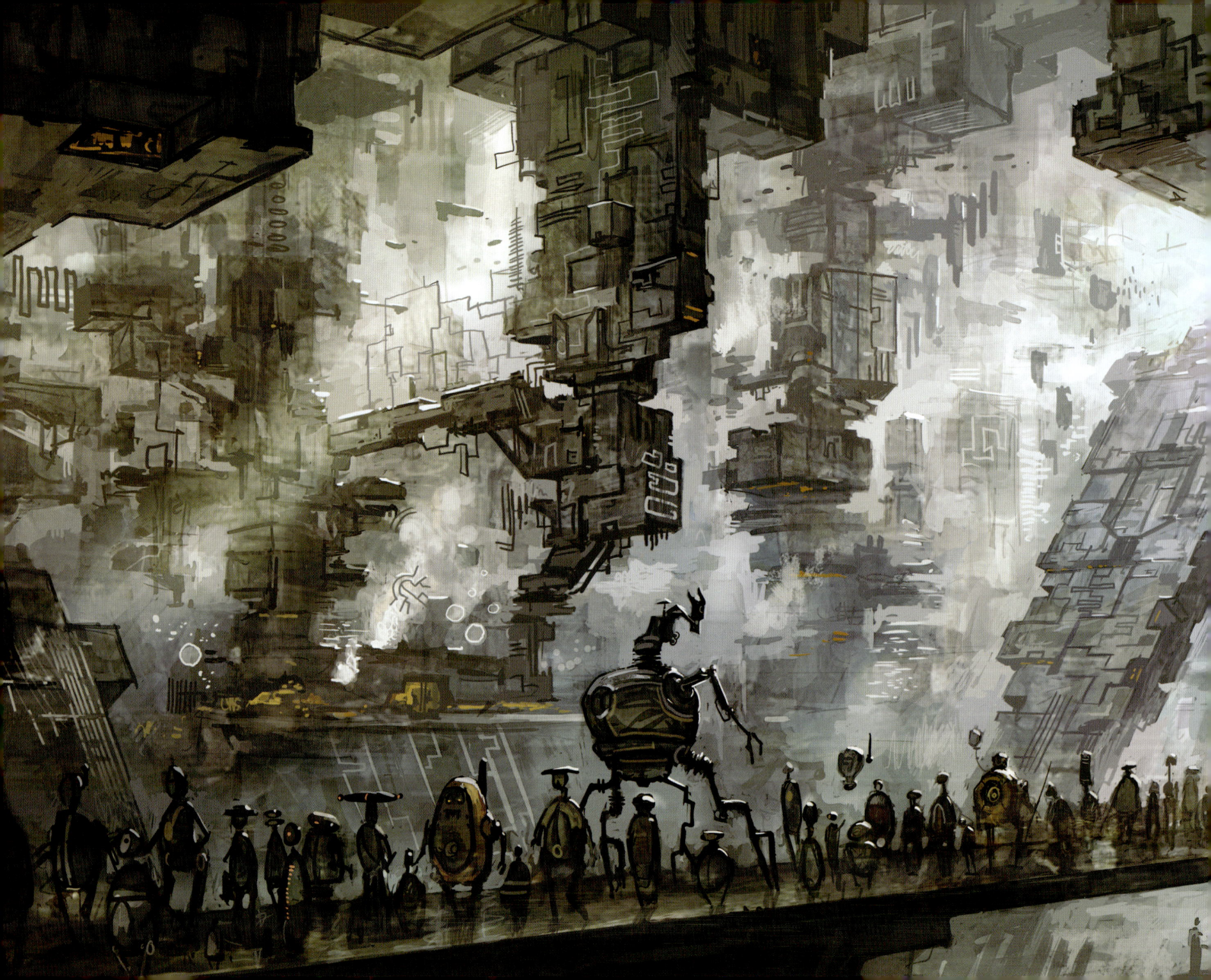

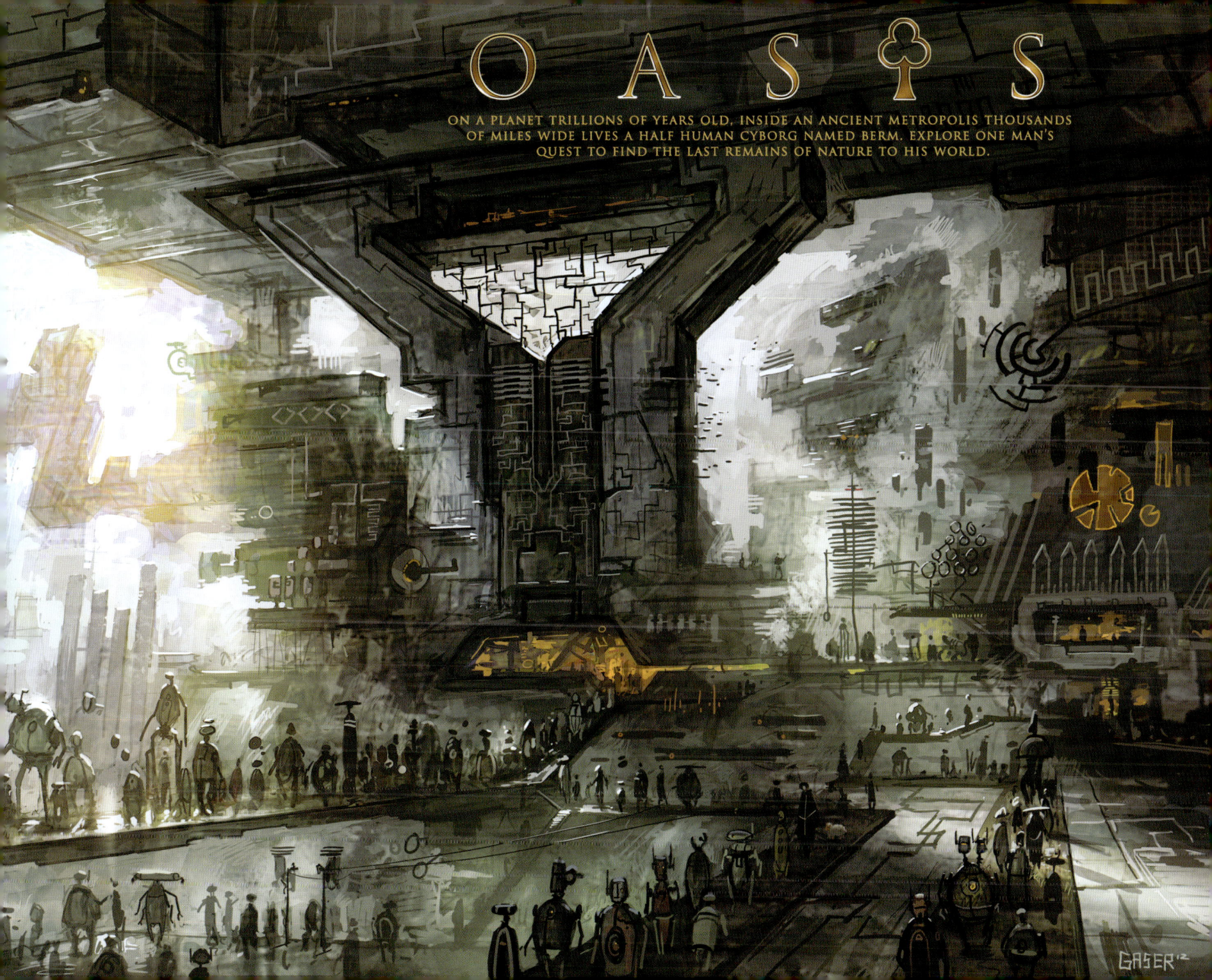

OASIS

ON A PLANET TRILLIONS OF YEARS OLD, INSIDE AN ANCIENT METROPOLIS THOUSANDS OF MILES WIDE LIVES A HALF HUMAN CYBORG NAMED BERM. EXPLORE ONE MAN'S QUEST TO FIND THE LAST REMAINS OF NATURE TO HIS WORLD.

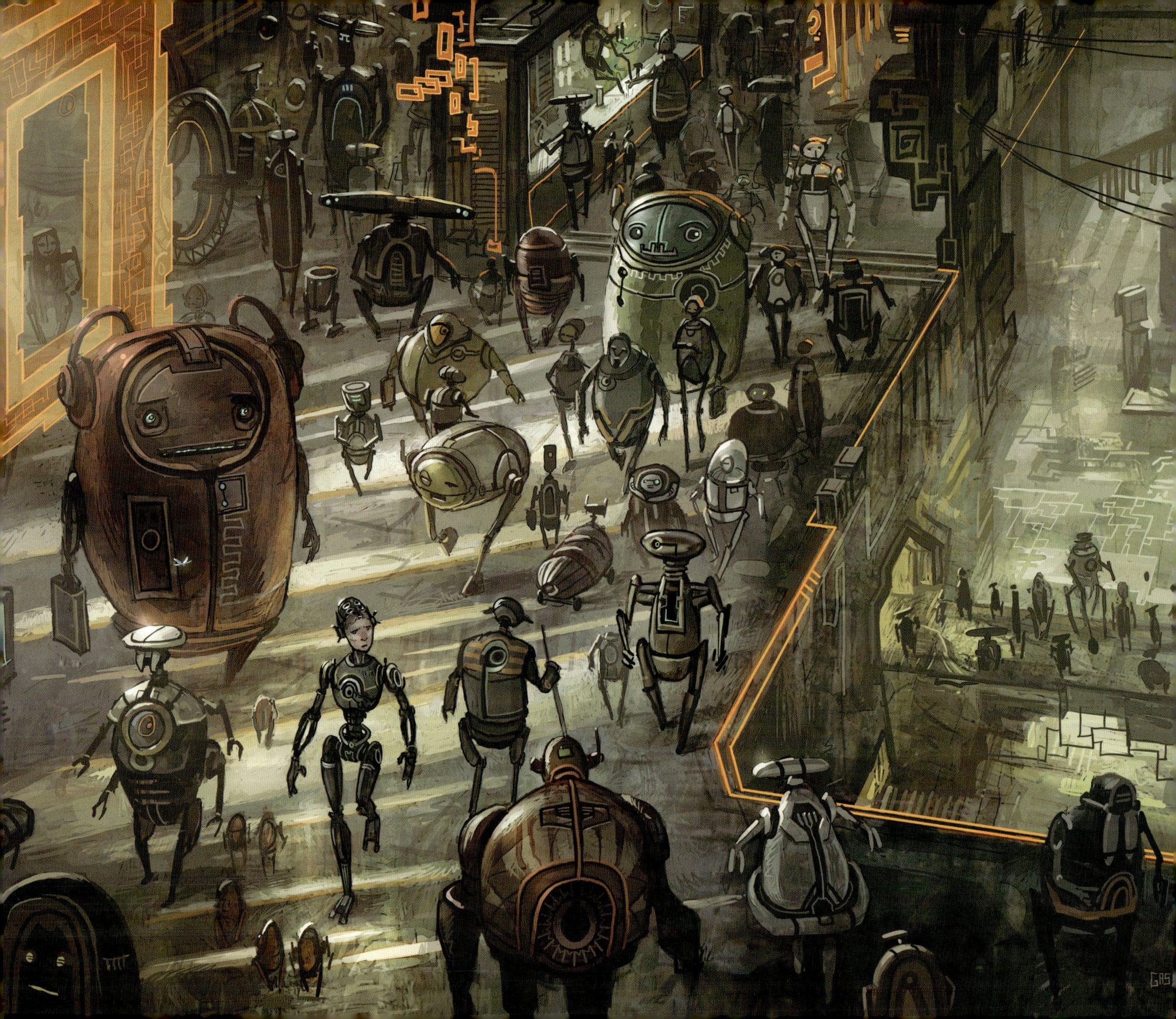

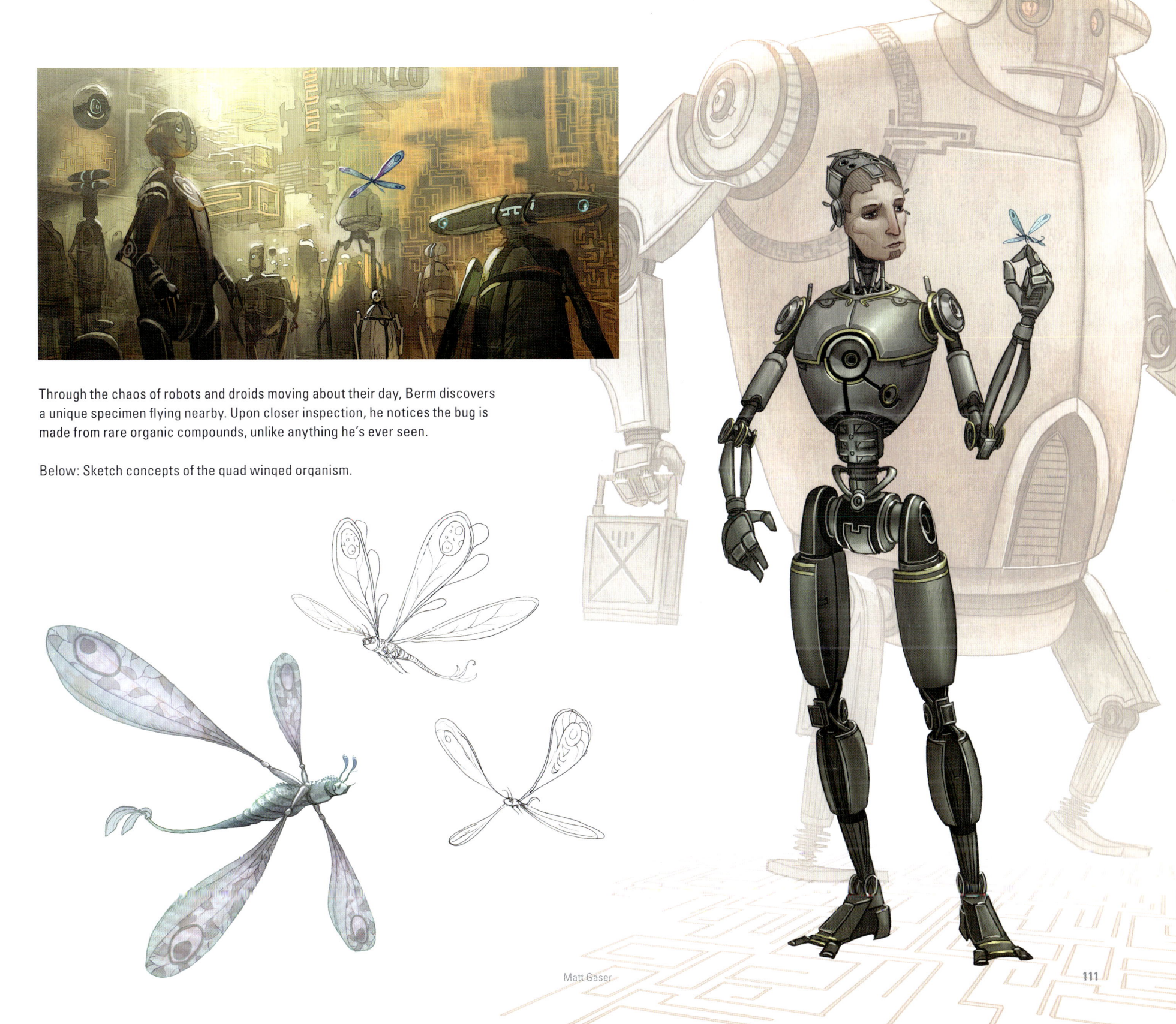

Through the chaos of robots and droids moving about their day, Berm discovers a unique specimen flying nearby. Upon closer inspection, he notices the bug is made from rare organic compounds, unlike anything he's ever seen.

Below: Sketch concepts of the quad winged organism.

Matt Gaser

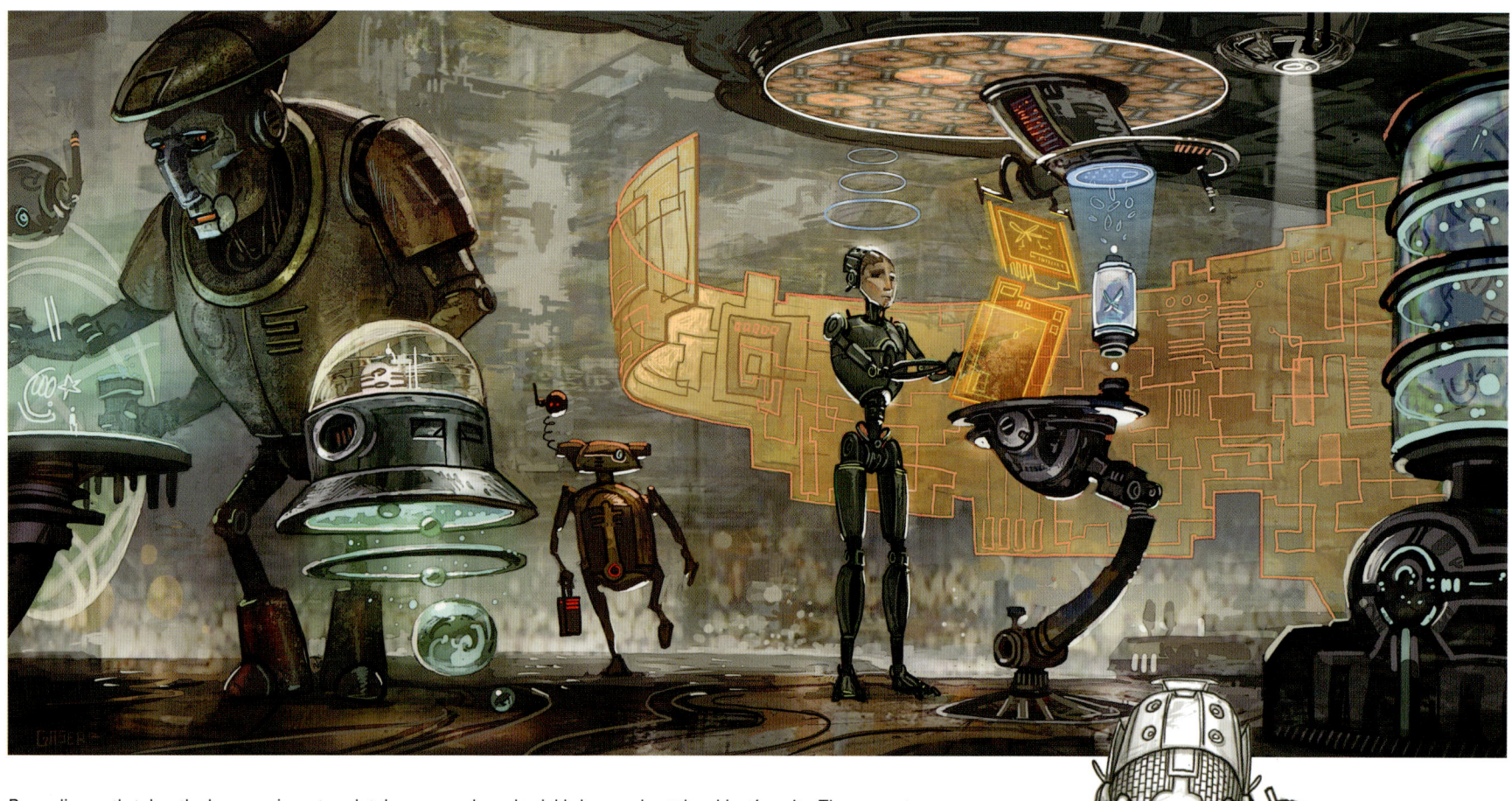

Berm discreetly takes the bug specimen to a database console and quickly learns about the object's rarity. The computer database searches for a history to the "organic life form." The compound went extinct 4,000 years ago in a revolution called the Great Migration to Synthetic Consciousness (GMSC).

During this singularity, the humanoids collectively agreed to mind-transfer from their organic host bodies into synthetic replacements. The GMSC erased all traces of their former race, including turning all life on their planet to a robotic form. Celebratory bonfires were lit around the globe to burn their leftover bodies, all in the hopes of preserving their minds forever. They wanted to become immortal. The computer gives Berm a map of the last known origin of life. It points to a location far away from his home inside the Sepo Quad, beyond the Fragmented Zone in the unknown Deleted Territories of Keplica. Berm downloads the map and decides to investigate further.

Opposite: The 3-D virtual map Berm researches from the kiosk.

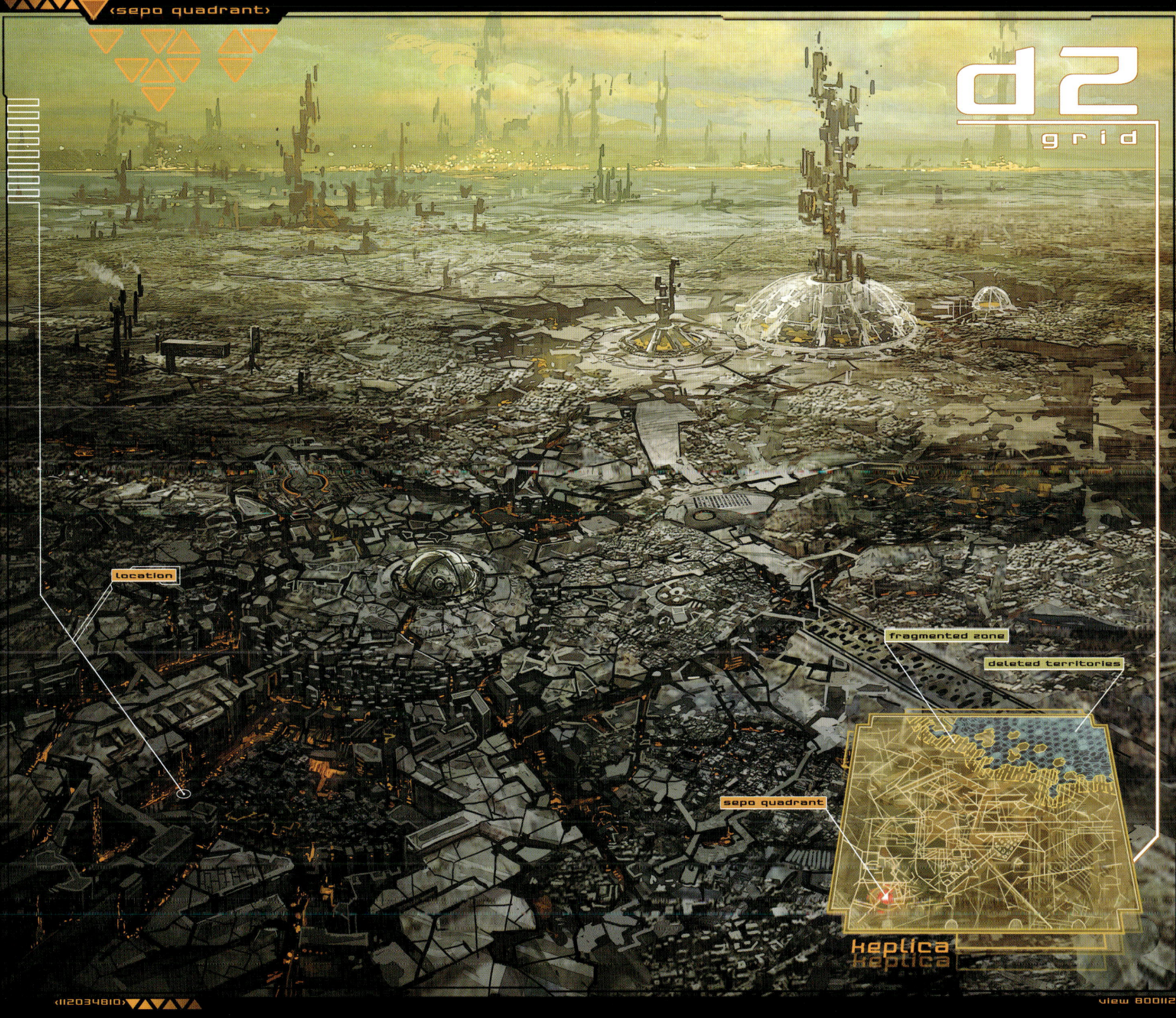

d2
grid

location

fragmented zone

deleted territories

sepo quadrant

replica
replica

battery
transport

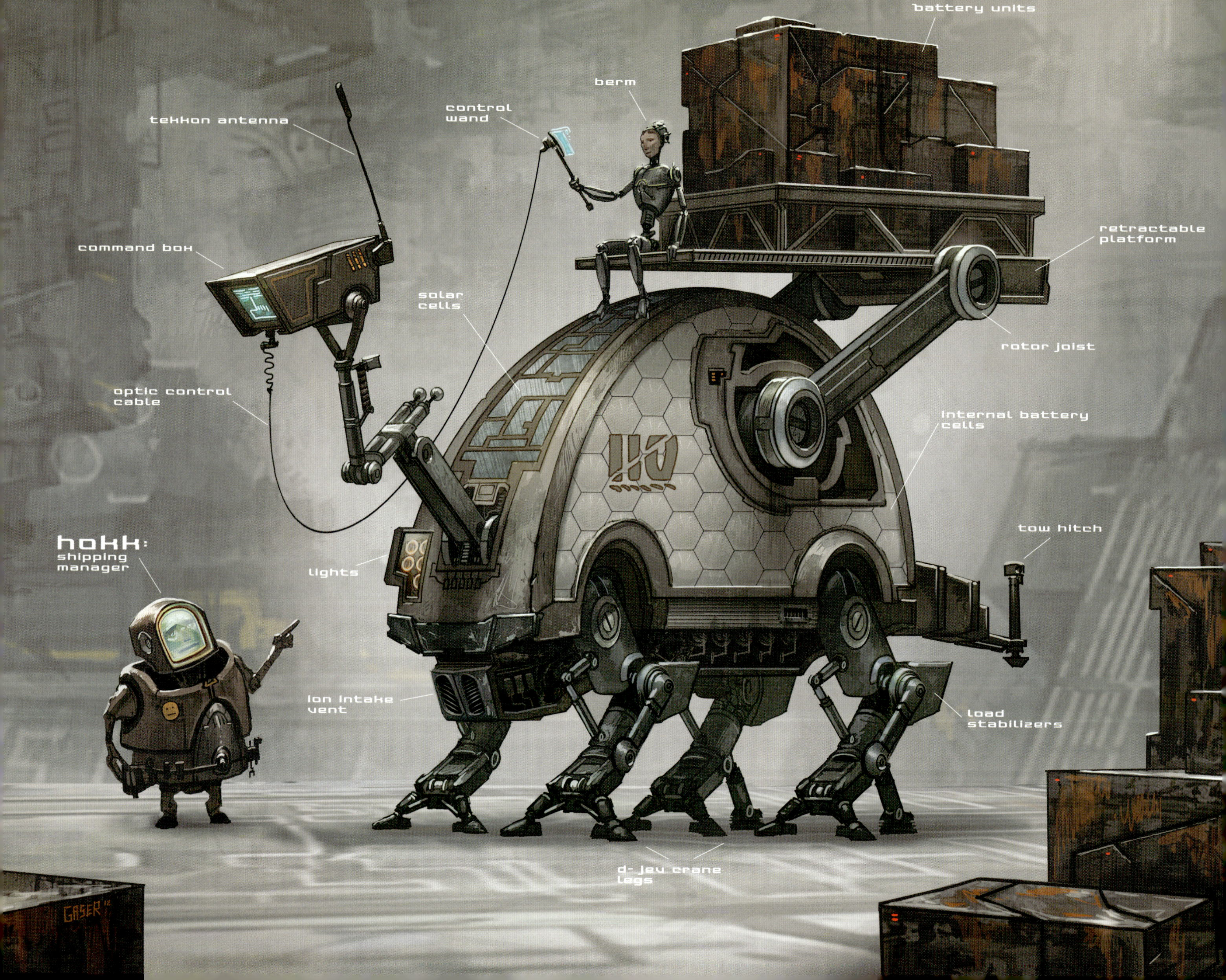

battery units

berm

control
wand

tekkon antenna

command box

retractable
platform

solar
cells

optic control
cable

rotor joist

internal battery
cells

hokk:
shipping
manager

lights

tow hitch

ion intake
vent

load
stabilizers

d-jev crane
legs

GASER 12

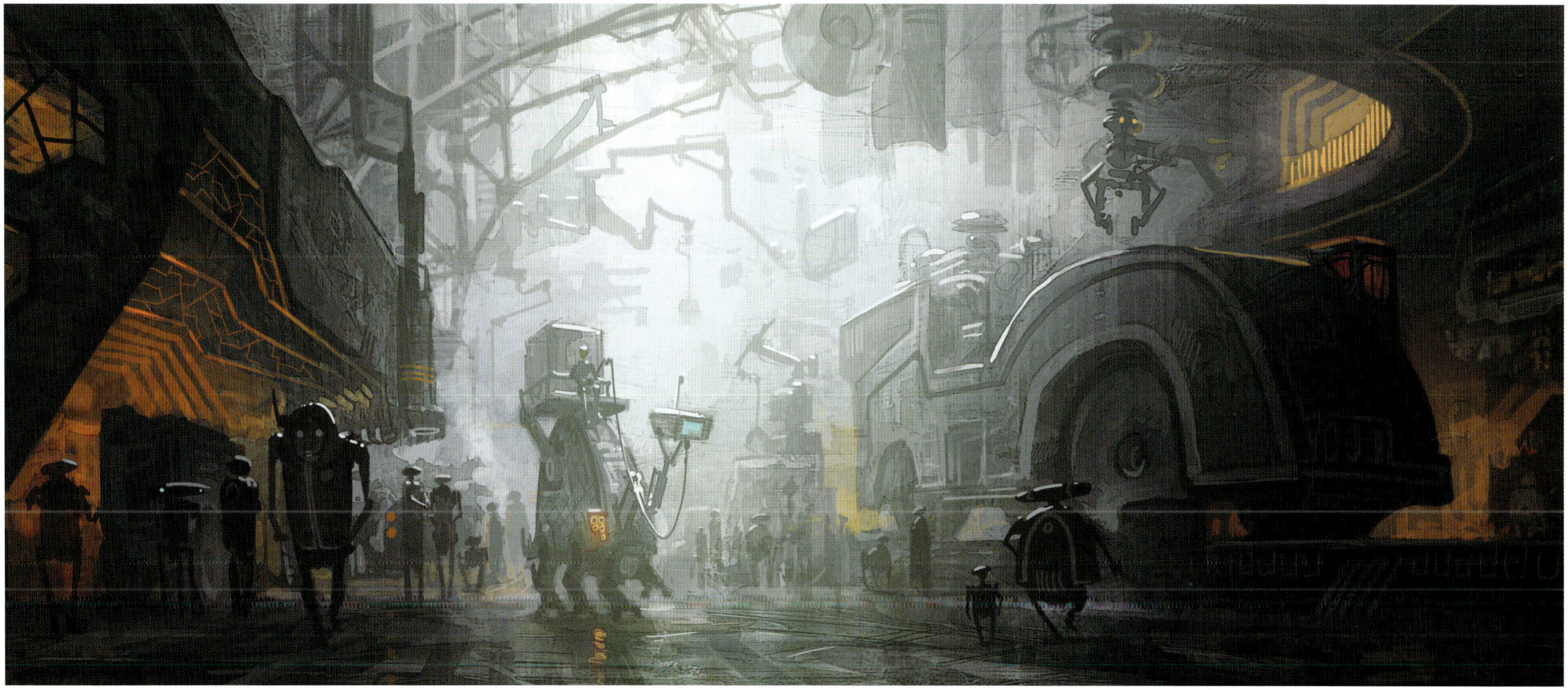

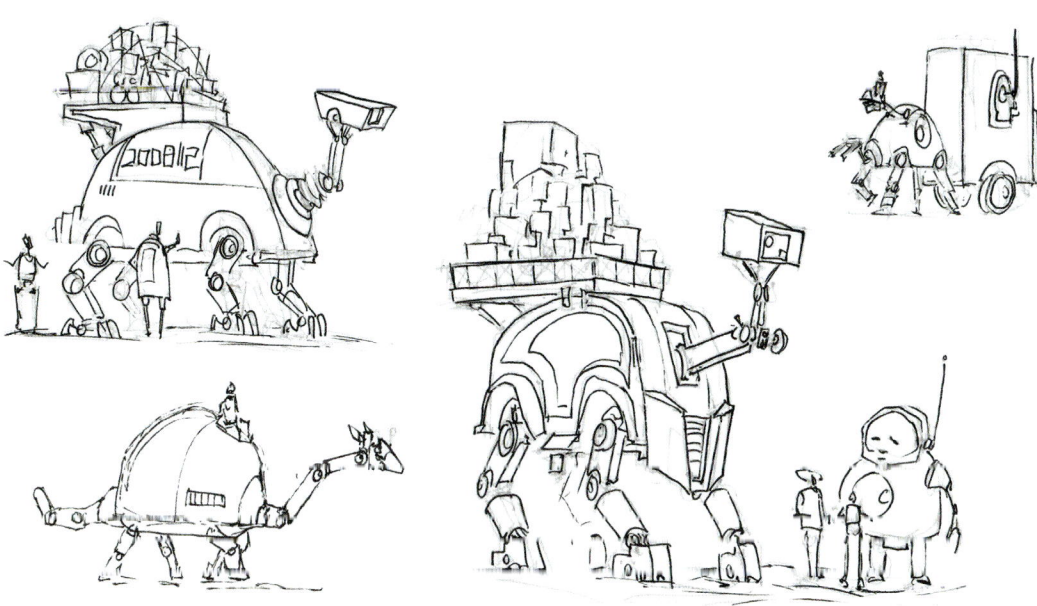

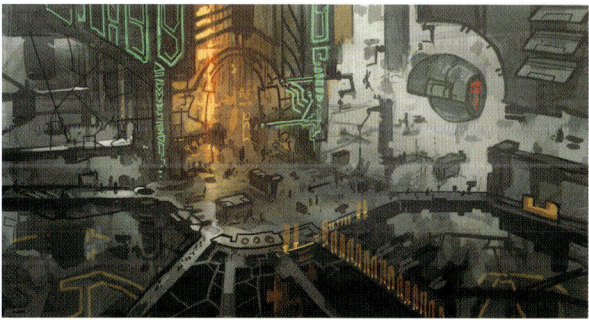

After deciding to follow the map into uncharted lands, Berm haggles with a shipping manager by the name of HOKK to borrow a battery transport (opposite). HOKK agrees to loan the rig in exchange for 10,000 hours of free labor. Berm considers the trade a deal, signs a contract, and starts his journey.

As he begins the long trek forward, he must navigate the labyrinth of machine cranes and cargo holds through a massive trading port.

Left: Sketch designs of the battery transport

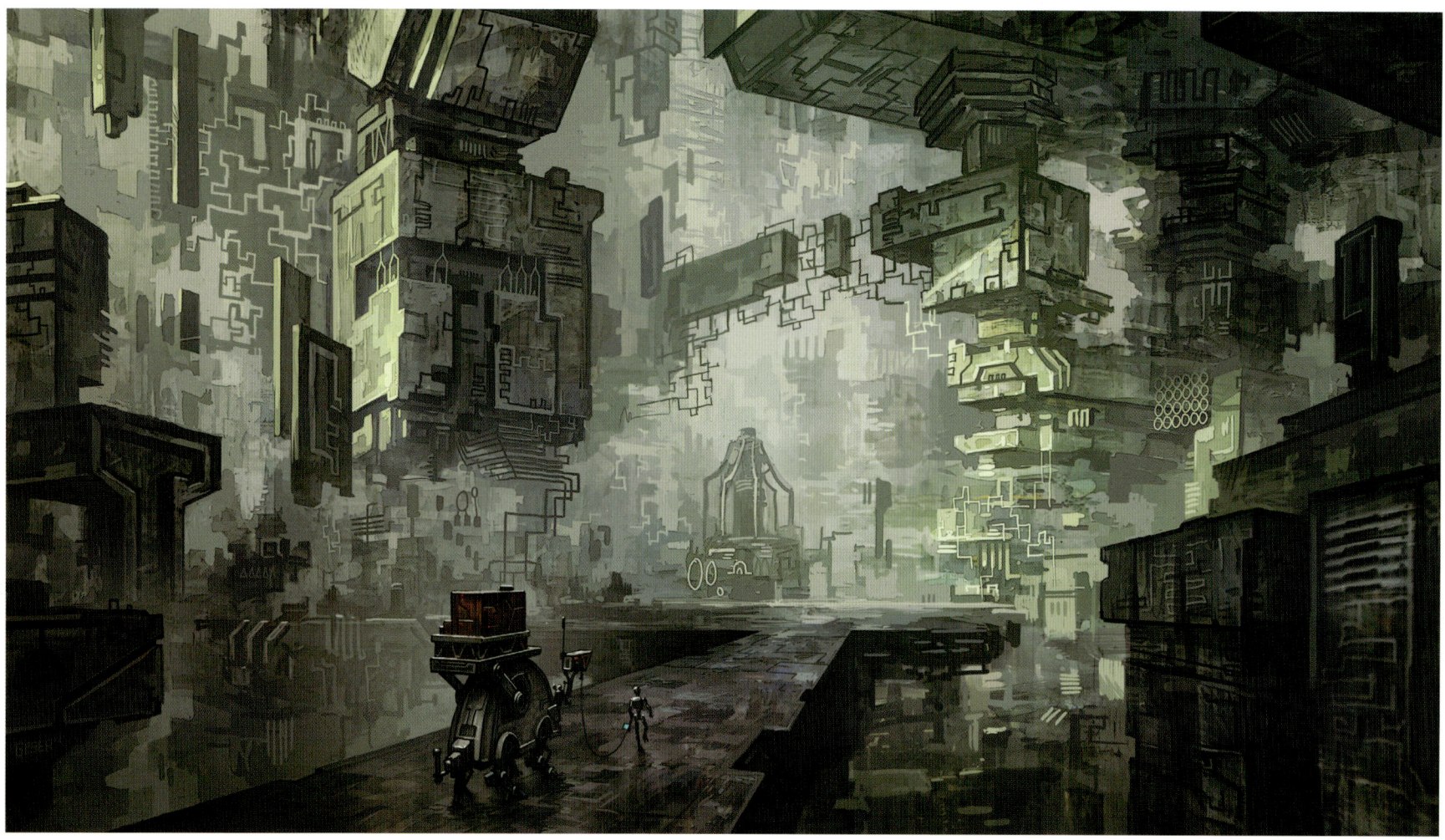

Before long, Berm finds deserted sectors of the city, void of activity. As trends and higher standards of living come online, entire communities relocate, leaving places like this to rest and possibly one day to be restored. These changes can happen rapidly, and over time have caused the entire planet to be completely swallowed in urban/industrial architecture.

Outcasts and corrupted bots hide themselves in these areas; Berm treads lightly. A stack of free energy units would be a tasty prize to any cyborg pirate. Fortunately, HOKK tipped Berm on a trade route with minimal risk.

Opposite page: As the landscape begins to open, Berm picks up speed and enters the fiery zone of Zeta Plat, an uncontrolled land of burning fuel pits left over from a vast war that occurred a millennium ago. Old soldier drones from the war still roam the skies in this sector. Carefully, Berm takes refuge during nightfall inside the wreckage of a hangar.

After many days of traveling, Berm discovers an outpost and meets Giggins, a research droid sent out to study weather patterns near the fragmented zone. Giggins, or "Gigs," as he prefers to be called, learns of Berm's quest and tells him of a strange land beyond the horizon: "Old-timers in these parts say it's a myth, a place of dreams!"

The next morning, Berm sets out on a three-day journey unlike any other, crossing into the Deleted Territories.

Bits of vegetation covering the ancient landscape begin to appear. After many grueling miles, brush of vibrant color and streaming waterfalls surround Berm. His mind is racing with excitement as he comes to a gigantic wall. He uses a half-fried control panel to begin to open a massive door. The sound of an oasis can be heard through the crack as warm air rushes over his face. With a couple steps forward, his senses are overloaded. It is a sight beyond anything he has previously known. Berm has arrived!

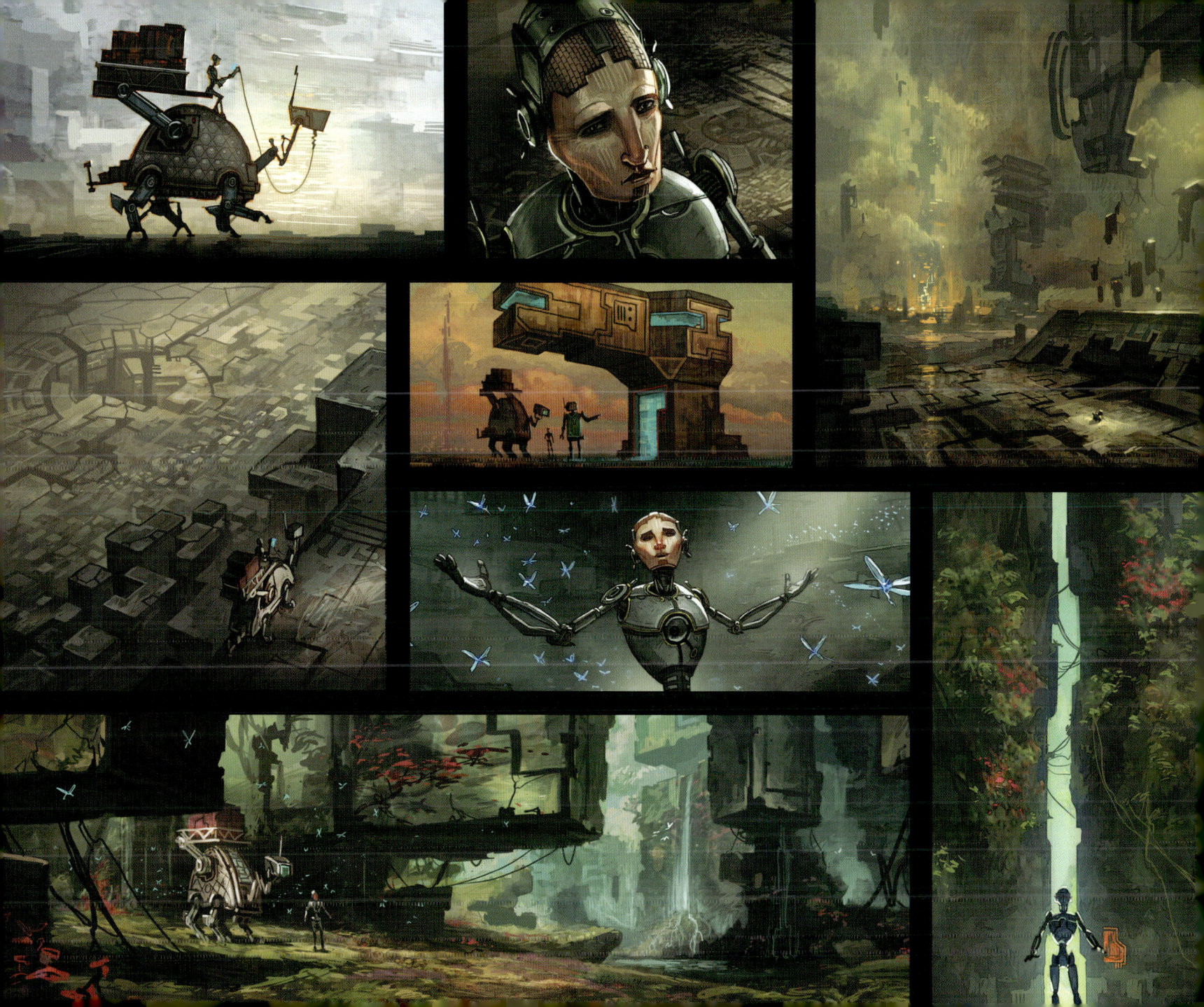

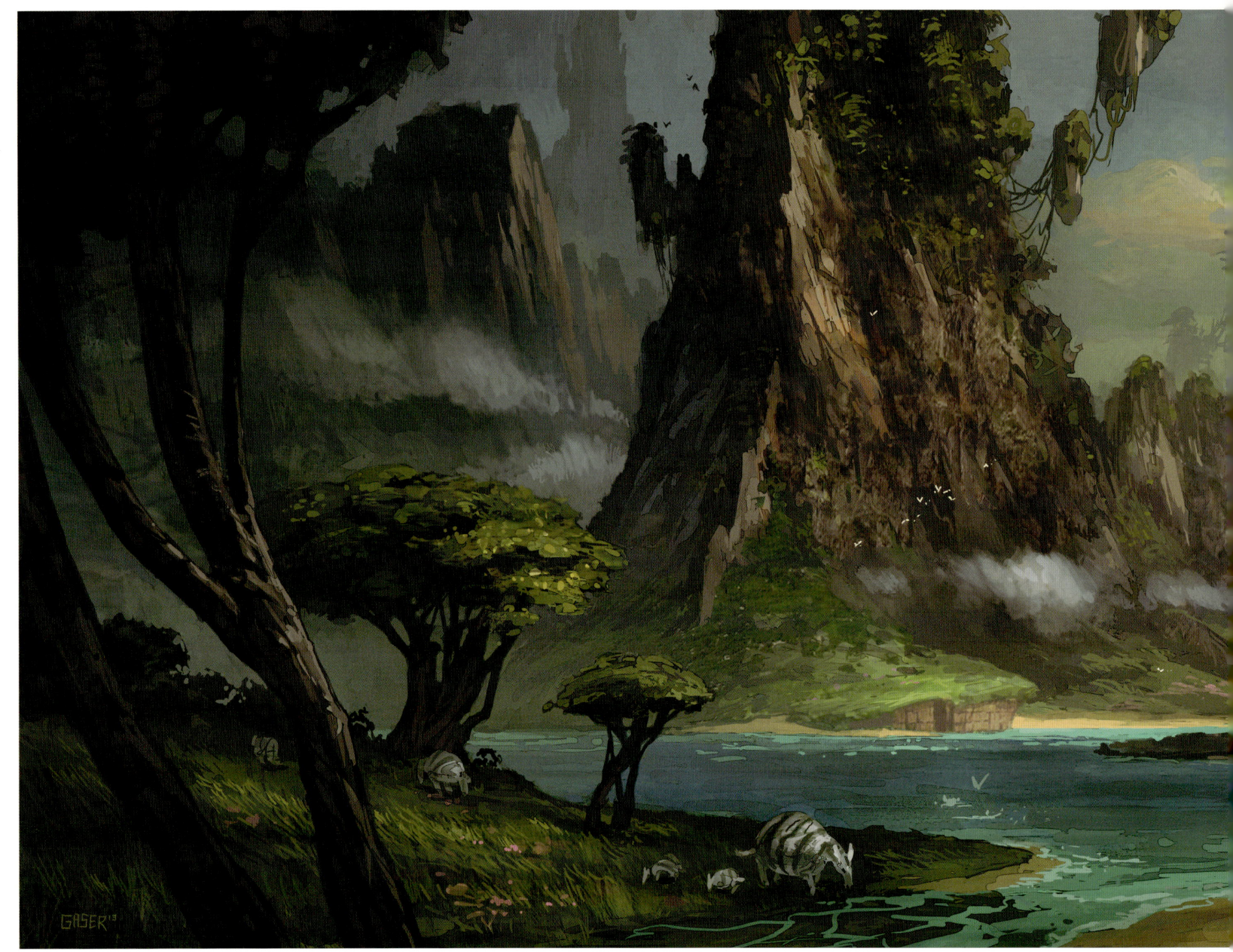

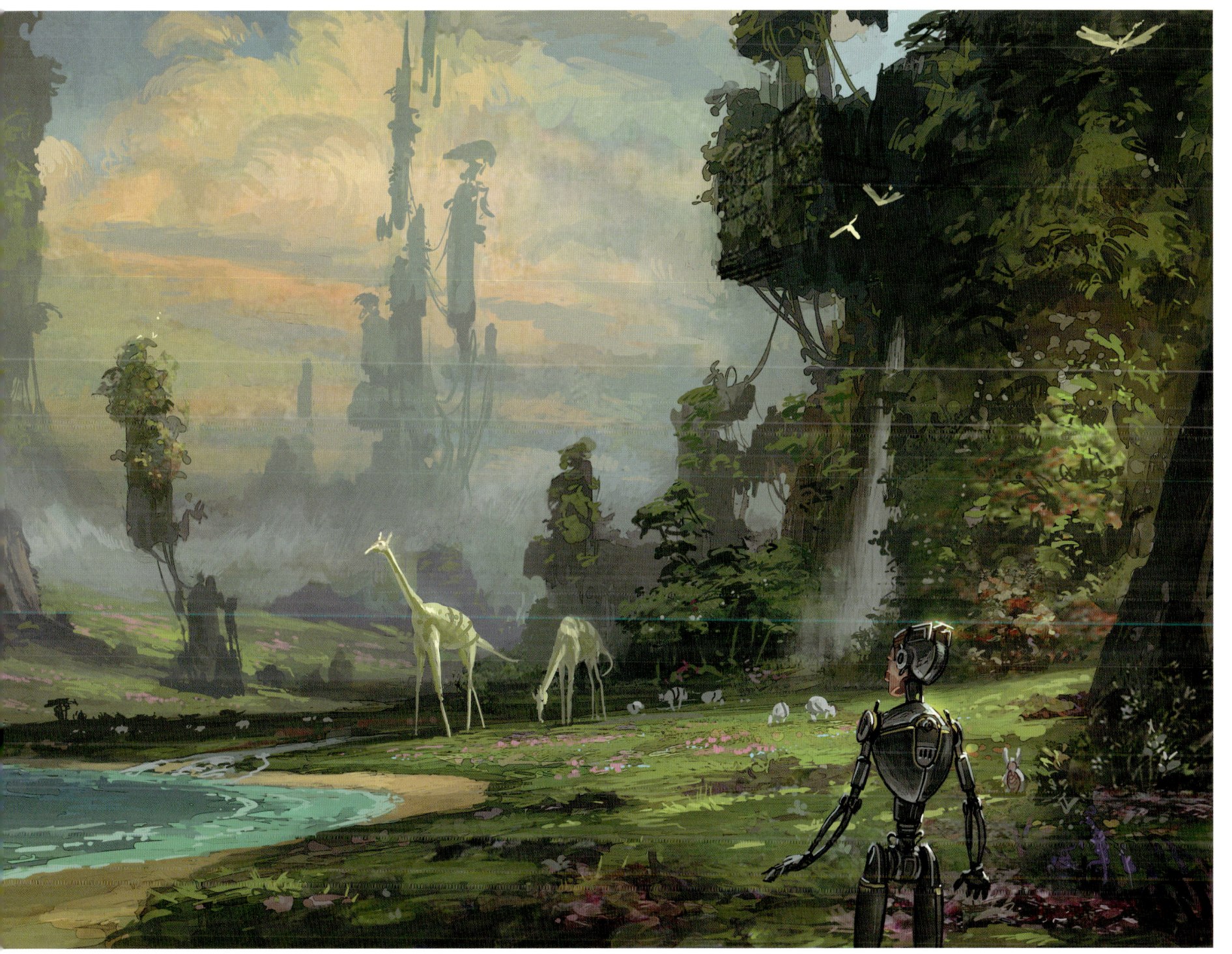

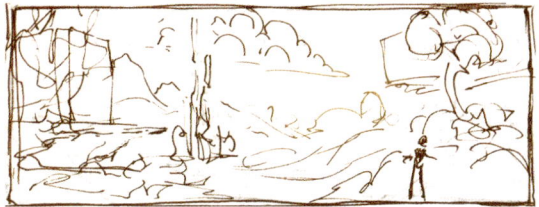

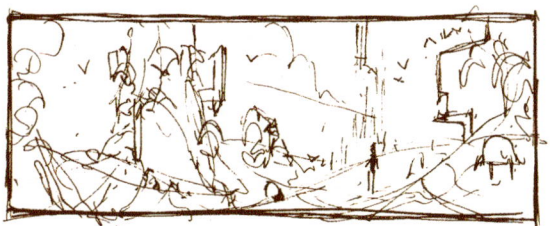

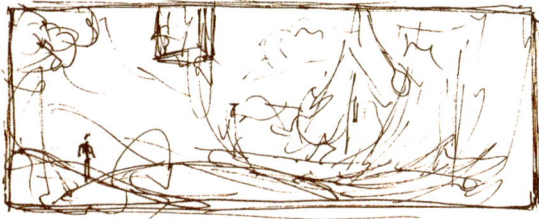

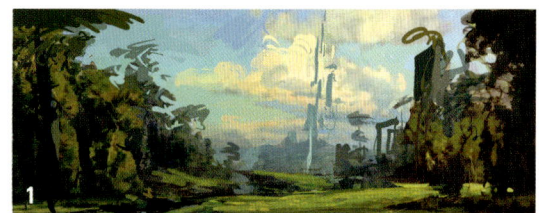

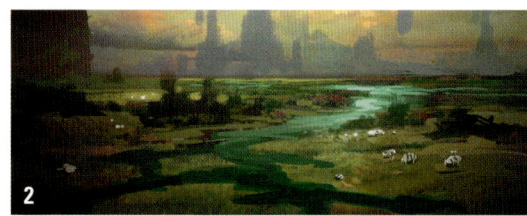

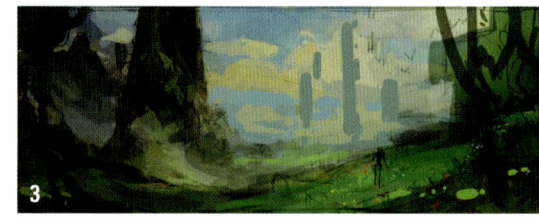

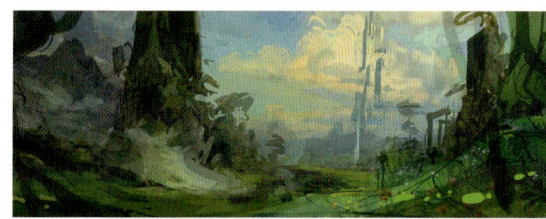

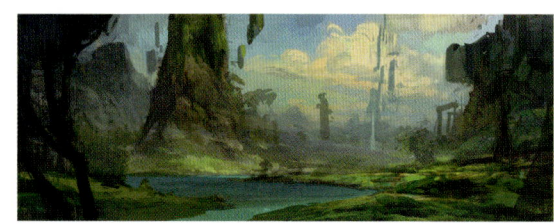

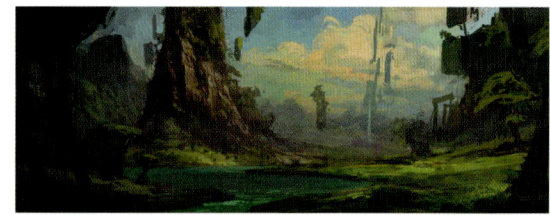

Step 1: Thumbnail Sketches

During the process of creating my previous page, I knew that the last visual of the oasis had to be grand in scope—a wide shot showcasing an epic vista that would become a two-page spread. It had to seem breathtaking to the main character. With a plan in mind, I generally like to start with pen on marker paper—just start doodling and see where things go.

As I finished three comps, number two was the most interesting—some kind of towering mountain with ancient ruins far away in the distance.

Step 2: Color Sketches

Once I scanned in the thumbnails, I began to sketch out color thumb ideas in Photoshop.

When starting these quick color studies, I like to use photo ref—stitch a variety of elements together and paint on top for a desired effect. The process is fast and sometimes creates unexpected results that become useful.

With number one, the mood was working but seemed too balanced on both sides. Number two was feeling more like a vast plain—not enough interesting elements. Number three was utilizing the pen sketch of number two as an underlay. Something about this comp was working for me. It had multiple points of focus and seemed to draw the eye into the scene. Perhaps I could combine color sketch number one with number three. Hmmm...

Step 3: Defining the Painting

After combining the two color sketches, I decided to explore the rest of the landscape. Along the way I discovered a lake of some kind. This could be a unique element in establishing a breaking point between the foreground and middle-ground plains.

I continued to add more bits of detail. I began to darken the left side of the scene to help pool the light towards the right, knowing I would add the main character in this area later in the process.

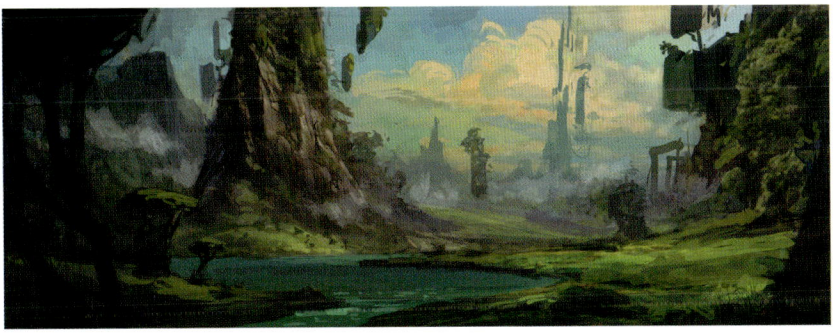

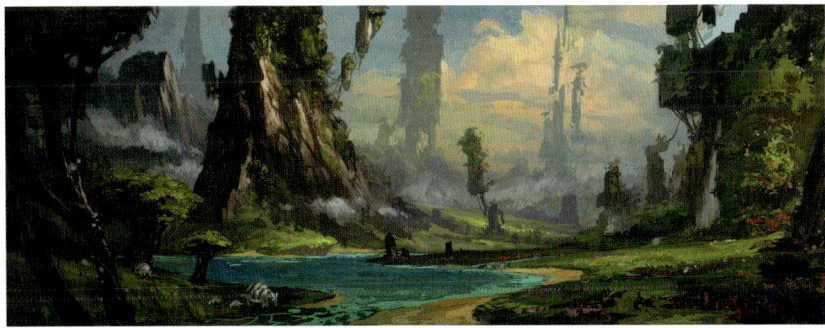

Step 4: Rendering

At this stage most of the components to the painting have been ironed out. It's now time to work on bringing the image to life. I added cloud layers to separate various fields of atmospheric depth. I decided to erase the tree on the right, swapping it out for a small grove of hanging brush. But the image was still fairly dry in terms of content; it needed more flowers and vegetation. Also, some wildlife would be interesting...birds and mammals grazing on the land. Adding elements like these into a scene can help with scale and give the viewer something to relate to.

Step 5: Details

Now comes the real fun: making the painting come alive. This stage involved making sure all of the highlights and textures read properly; pinpointing areas of interest with a strong light source; adding floral detail, a cascading waterfall on the right, and a family of animals on the left; and creating a beach around the lake, using its perimeter to help train the eye into the painting, establishing more depth.

I noticed the center of the painting (from step 4) in the sky seemed to take over the view. So, I covered it by creating another colossal ruin structure in the distance. This helped the eye move back down to the middle ground, into the painting, while creating a visual tunnel to the grand ruin towers on the horizon.

All that's left are a few more critters, layers of birds, and the main character in the foreground.

PAT PRESLEY

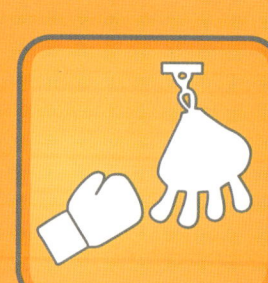

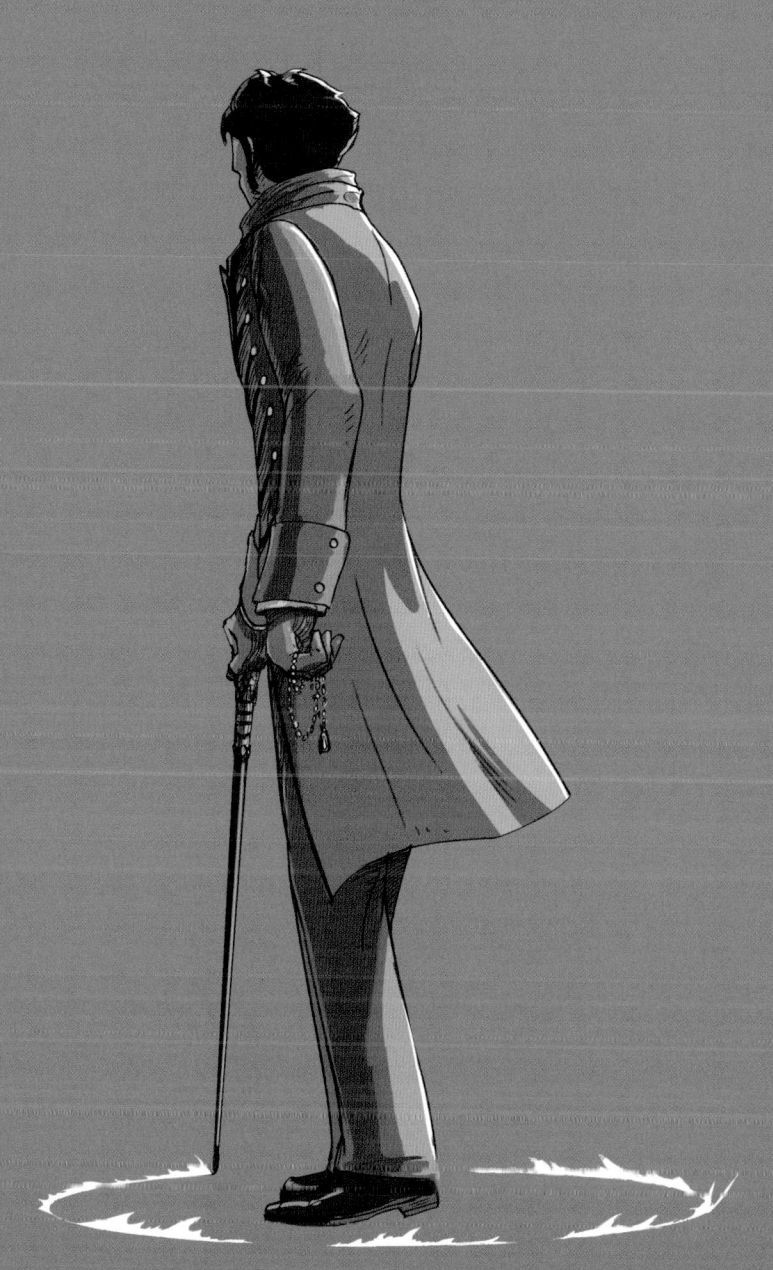

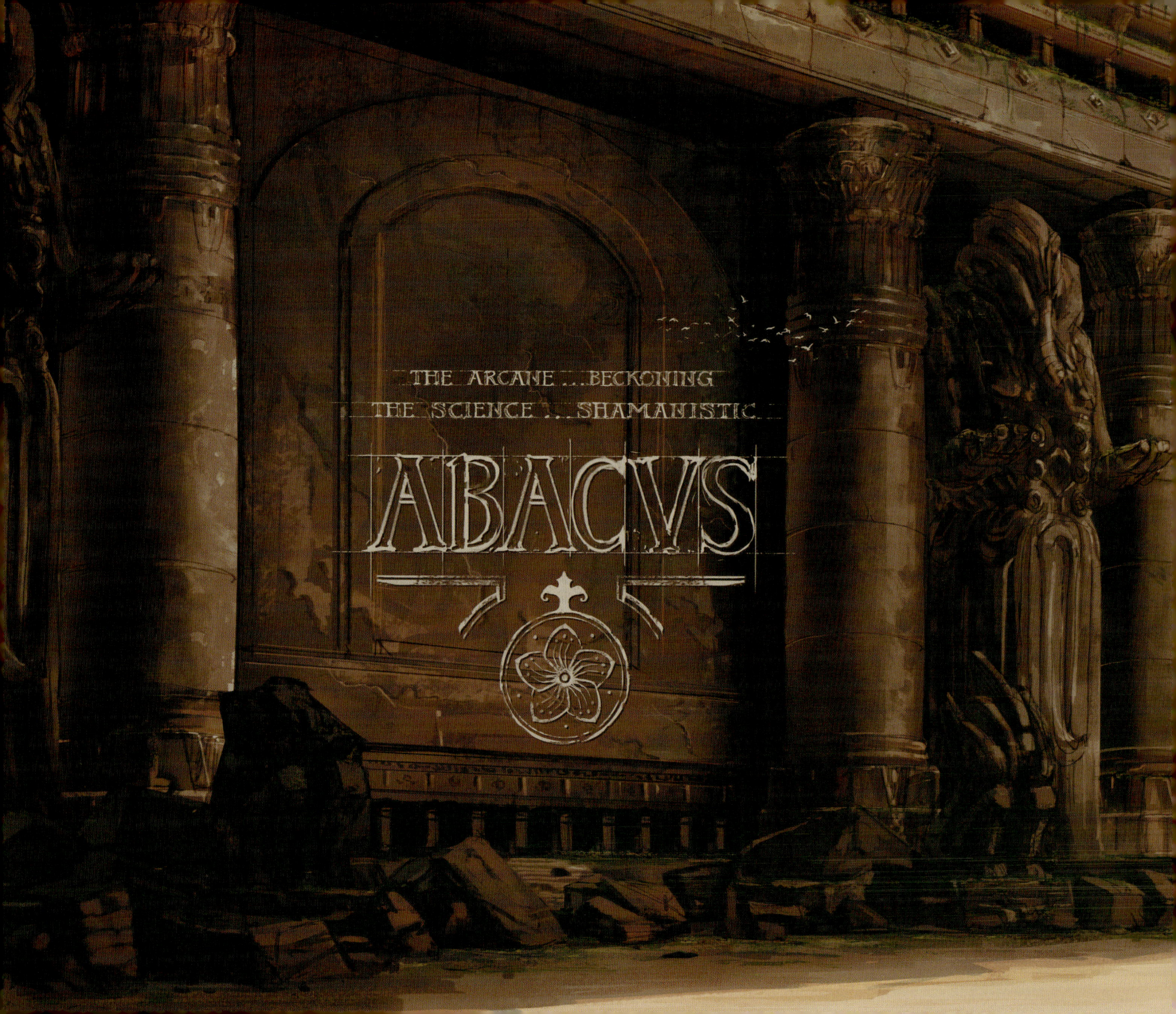

THE ARCANE...BECKONING
THE SCIENCE...SHAMANISTIC

ABACVS

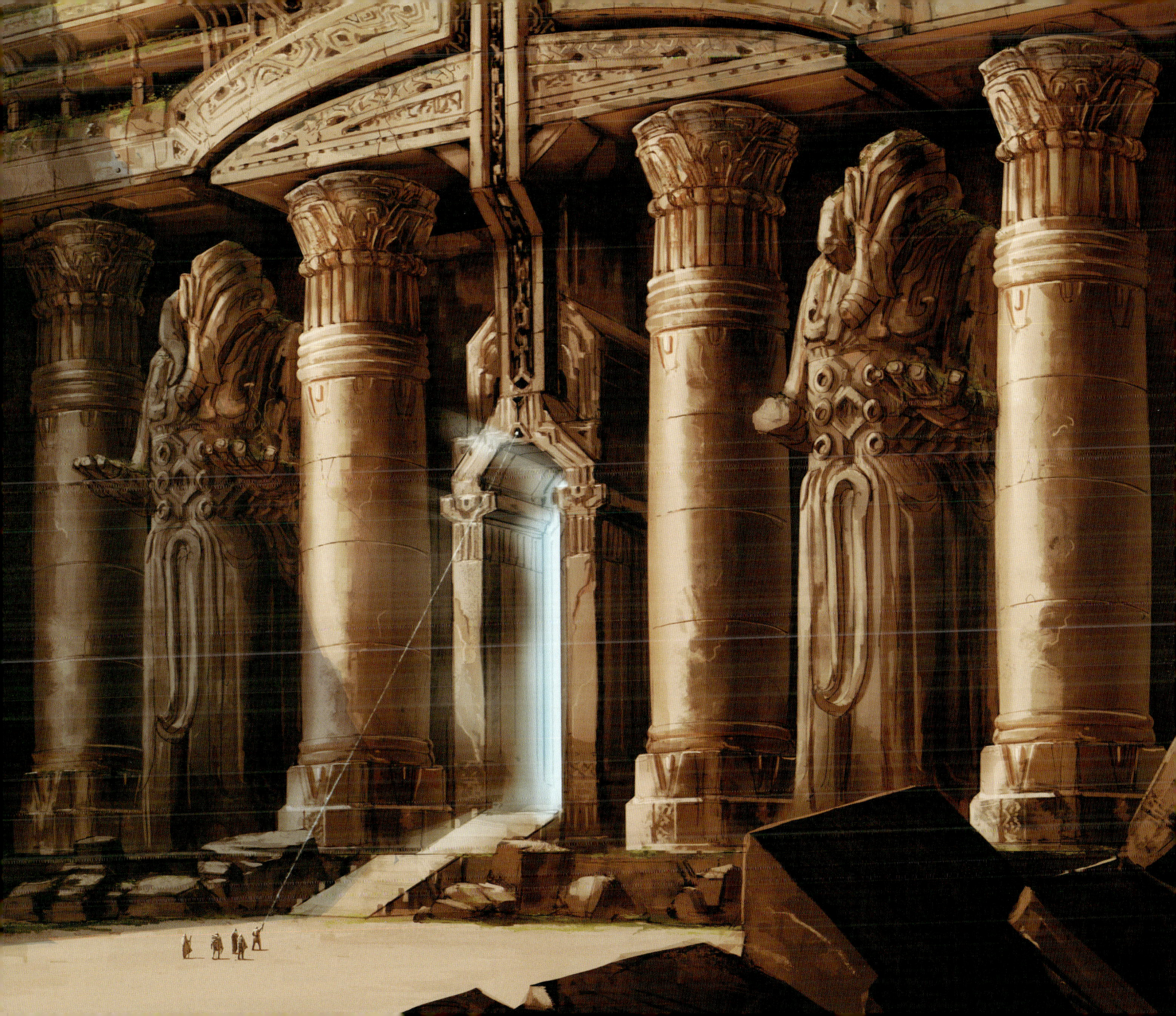

A Child of the Sea

On the high seas in the Indian Ocean, an infant boy is found adrift on a lifeboat. Covered in strange body markings, the boy is wrapped in a red cloth along with three artifacts. There is no report of a lost vessel. His origin unknown, the boy is raised as Abacus by his rescuer, Captain Atticus of the East India Trading Company.

Growing up on the sea in the Age of Sail, Abacus learns with the trade winds. His adopted father exposes him to worlds beyond the deck, from Persia to Batavia, Bengal to Siam. In a time when the ancient beckons to be found, while the new science speaks with a shamanistic tongue, Abacus is shaped into the rarest of all steel.

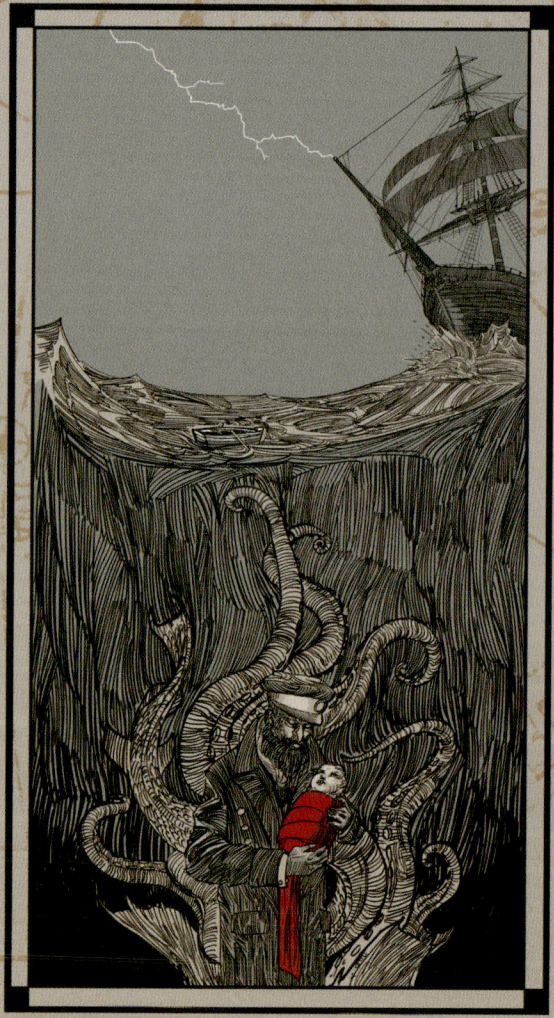

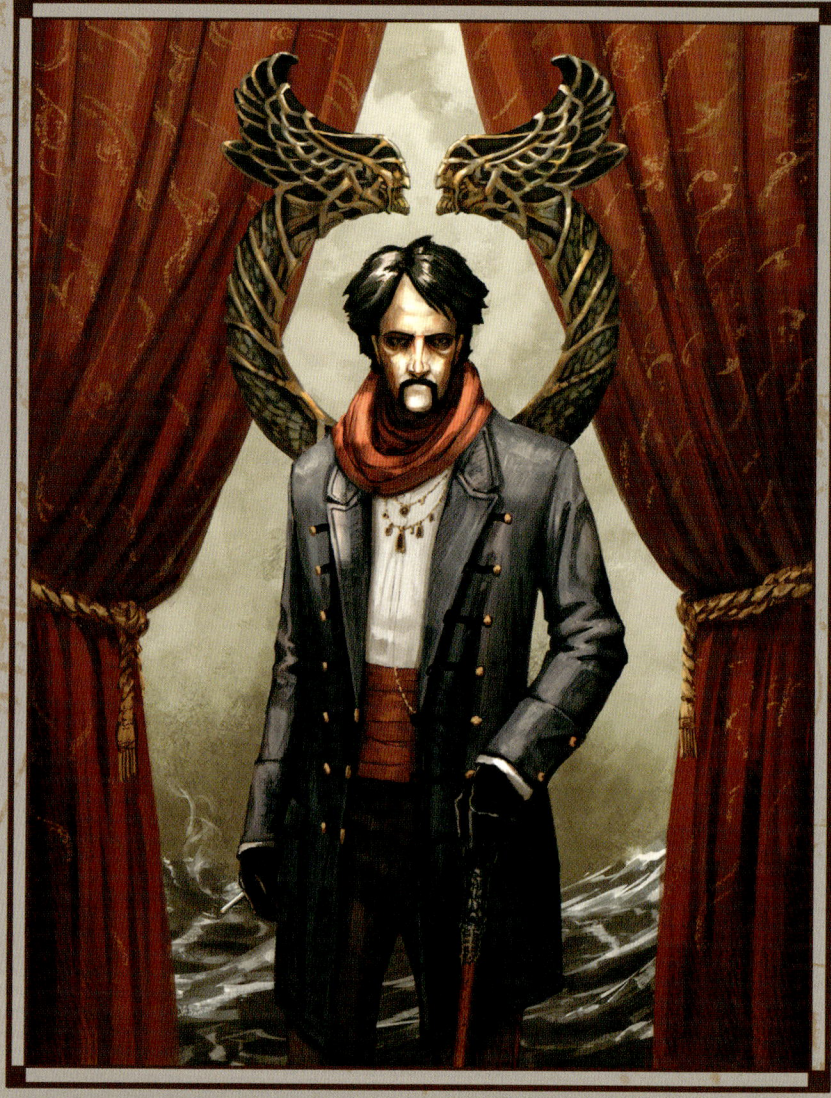

Discipula Artium Arcanorum

After traumatic events during his teenage years in the Khmer, Abacus discovers the world of dying ancient rites and incantations, giving him clues about his body markings and the three artifacts. He develops an affinity for the arcane. Conscious of his markings but without understanding their true nature, he covers himself from the neck down. Abacus always carries a cane, one of the three artifacts found with him on the lifeboat.

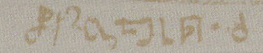

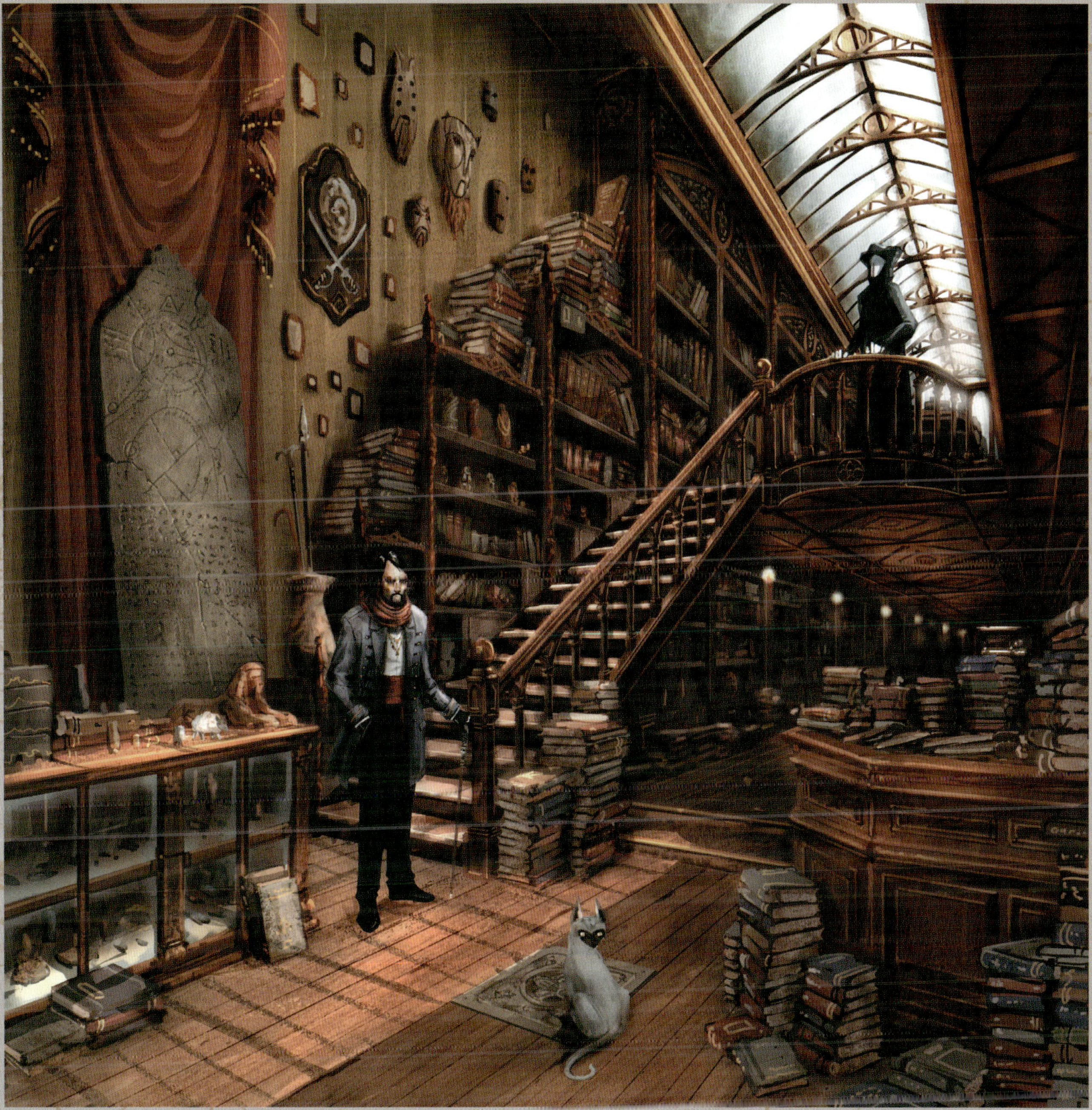

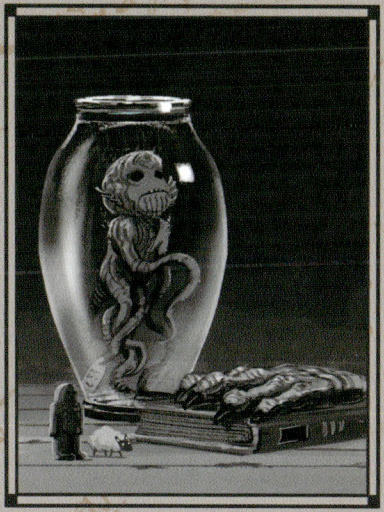

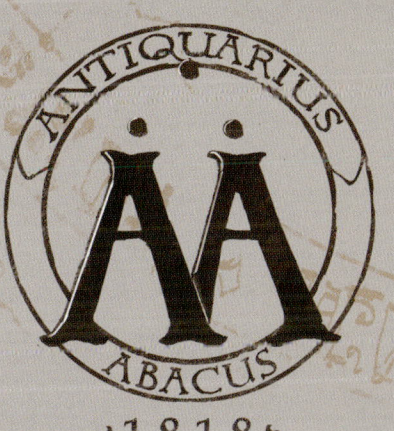

The Antiquarian

After his adopted father's mysterious death, Abacus uses his wealth to establish Abacus Antiquarius, a trading post for ancient tomes and artifacts. He builds the shop on top of an old lot. Abacus Antiquarius is constantly filled with uninvited occupants, strange objects, and books of forgotten time.

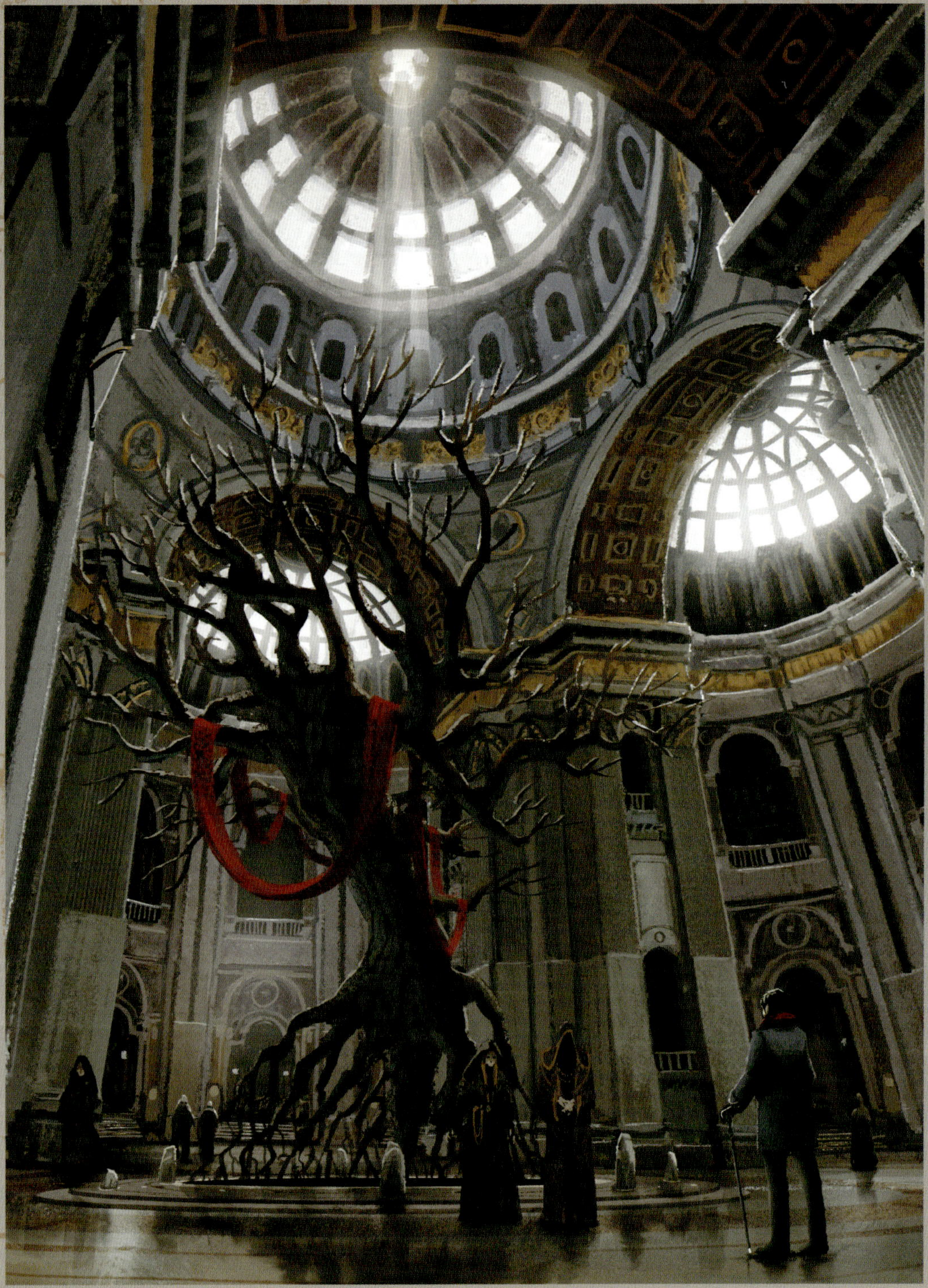

The House Plumeria

Early in his career as an antiquarian, a client asks Abacus to seek out a terma, a Buddhist relic believed to have fallen from the sky. To find the relic, Abacus must seek out a fifth-century scripture written by a tertön, the protector of this ancient relic. During his search, Abacus encounters The House Plumeria, an ancient fraternity who created a nexus in which all opponents and allies of the arcane congregate.

A neutral ground for all, the house allows all types of orders, covens, and sects to make transactions. Disputes are settled and the game for one's soul is played under the plumeria tree. The house keeps a close eye on all, while secrets and knowledge echo among its cavernous halls. Yet the true nature and intention of the house remain unknown to Abacus. His relationship with the house is tenuous at best.

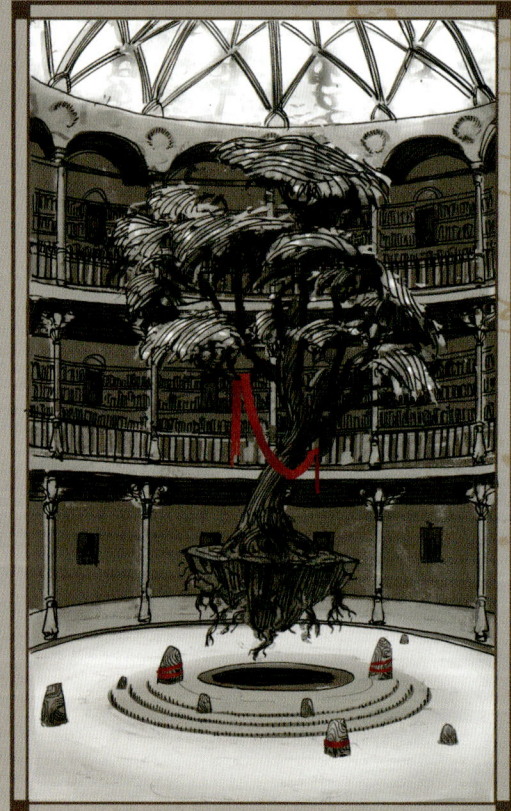

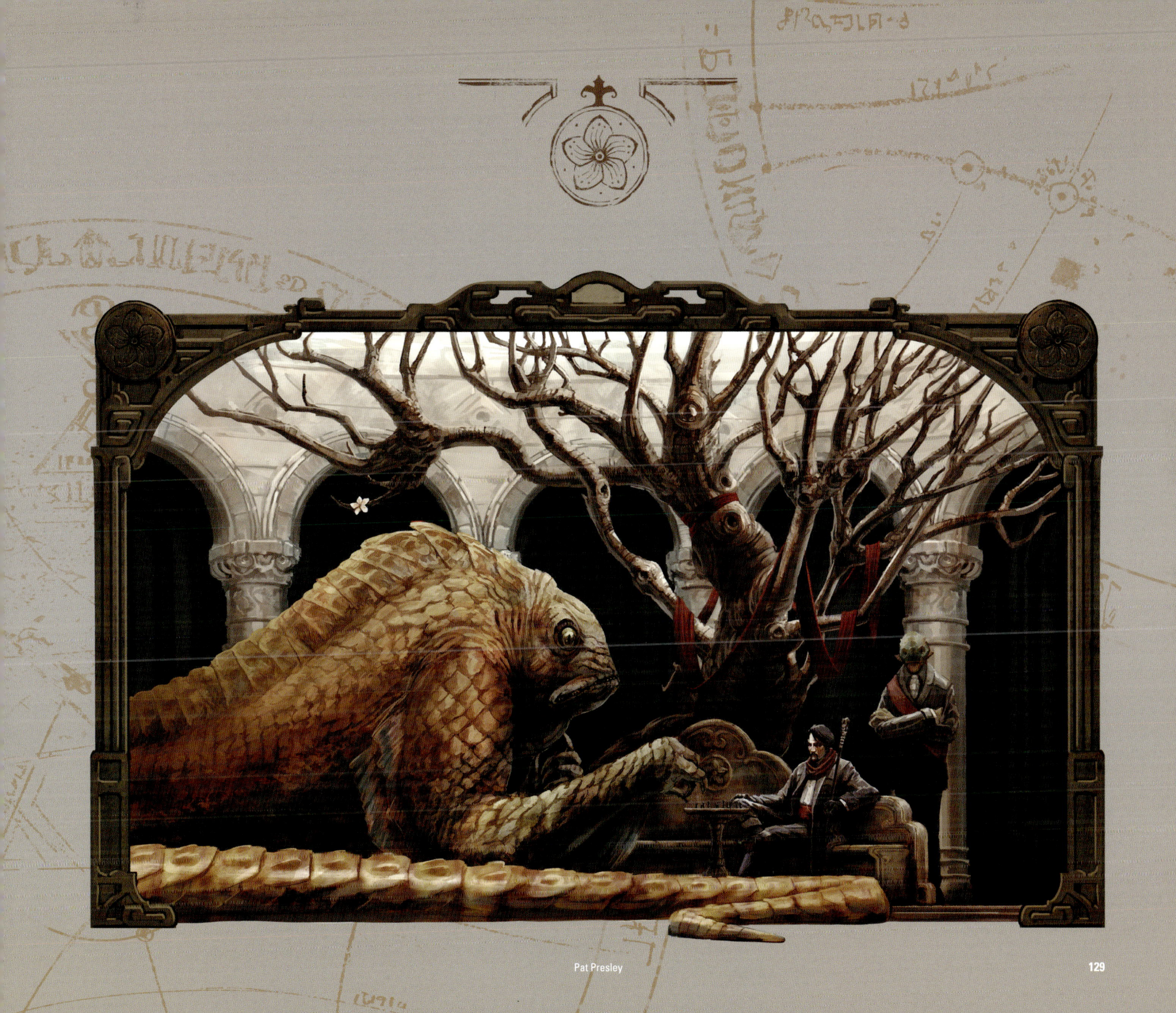

Pat Presley

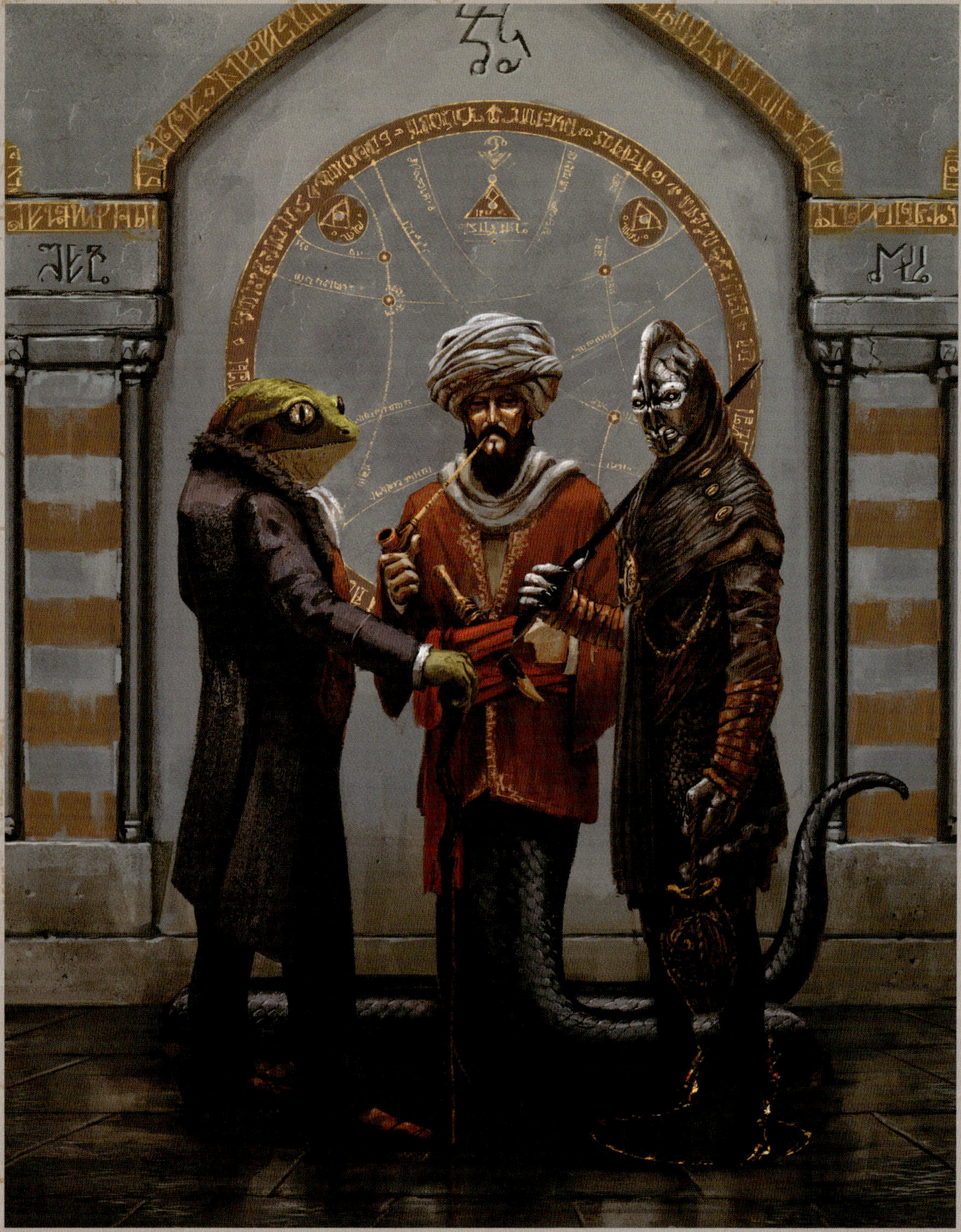

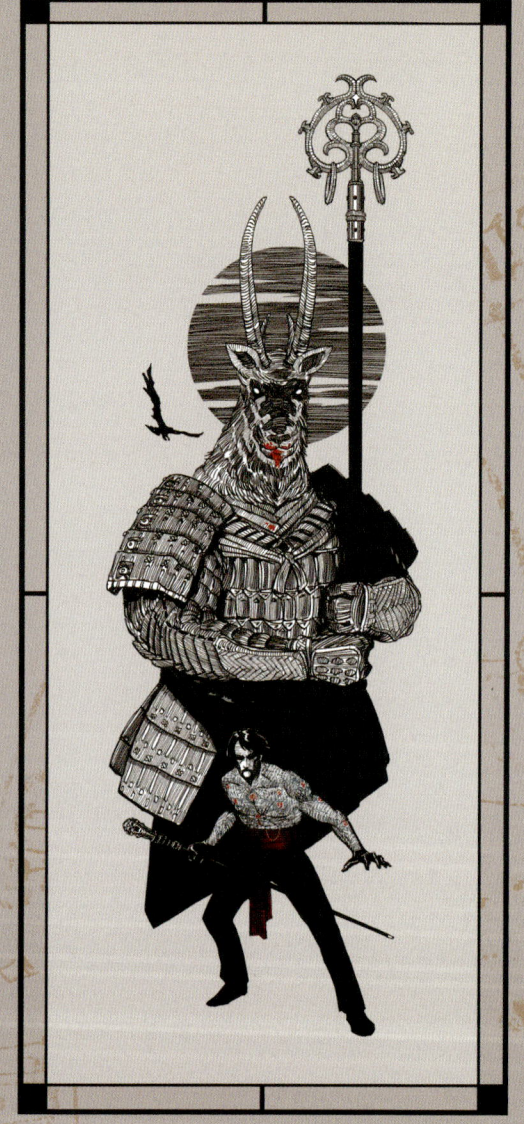

Friends or Foes

During his journeys, Abacus encounters many individuals who play a part, large or small, in the puzzle of his life. Some are chance meetings that grow into lifetime friendships, while many confrontations alter Abacus forever.

Facing page left: At times, exiled demons are said to have taken refuge under its roof. The House Plumeria has seen many souls walk through its dark corridors. But beyond the threshold of the house, are they friends or foes?

Facing page right: Abacus travels to Aokigahara, the Sea of Trees at the base of Mount Fuji, seeking the scepter said to belong to Kamoshika Demon. Barely escaping with his life, Abacus returns home empty-handed. Did he encounter the demon or did the myth of Aokigahara almost destroy Abacus?

Below: After a vessel from a small fishing town drags an obelisk marked with strange glyphs from the ocean, an outbreak occurs. Those who come into contact with the stone are left with a mysterious affliction. Abacus is called in by the town mayor to study the obelisk. While uncovering the mystery, Abacus is stalked by a strange creature who warns him of the town's secret history, which may very well hold a key to Abacus's past.

Right: While looking for the legendary forest Himavanta, Abacus searches for clues about his real parents and his origin. At the edge of the mythical forest, he encounters a half-bird girl who becomes his loyal guide in the ever-shifting forest, but at what price?

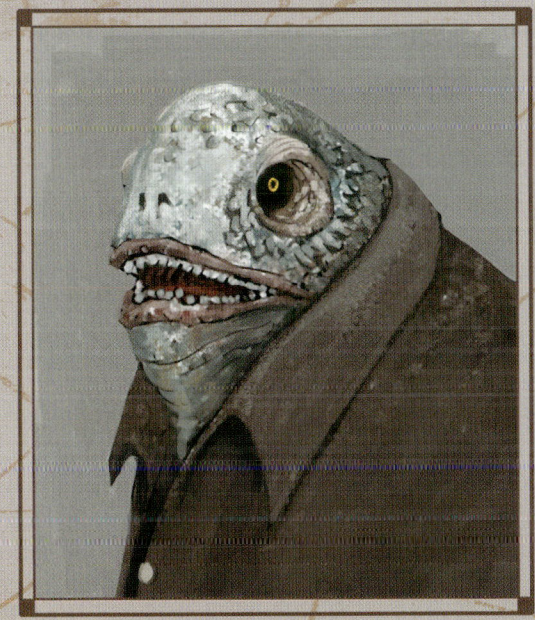

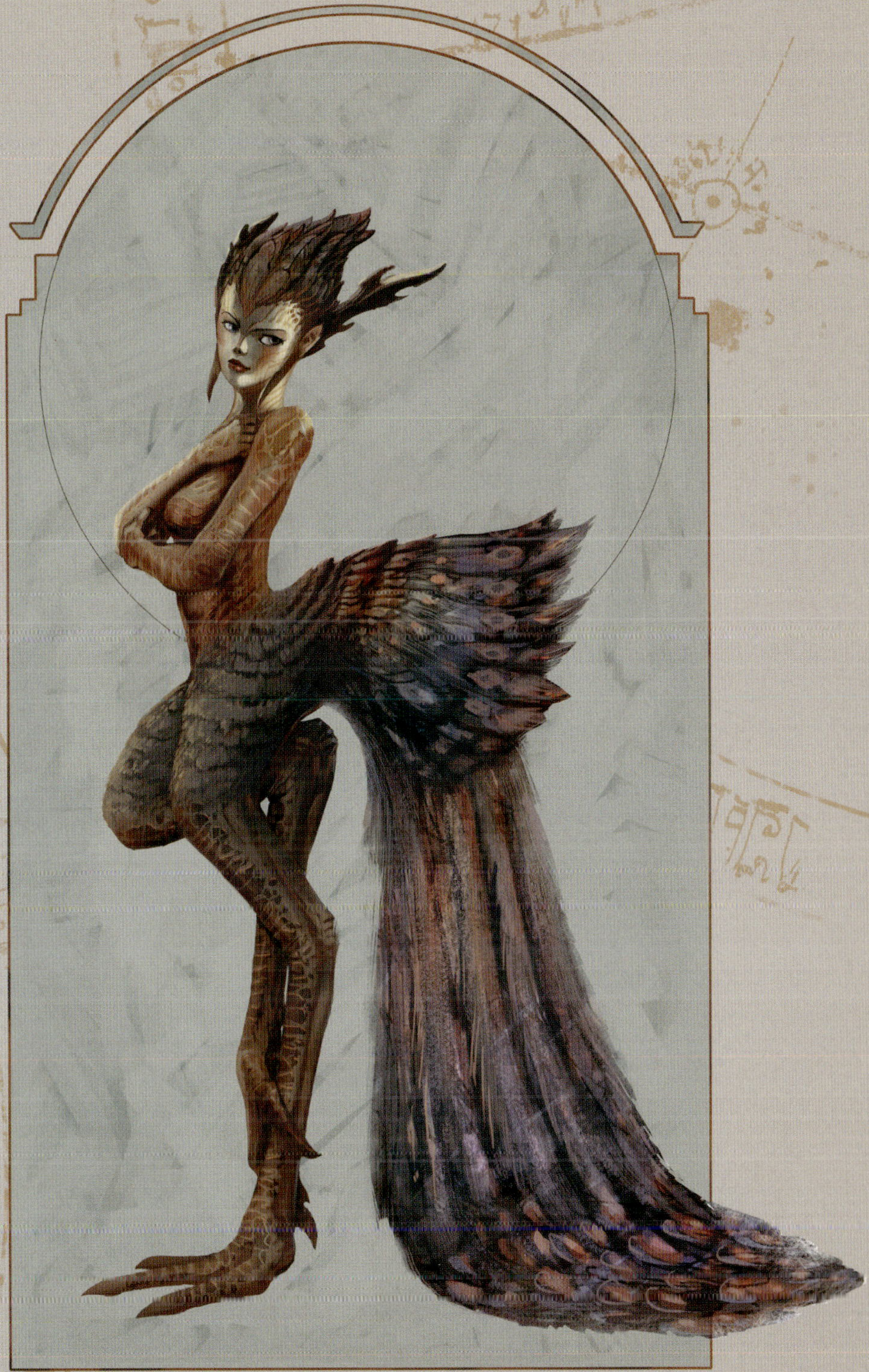

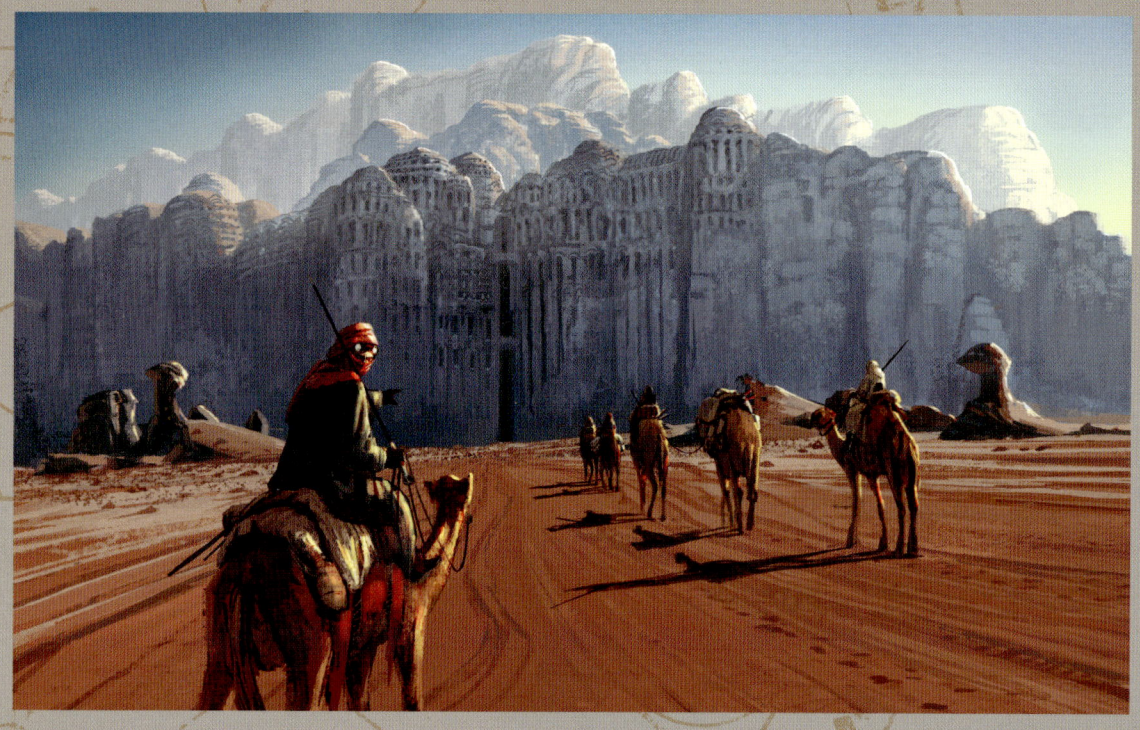

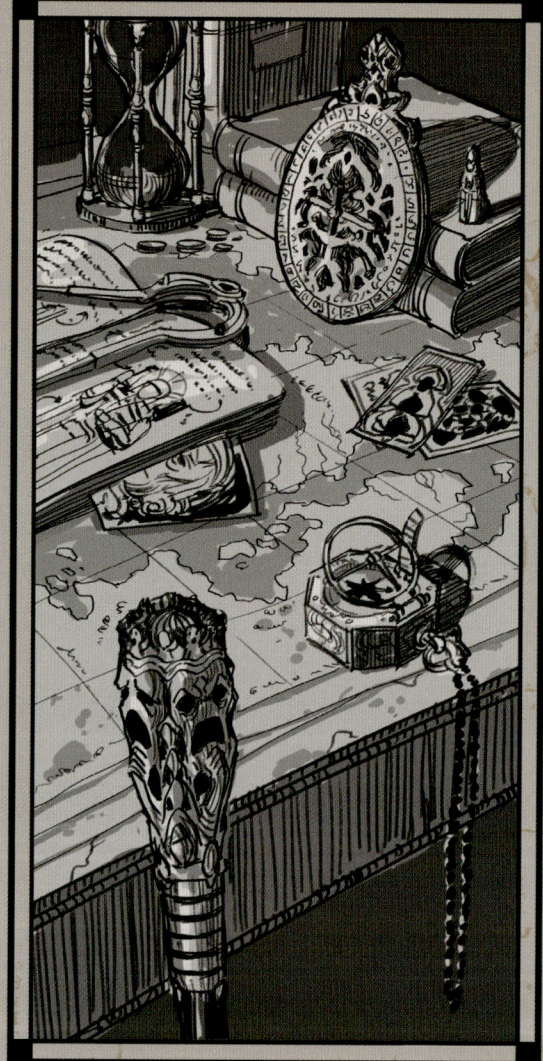

Terra Incognita

The journey takes Abacus to places both familiar and unknown. While traveling the world seeking the odds and the olds, he will discover the pieces of the puzzle that will dictate his life and propel him towards the inevitable revelation of his origin and his return to the ocean.

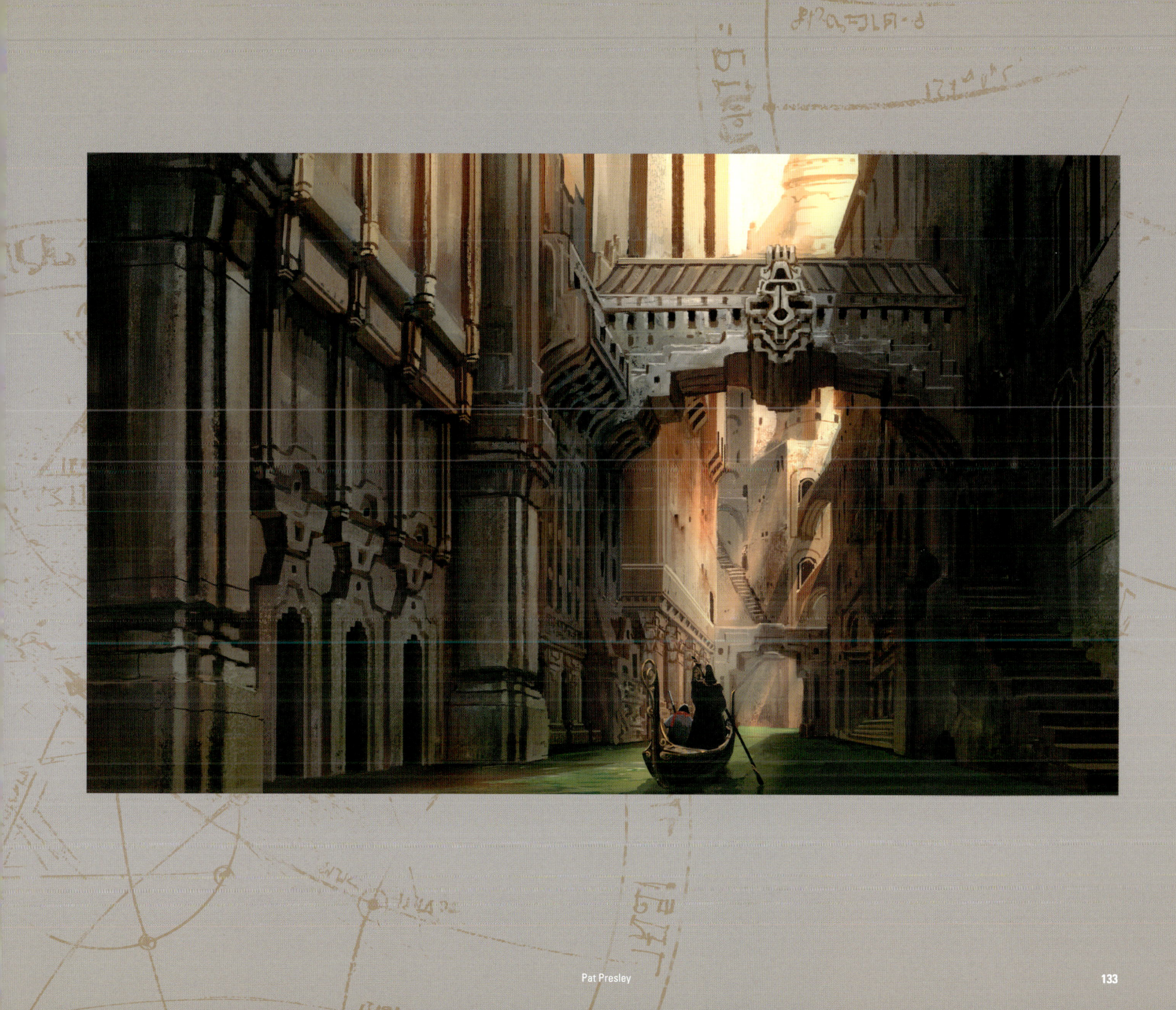

Pat Presley

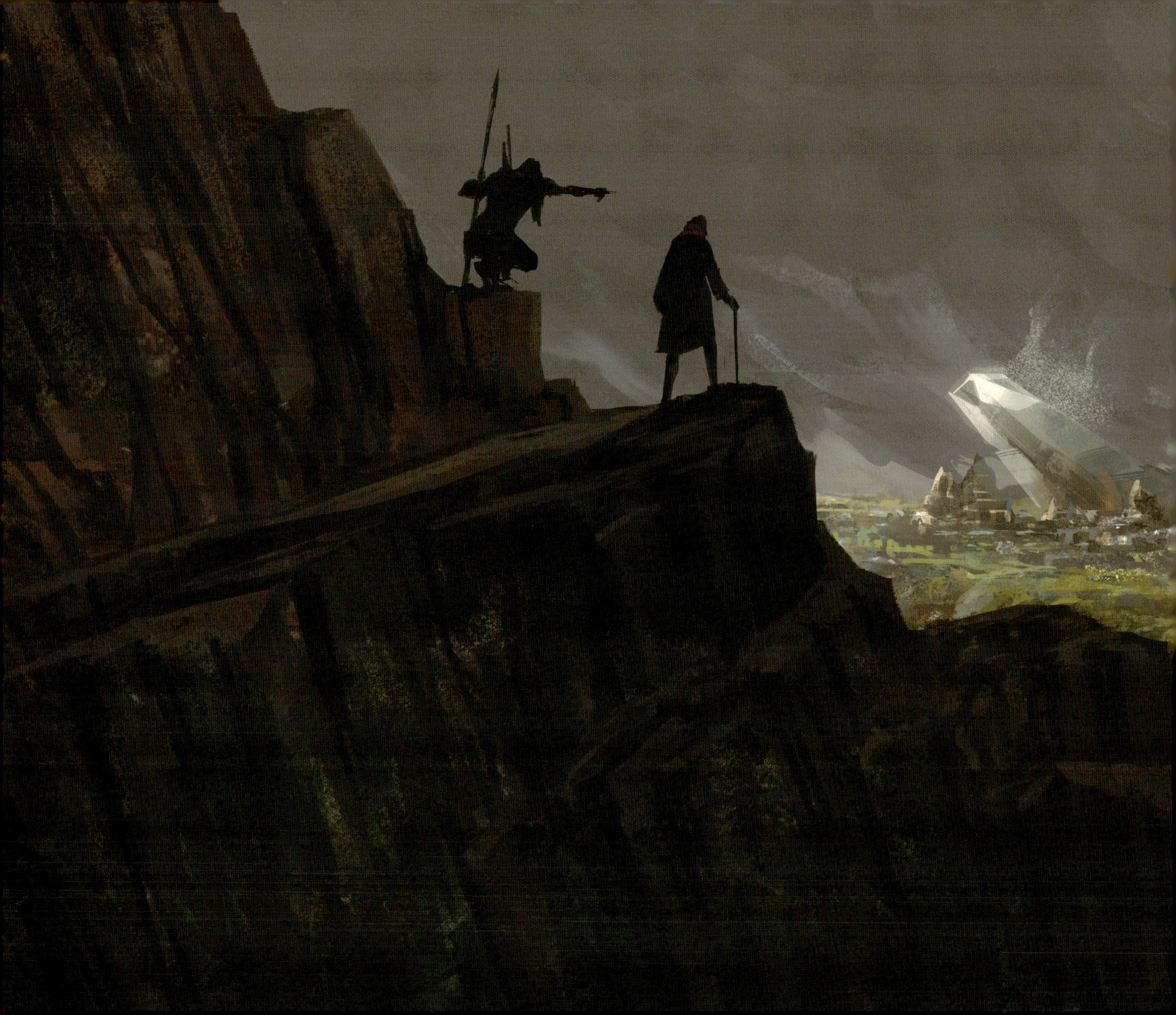

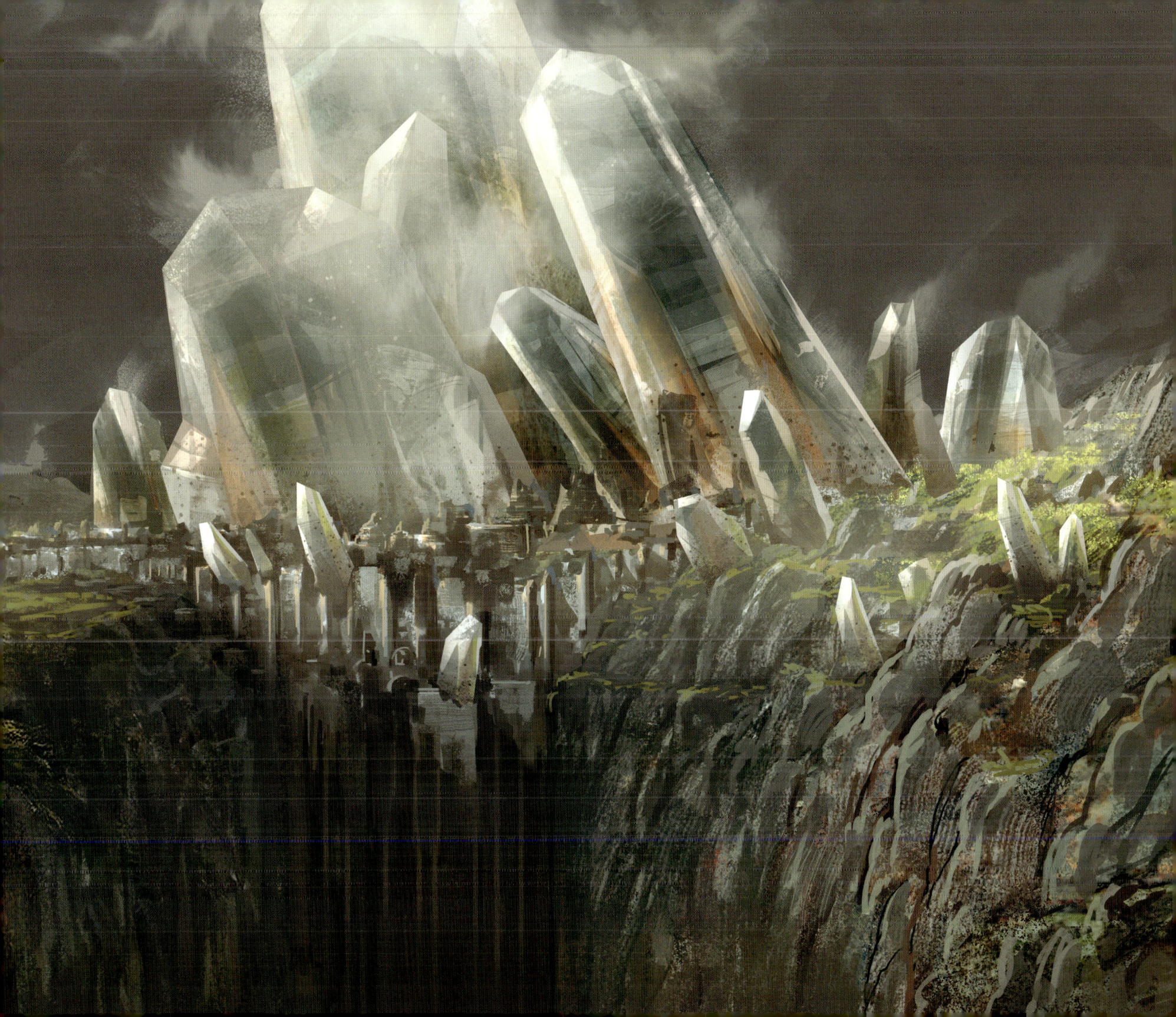

Genesis of Abacus

Abacus was born out of my love for old-fashioned adventures. Before starships and robots, there were weekends spent reading *The Count of Monte Cristo, Mysterious Island,* and *The Fall of the House of Usher.* I remember how Aramis was my favorite of all the musketeers, and that I preferred Solomon Kane over Conan and Doc Savage.

When the *Battle Milk* team gave me the honor of joining them in their continuing adventure, I saw nothing more fitting than to pay homage to all the serial adventures that took me away to the uncharted all those afternoons. For Abacus, I wanted to fuse the inspirations from Dumas, Lovecraft, Poe, and others to create a rich world that Abacus and a cast of characters and places could occupy. With that thought in mind, I set out on a mission of world-building. Through a series of images enhanced by backstories, Abacus finally came to be. It's my hope that he will continue to take me on many more journeys.

After all, this is only the beginning of *The Adventures of Abacus.*

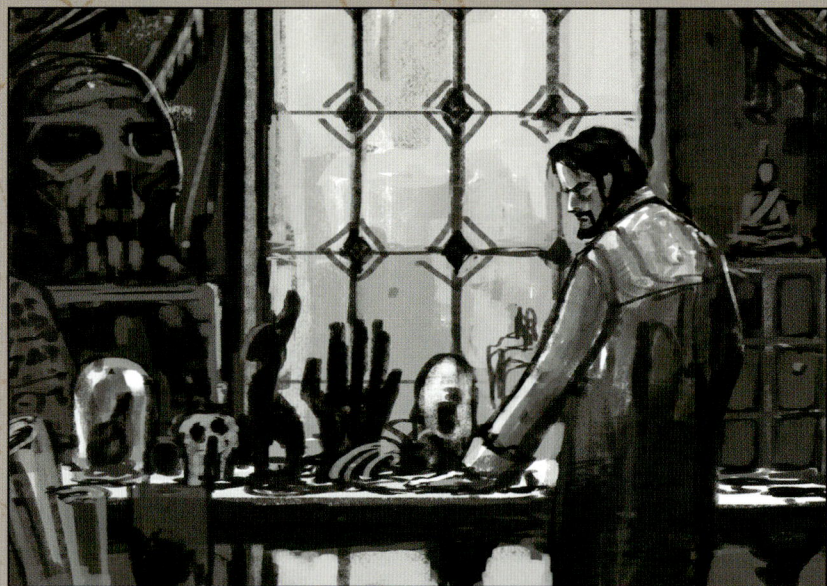

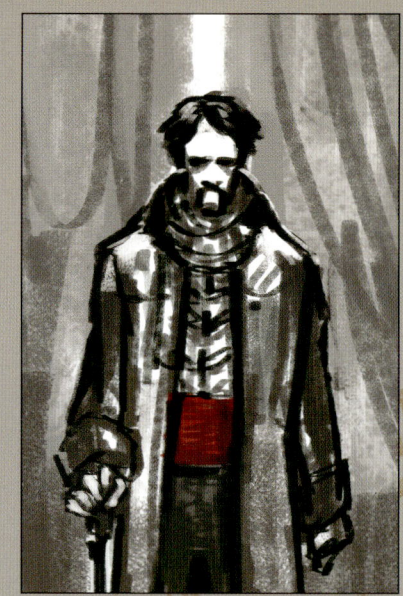

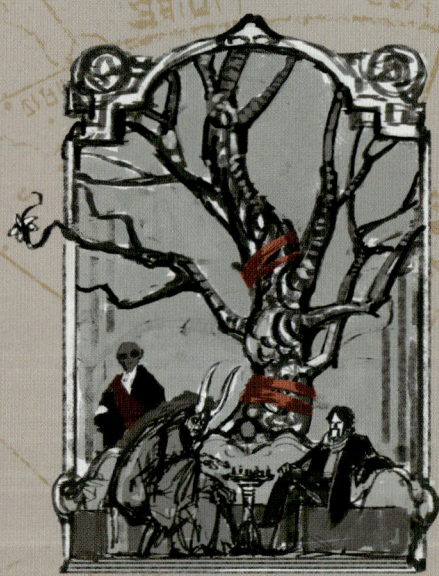

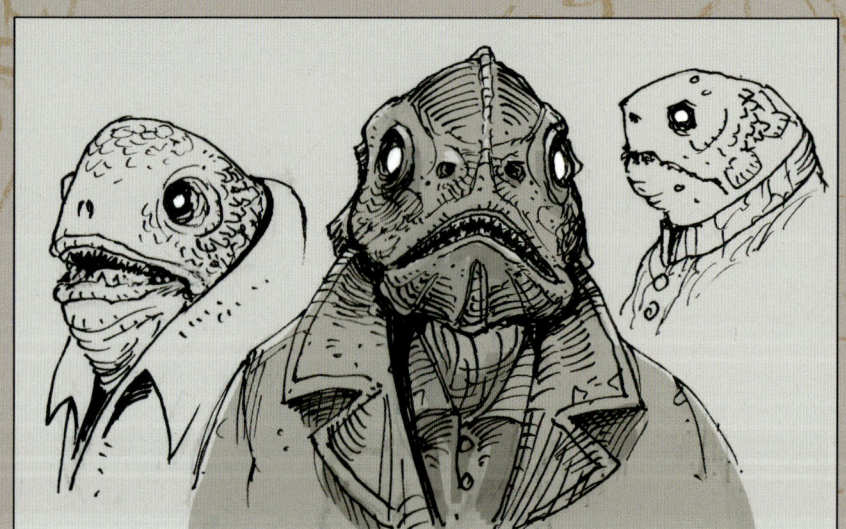

Process for the Ancient Ruin

Step 1: Composition

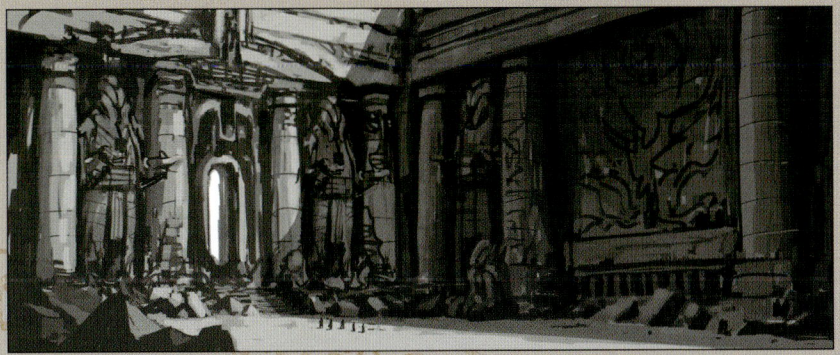

Like most of the work done here, the first step is to find a visual bearing for the image. I created a rough gray-scale composition. At this stage I didn't worry too much other than to make sure that I kept important visual elements away from the center of the image. I decided the focus should be at the central massive doorway.

Step 2: Line Work and Color Palette

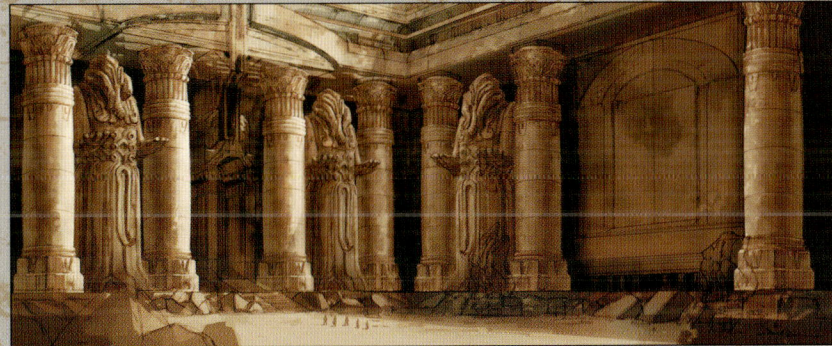

At this point I knew where the overall image was going. I then shifted focus to designing the rest of the image with some loose line work and then laid down a rough color palette.

Step 3: Shapes and Rendering

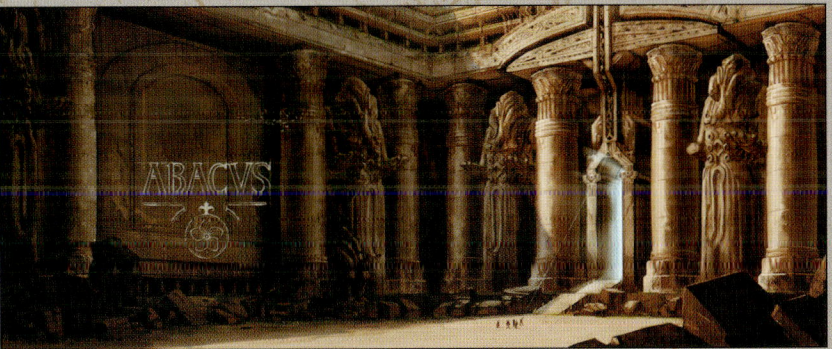

This is an execution stage where I identified major shapes and then tightened the rendering toward the final image.

Step 4: Final Image

For the final image I flipped the image to take advantage of the shadowed side of the composition, where the title and symbol would be placed.

Pat Presley

THANG LE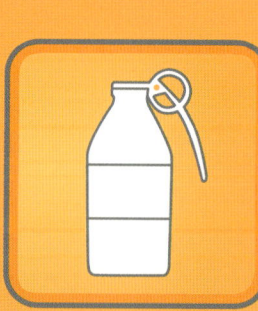

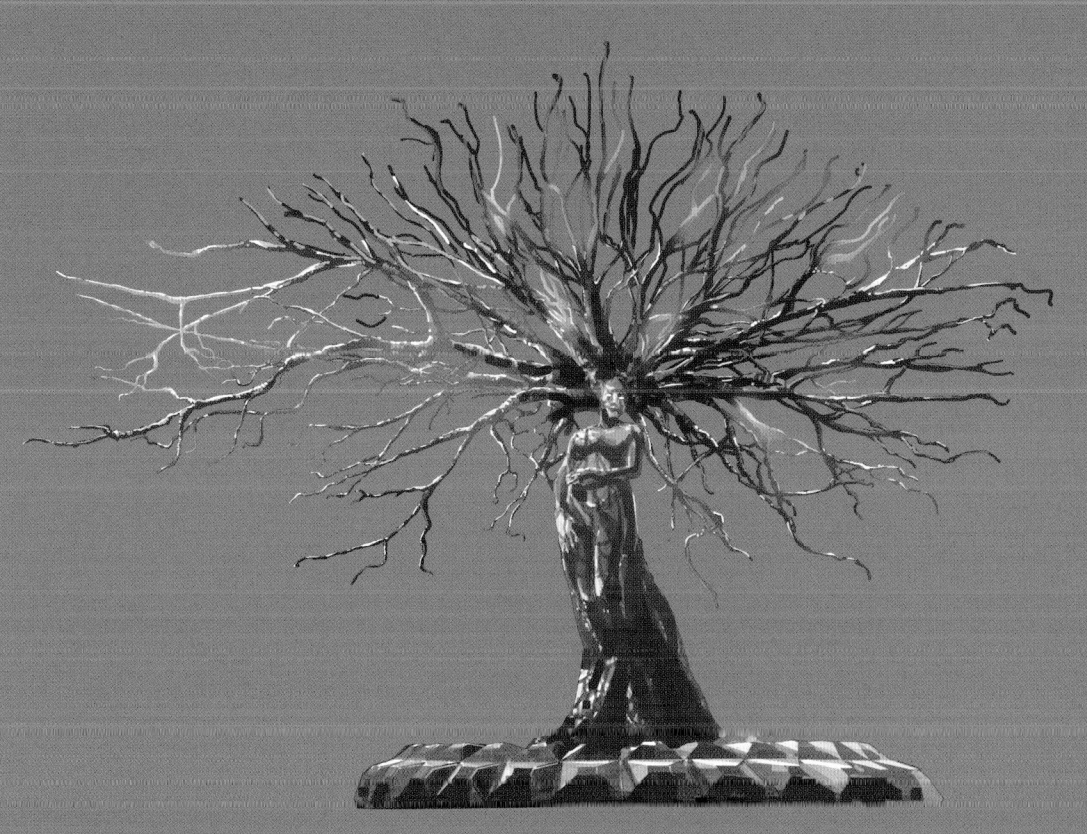

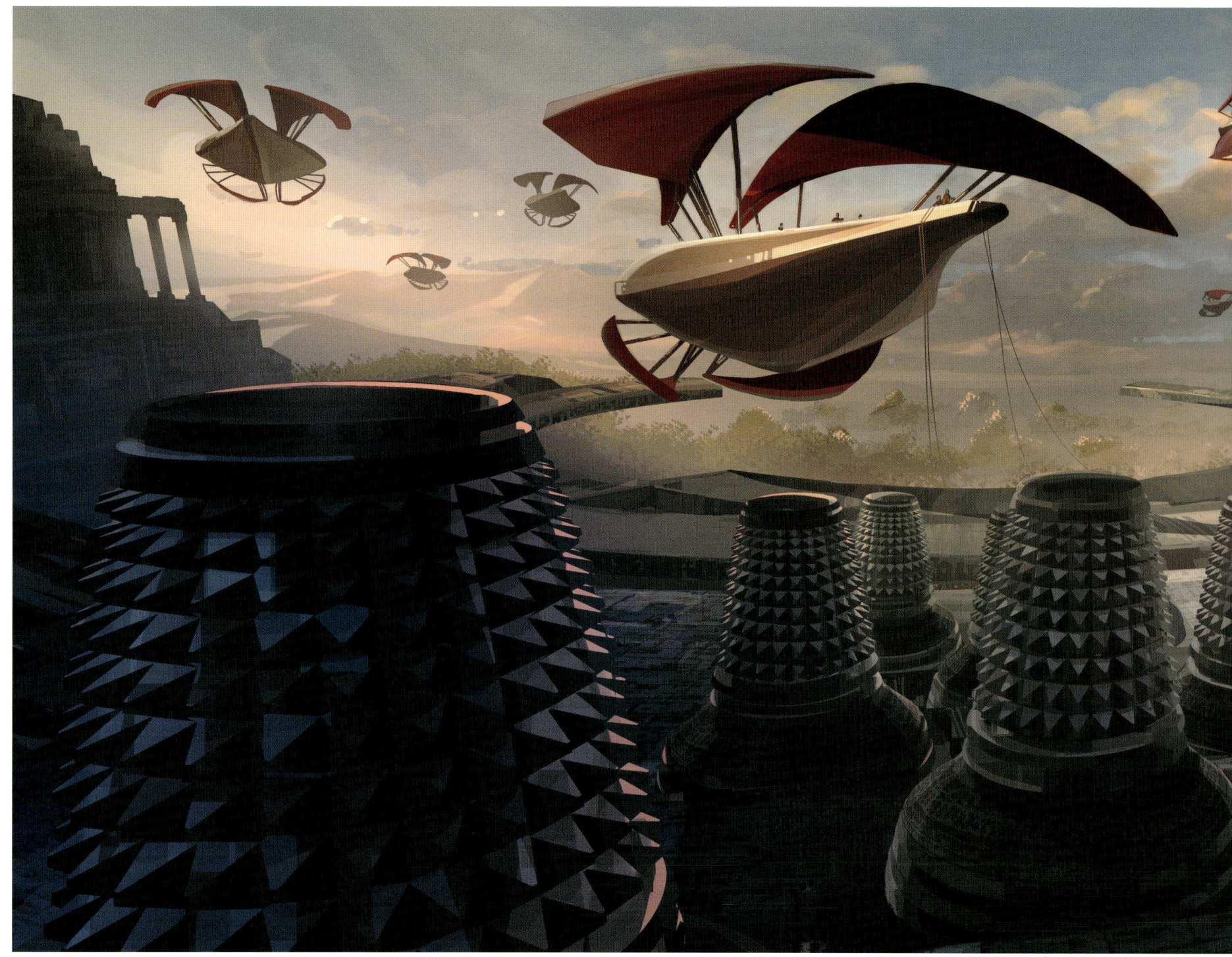

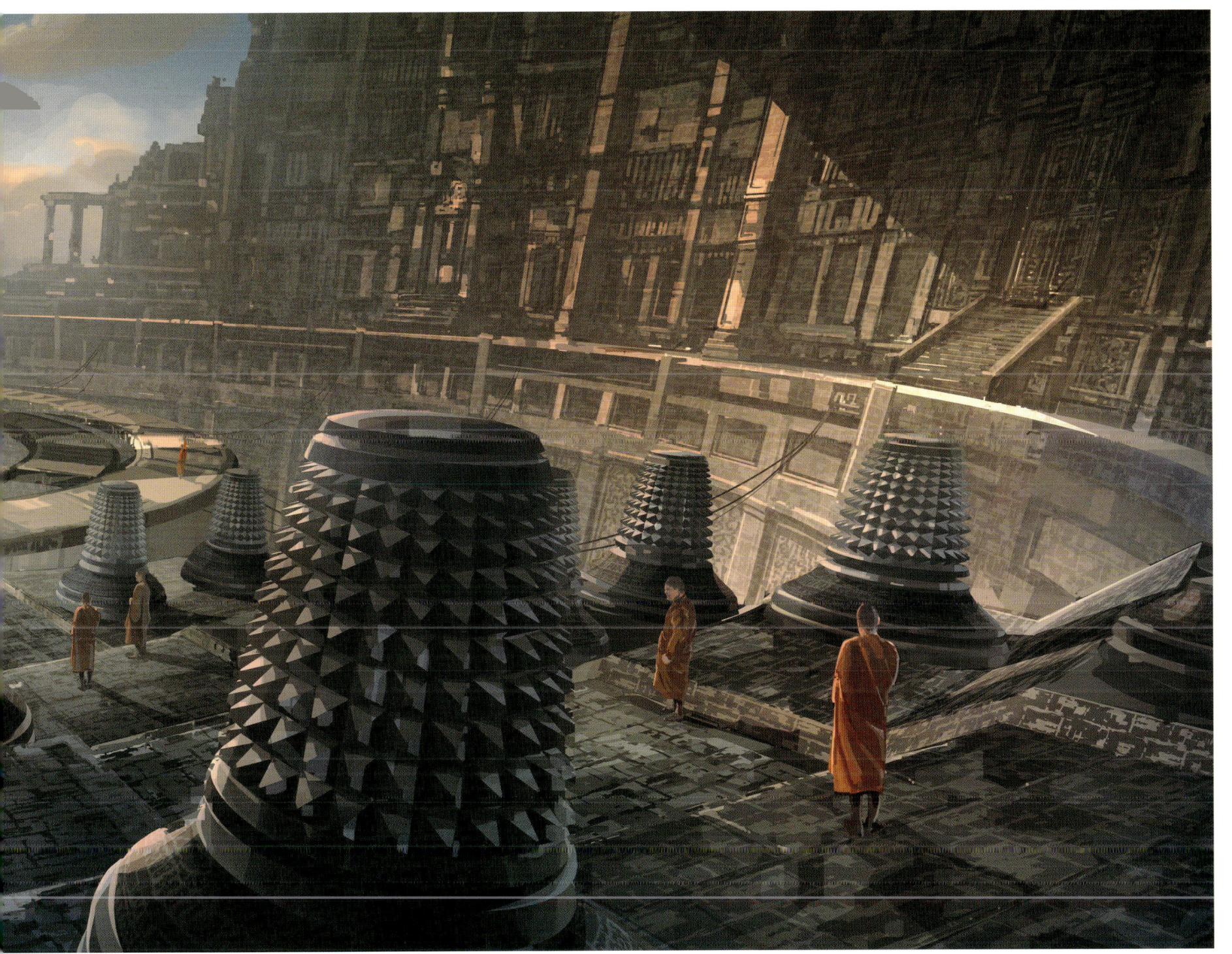

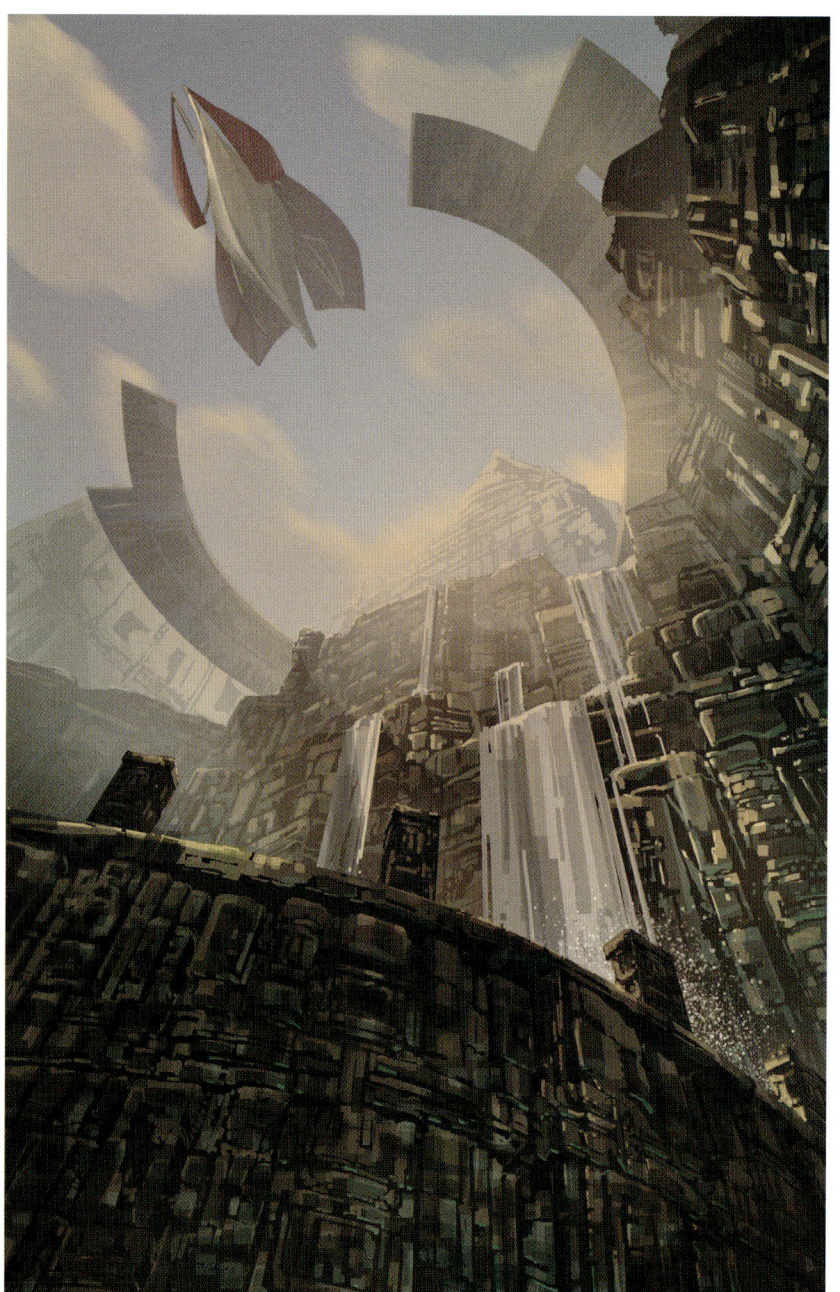

The Arrival (previous page)

Within the mountains of the Jinean Kingdom lie the temples of the Order of the Bei. The followers of the Bei would set off from distant lands to pay homage. Oftentimes their journey was demanding and arduous. The Bei would travel by air ships or the long, winding paths of the mountain trails.

The Walking Trail (left)

The trails leading towards the temples' entrances are surrounded with walls that are etched directly on the facade of the mountain. Flowing streams weave a watery tapestry throughout the Bei sanctuary, creating a peaceful atmosphere for those who visit. The sounds of the cascading water serve as a comfort to returning visitors.

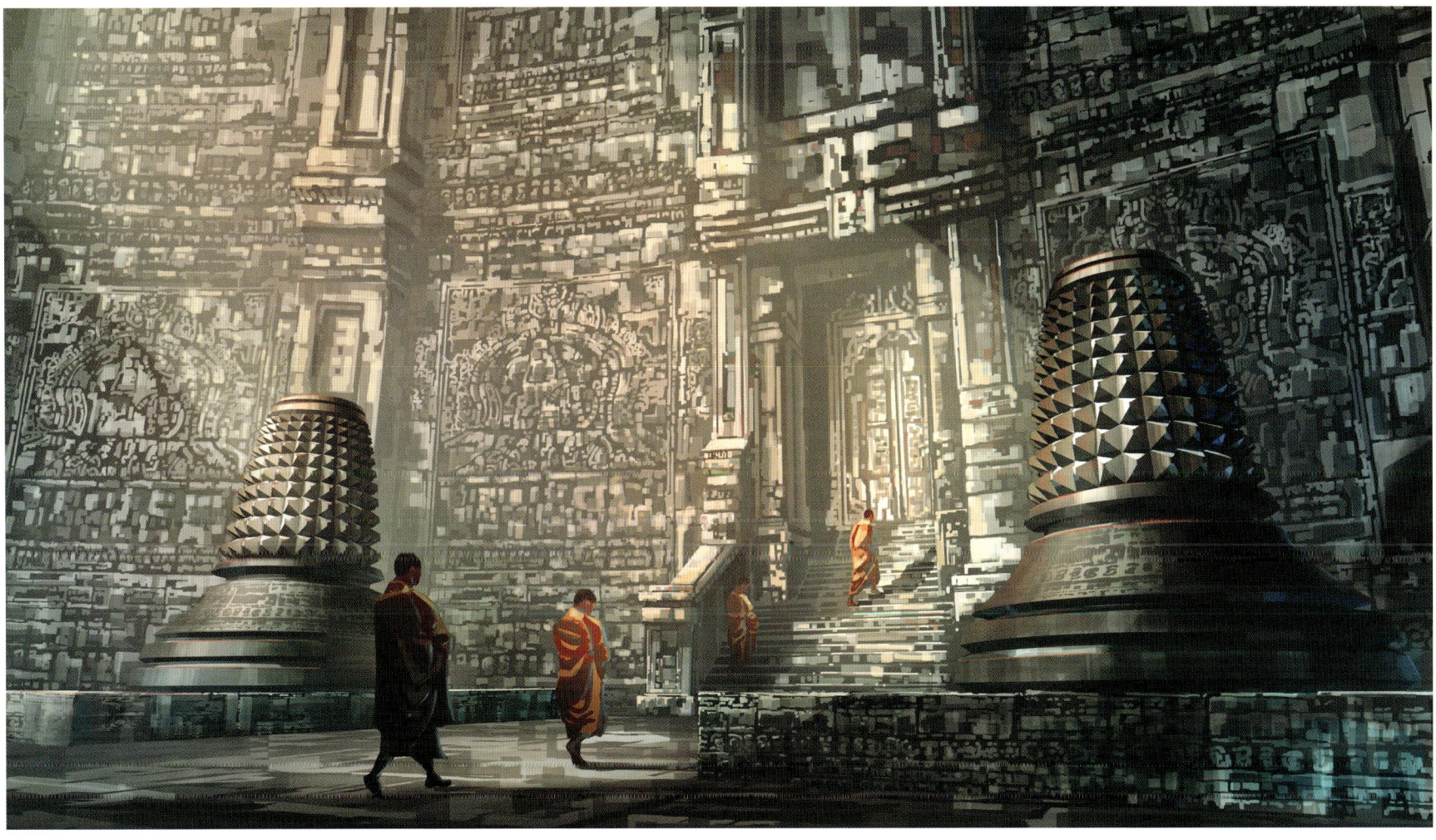

The Gate

There are 100 gates that lead to the interior of the temples. Each gate is bordered by intricately carved walls, which recount the history of the Bei. The walls describe how the Order of the Bei came to be over millennia. Those who make the journey attentively reflect upon the past events before proceeding further.

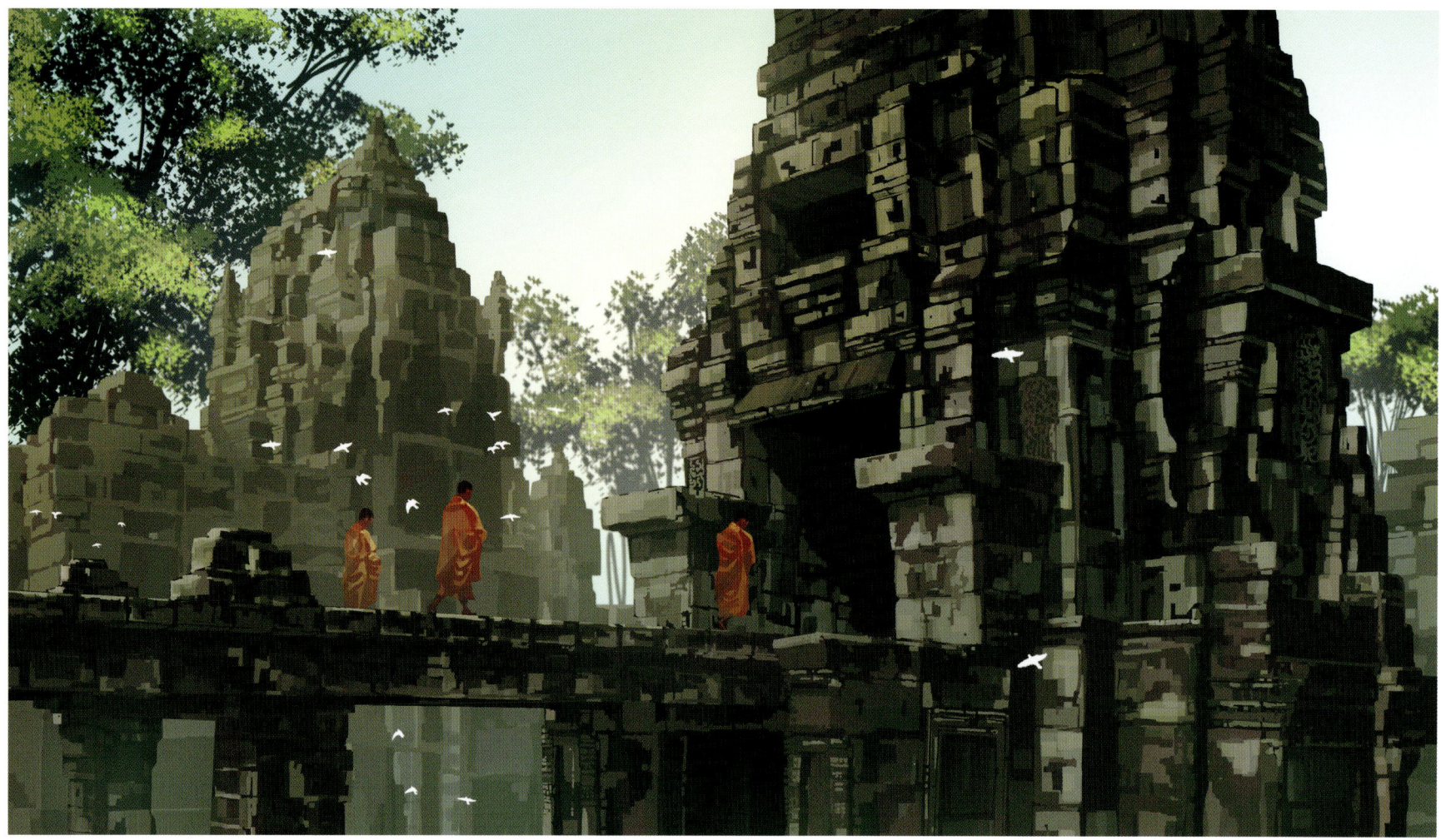

The Garden Entrance (above)

Within the confines of the temple walls, the followers of the Bei cultivate a self-sustaining garden of fruits and vegetables. They are known to be completely independent and self-reliant people, living on their own resources. Aside from being self-sufficient, the followers are generous and will share their resources with those who pass through or the people of neighboring villages.

The Gardens (right)

Gardens lined with towering trees provide much-needed shade on warm days for travelers. The temples of the Bei are built harmoniously with the existing landscape. The vegetation and manmade structures exist in tranquility as a way for the Bei to exhibit their appreciation for nature.

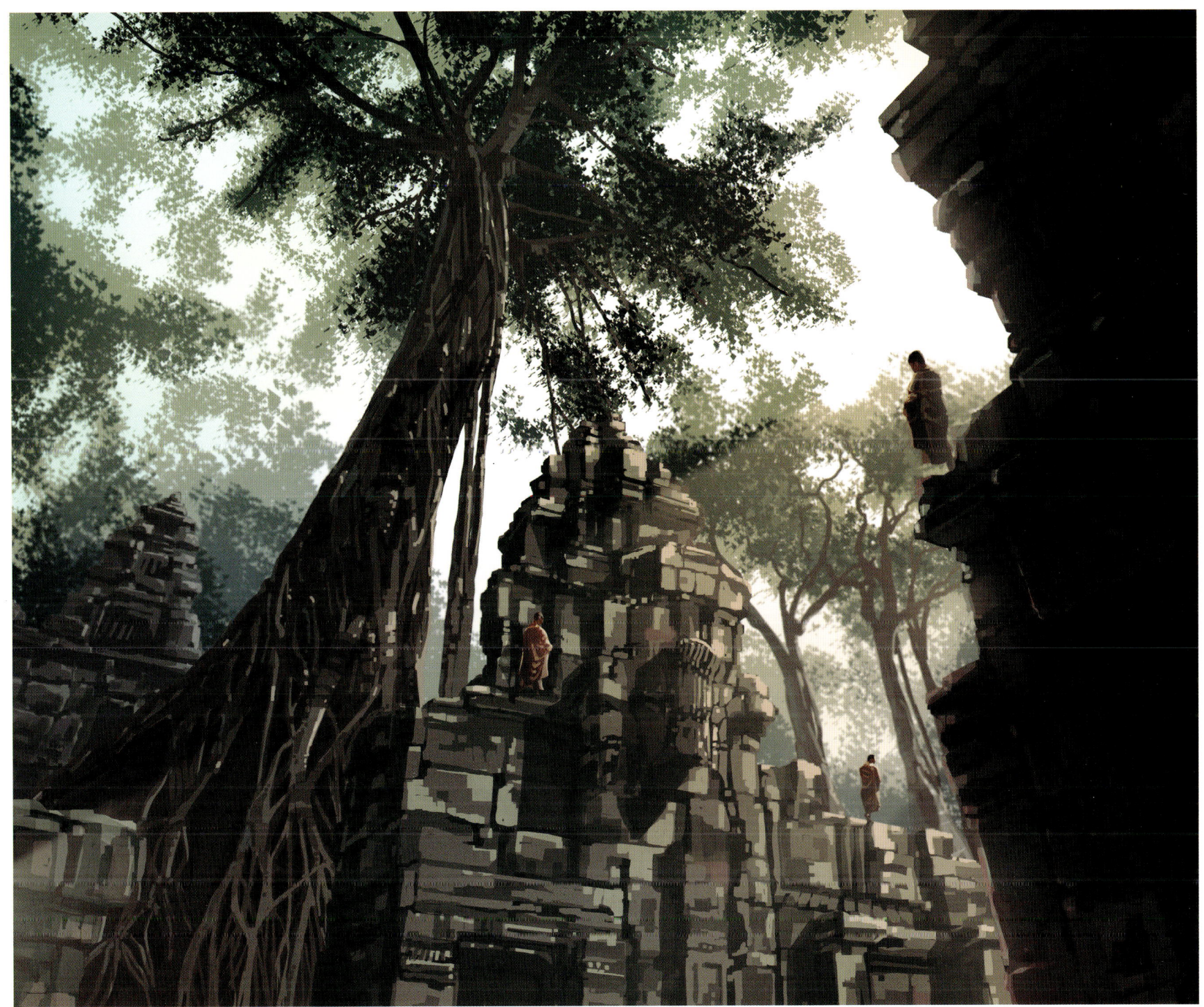

Thang Le

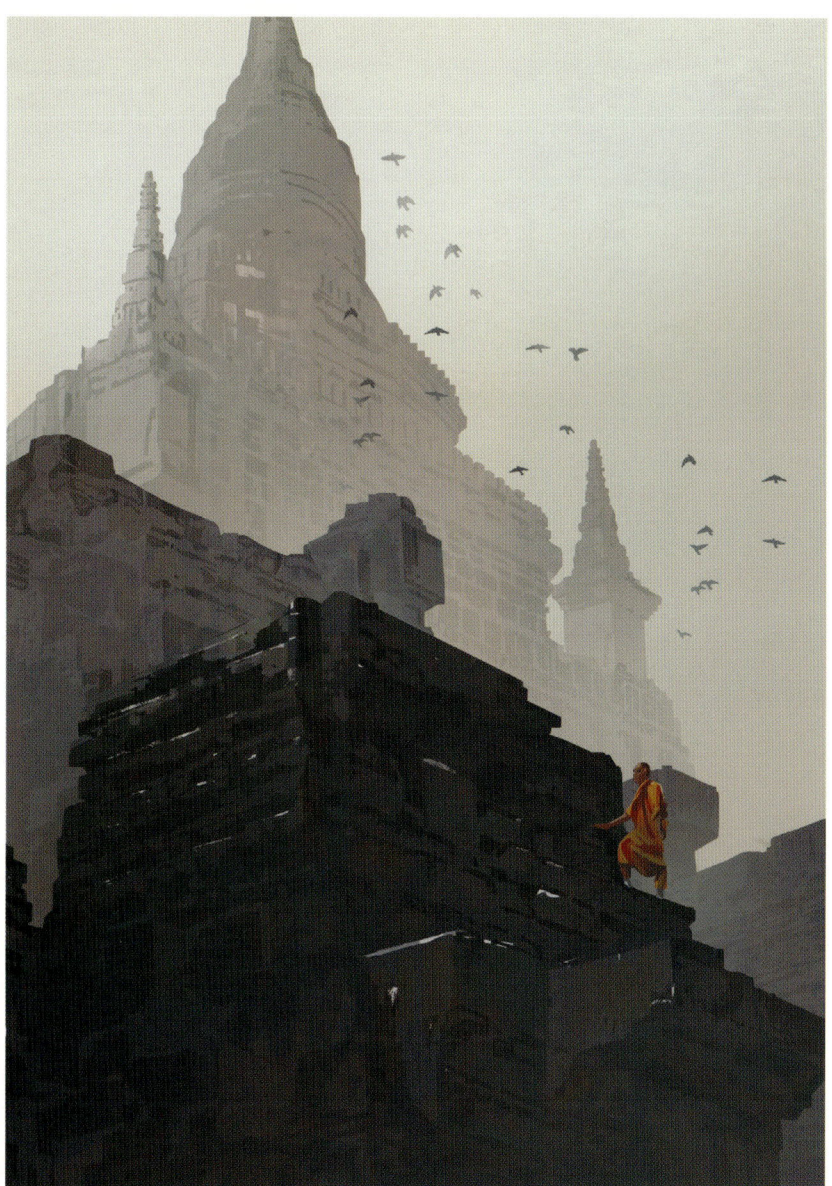

The Climb (left)

Inside the walls of the temples, the interior structures are terraced into the side of the mountain. The terraced sides contain stairs that must be climbed in order to reach the main temple. The ascent up the mountain is long and difficult, taking much time to complete. Only the most earnest will be able to complete the journey.

Temple Interior (right)

The Bei architecture is not only ornate in detail but rich in history. Each carving describes an event that is significant to the order of the Bei. The temple itself serves as an archive that reveals itself to its followers as they ascend closer to the main temple. To grasp the entire history of the Bei would take a follower's lifetime. Oftentimes, when a follower ventures to the temples, there they will remain.

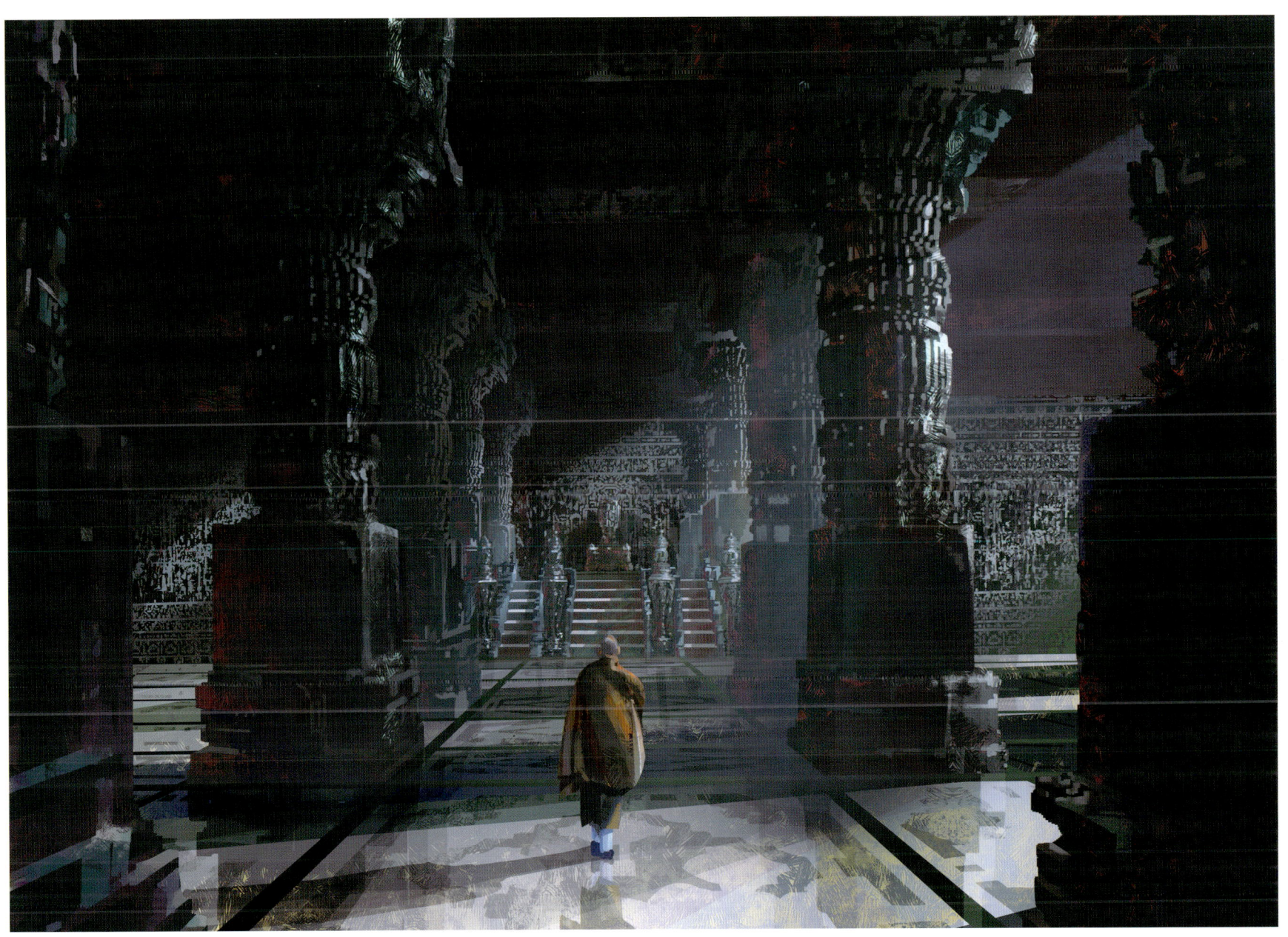

Thang Le

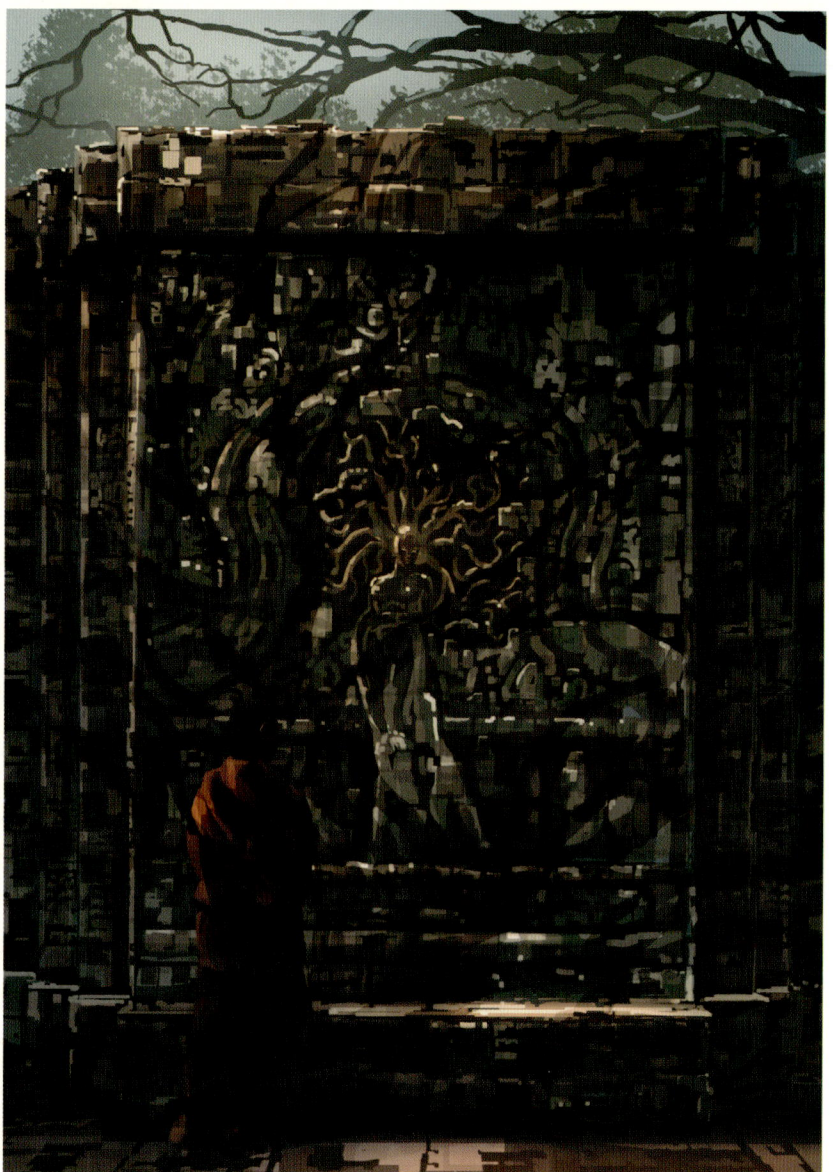

History of the Bei

The walls of the temples are covered with intricate carvings. Each carving depicts a moment in the history of the Bei. The temple structures are like a collection of books, with their walls being the pages.

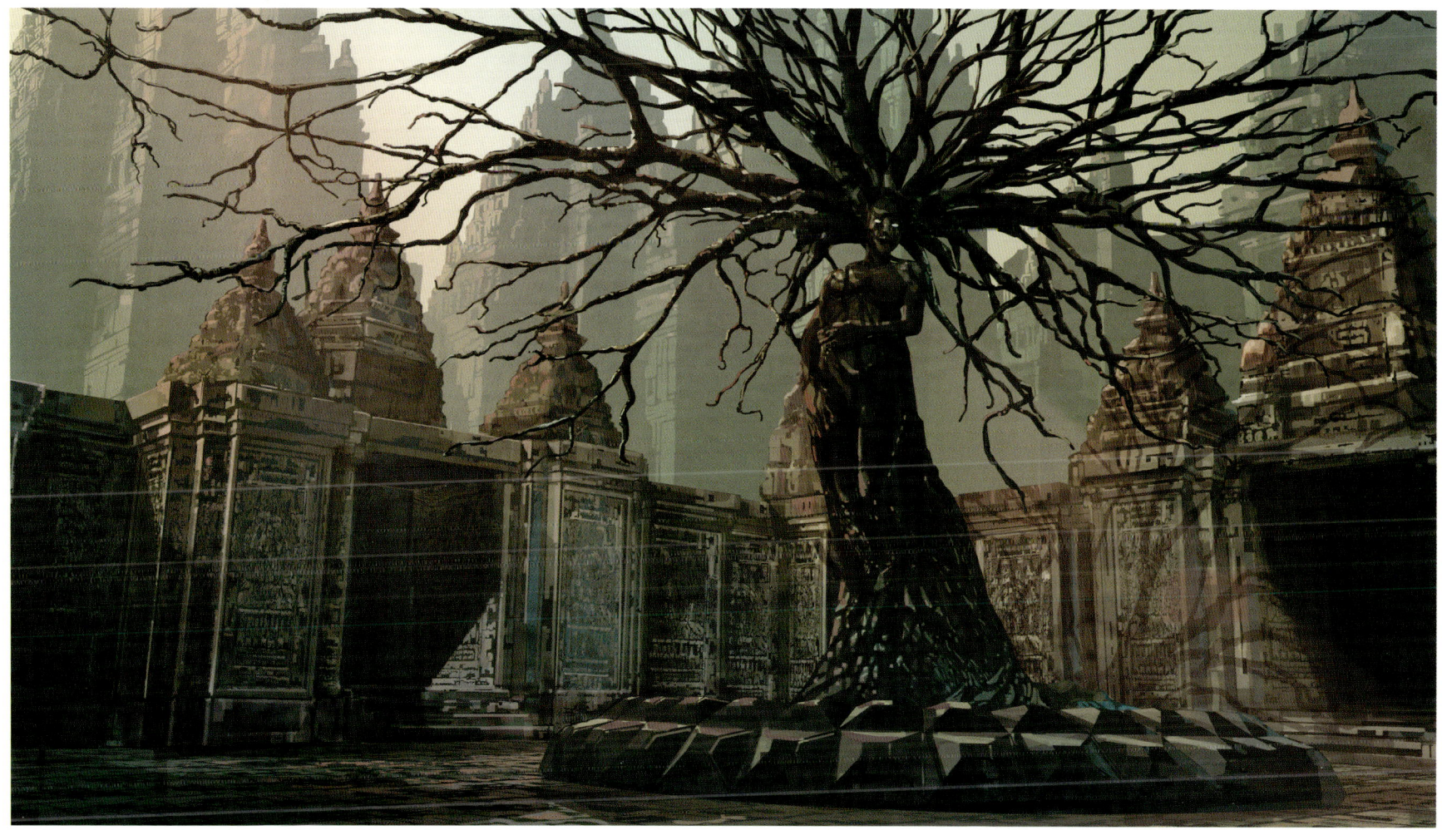

The Spirit Tree

The spirit tree, also known as the tree lady, is as old as the Bei order itself. Legend has stated that the tree is actually the spirit of the mountain. The Bei have built the temples to pay tribute to and serve as protection for the spirit tree. It is common for followers to collect the fallen leaves and wear them as a necklace under their robes as protection and luck when embarking on a long journey.

The Courtyard

There is a central courtyard located in the main temple of the Bei. This is where the followers would gather and perform their ceremonies. Many members who traveled from afar would stay the entire day to pay tribute to the order in the courtyard. Some would place relics from their journeys at the root of the spirit tree as a gift for her protection.

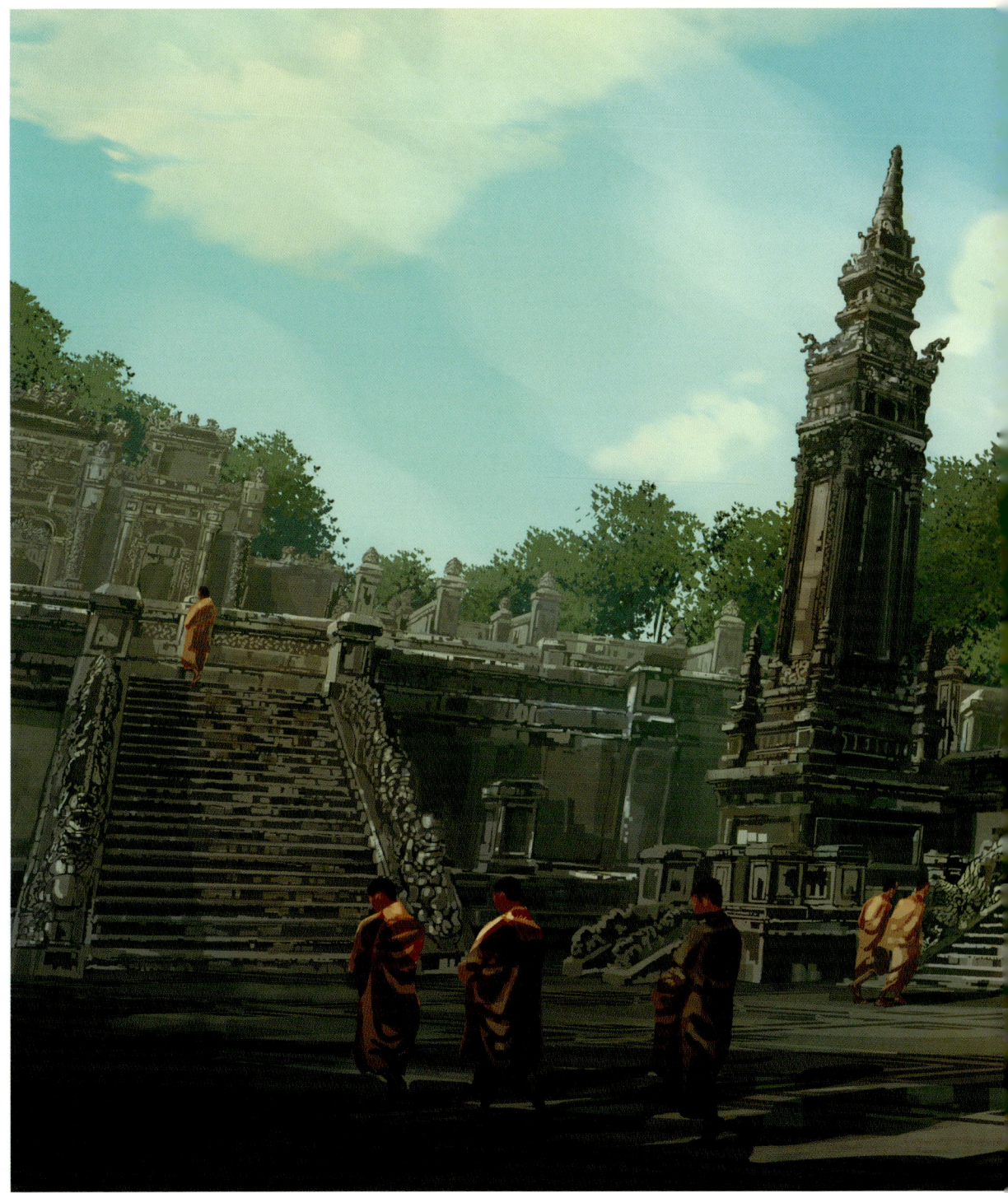

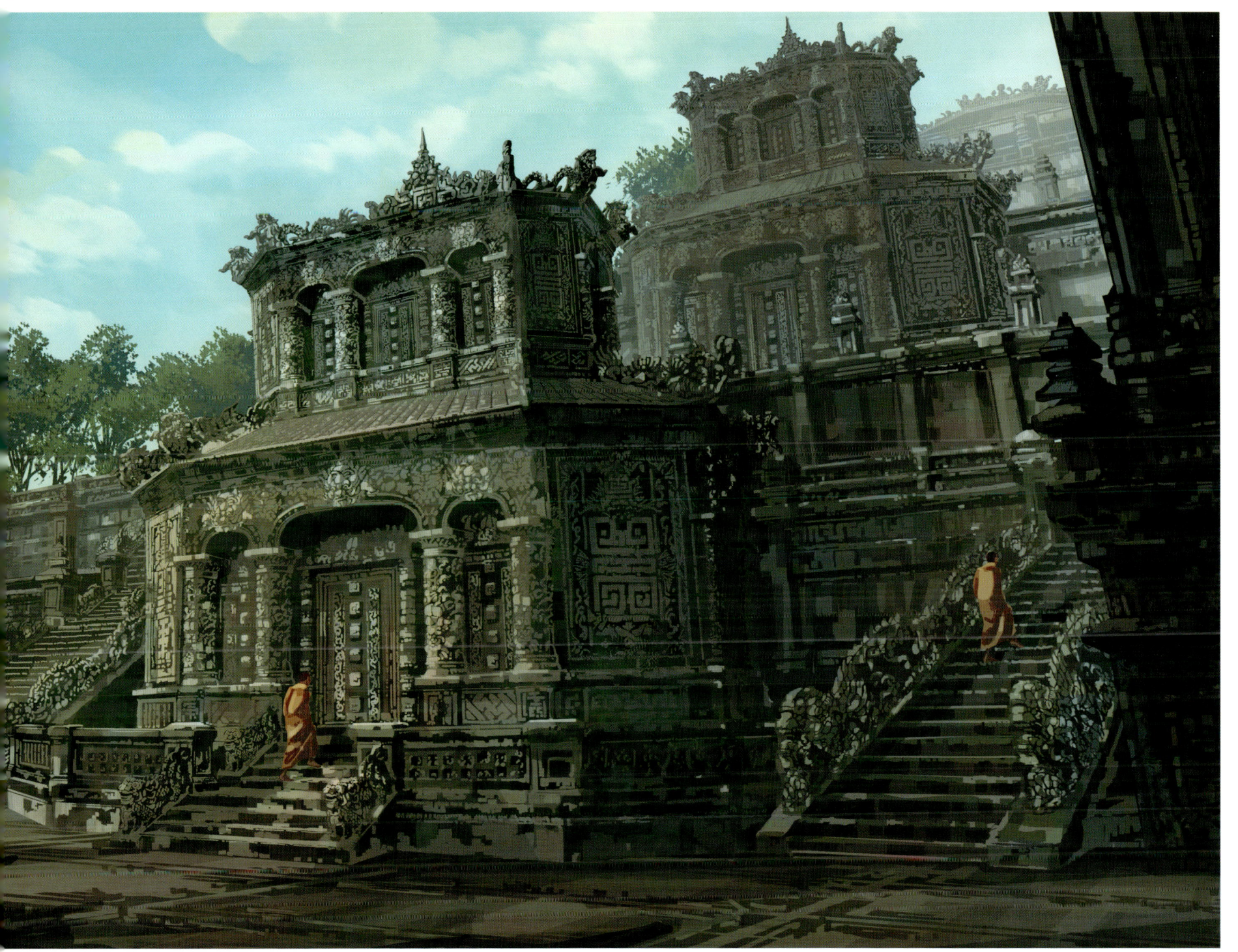

Thang Le

Intro

As artists and designers, we are influenced by our experiences. I have been fortunate enough to have spent the last few years traveling to various parts of Asia. This collection of art represents the influences of different countries I've visited, monuments and structures I've seen, stones and rocks I've climbed, and stories I've been told.

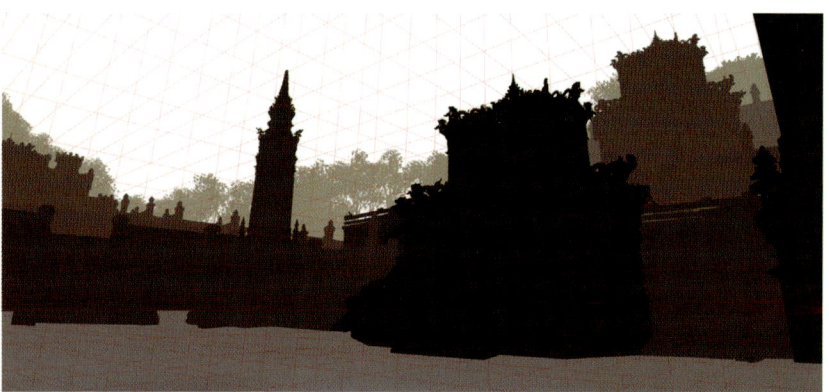

Step 1: Blocking in Shapes

I begin by blocking in the initial shape of the structure, then separating between the foreground, middle ground, and background, while keeping the perspective in mind.

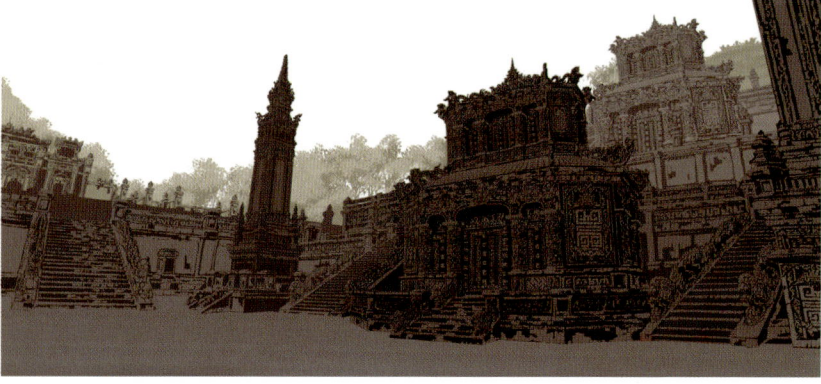

Step 2: Simplified Detail

I was aiming for a more graphic and simplified approach. For this, I started to add in the details of the structure, focusing on where the light and dark areas of the structure would be. The process was similar to that of etching.

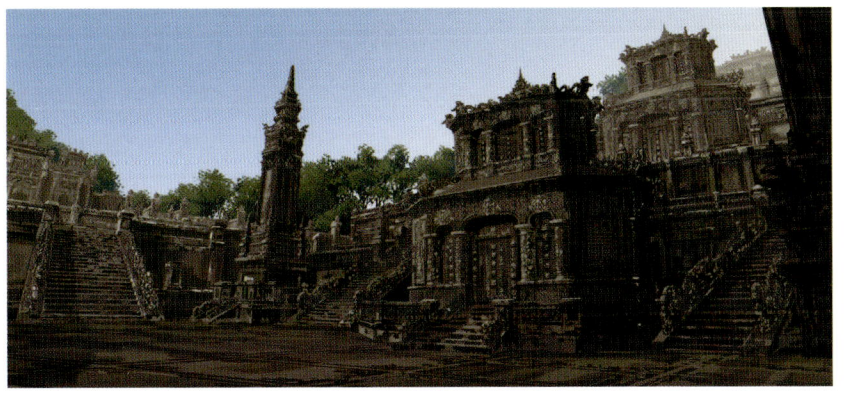

Step 3: Lighting

With all the elements in place, I begin to think about lighting. For this image, the light is coming from screen left to right. I begin to define the sides of the structures, remembering which sides face directly to the sun, which sides face the sun indirectly, and which are in shadow. At this stage, I am also minding foreground, middle ground, and background.

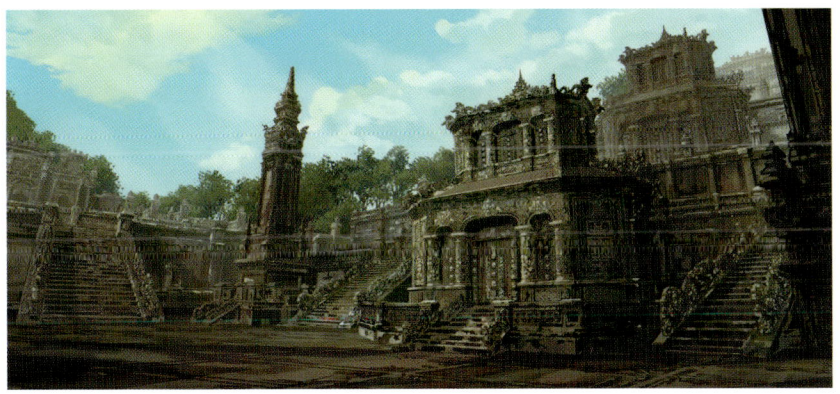

Step 4: Warm and Cool

With the values in place, I begin to add the warm and cool, adding warm to areas that are exposed to sunlight and cool to areas in shade or shadow.

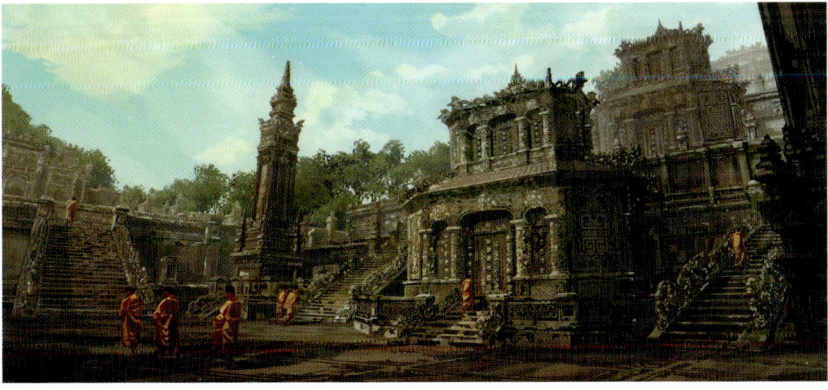

Step 5: Finish

I finish by populating the scene and adding areas of saturation and contrast to direct the viewer's eye.

Christian Alzmann

It all started in kindergarten. One day during arts and crafts, I developed the urge to draw Darth Vader in finger paint. At 24, I decided to go to Art Center and study illustration like two of my childhood heroes, Ralph McQuarrie and Syd Mead. There I tried everything from children's book illustration to fine art, and I learned that all of these paths have great possibilities for an illustrator. I also found out that the purpose of every one of them is to tell a story, which is what I really love doing. Upon graduating, I got a job as a production assistant in the Industrial Light & Magic art department. Within a year, I began work as a concept artist on Steven Spielberg's *Artificial Intelligence*. Still there 13 years later, I'm a senior VFX art director. I am still having fun working in film and illustrating for print.

www.christianalzmann.com

David Le Merrer

I was born in Paris, where I grew up and later studied graphic design at ESAG Met de Penninghen. After getting my degree, I spent a few years in the UK creating art for video games. But after a while I grew tired of the rain, and in 2005 the road took me to California, where I ended up in another video-game company. Now I am working at Lucasfilm on *Star Wars: The Clone Wars*, an animated television show where I met all these crazy folks and decided to join the Battle Milk team.

www.david-le-merrer.blogspot.com

Jackson Sze

I studied illustration at Art Center College of Design with an emphasis in entertainment arts. Since leaving school, I have worked in advertising, video games, television, and film. Currently I'm working at Marvel Studios as a senior concept illustrator.

www.jacksonsze.com
www.jacksonsze.blogspot.com

Justin Ridge

Born and raised in smoggy Southern California, I received my BFA from California State University, Fullerton, and have storyboarded and directed on several animated shows such as *Avatar: The Last Airbender, Star Wars: The Clone Wars,* and *The Cleveland Show*.

www.justinridgeart.com

ARTIST BIOS

Kilian Plunkett

Growing up in Dublin, Ireland, it seemed unlikely that I would one day end up gainfully employed drawing and painting the kind of robots, monsters, spaceships, heroes, and villains that appeared in my favorite entertainment. I moved to the U.S. in the early 1990s when the chance to work as a professional comic artist came along. Comics taught me the value of learning to draw as broad a range of subjects and settings as I could. I worked almost exclusively as a comic artist until 2005, when an opportunity arose to work at Lucasfilm Animation. I've been fortunate as lead designer on *Star Wars: The Clone Wars* to learn more from some incredibly talented artists, a few of whom have work in this very book.

www.kilianplunkett.blogspot.com

Le Tang

I grew up in Southern California but spent a few years as a story artist in the Bay Area working at Lucasfilm Animation. I have since returned to Los Angeles, where I told some kung fu fightin' tales at Nickelodeon. Currently I am doing my storytelling at Dreamworks Animation.

www.letang79.blogspot.com

Matt Gaser

I was born and raised in Northern California. Growing up, I ran around the woods pretending to be an Ewok while drawing my own characters, writing stories, and otherwise fueling my imagination at an early age. I studied illustration at Art Center College of Design, and interned at Klasky Csupo as a background/prop designer for the animated TV series *Rugrats* before completing my studies. After graduation, I worked in games for six years, which eventually led to an amazing opportunity working at Lucasfilm on the animated TV series *Star Wars: The Clone Wars*. After several years at Lucasfilm, I decided to shift gears and work freelance full-time out of my studio in the San Francisco Bay Area. Some recent projects I've been designing for include *Green Lantern* (animated series) and *Hop* (feature film). I'm currently working for Andrew Adamson on his new feature in development, *Fountain City*.

www.mattgaser.com

Pat Presley

was born in the oldest part of Bangkok, The Rattanakosin Island. He grew up in what he believed to be a haunted house full of snakes, trees, and ancient relics his great uncle collected. Besides attending an old French missionary school, he learned from watching his father. When it was the time to further his education he was hoping to become a doctor just to make a lot of money, but then decided he best be an idealistic architect. Neither one panned out, so he stopped making plans and relearned everything from scratch. He went back to drawing late into the night and remembered how great it was to be a kid who gets to stay up way past his bed time.

Although some people wonder about his age, he was old enough to see *Star Wars* in the theater.

www.phattro.blogspot.com

Thang Le

I was born and raised in Southern California. I was educated at the Art Center College of Design, majoring in transportation design. I started my career in entertainment working in television commercials and video games. This eventually led to working in animation, film, and theme parks. Currently I am working at Industrial Light & Magic as a concept artist. My credits include *The Avengers, Battleship, Tron: Uprising, Star Wars: The Clone Wars,* the animated series *Green Lantern*, and Disney Imagineering.

www.thangle.com

Many people have assisted, guided, mentored and, in general, helped us to become the artists we are today. We can't thank them all here, but there are a few people who specifically helped us out with this book: Michael Long, Scott Robertson and Tinti Dey.

Christian Alzmann. I would like to thank Thang Le for inviting me to participate in *Battle Milk Volume 3* and the entire Battle Milk crew for so graciously welcoming me into this talented collection of artists. I would also love to thank one of my biggest heroes and inspirations, Ralph McQuarrie, for inspiring a little kid to draw, make up worlds, and from that create one for himself.

David Le Merrer would like to thanks his family, his parents and sistor and of course his wife Johanna for her love and support.

Jackson Sze would like to thank his teachers and friends for their time and generosity. Thank you to Jacob Johnston and Edmund Liang for story support. To his family, for encouraging his passion in art. Thank you to Michael Long, Rob Leigh, James Gurney, Tinti Dey, and Scott Robertson for helping make *Battle Milk Volume 3* possible.

Justin Ridge would like to thank his family and friends for their love and support, the Battle Milk crew for letting me be among such an amazing group of talented artists, and lastly adrenaline, for never failing to kick in at the last minute.

Kilian Plunkett would like to thank George Lucas for the chance to help him tell more stories in his Galaxy far, far away. Further thanks to James Gurney, Michael Long of Transit Creative, Scott Robertson, Tinti Dey, his partners in crime in this volume of *Battle Milk* and his wife, Catherine.

Le Tang. I've been very fortunate to have a lot of supportive people in my life; people that have given me opportunities when very few other would have. Thank to James Gurney for honoring us with his words, to our designer Michael Long for his great work and artistry, and DSP for helping us get our voices out there. Lastly I'd like to thank my fellow Battlemilkers for inspiring and intimidating me all at once.

Matt Gaser would like to thank his wife for supporting all the time he put into this book. He also wants to thank the original Battle Milk team for inviting him to participate, Michael Long of Transit Creative for the book design, and Scott Robertson and Tinti Dey from Design Studio Press for all their help. A super special thanks to James Gurney for supporting this book with his foreword.

Pat Presley would like to thank his parents and his sister for a lifetime of love and support, to the Battle Milk crew for the endless inspiration and the invitation to join the fun, DSP for the help making our ideas into reality, Michael Long for awesome book design, James Gurney for the wonderful foreword, Brian Kalin O'Connell for ideas and suggestions, and finally to Annika, the pillar of his world, for her infinite patience and strength that help him in this adventure.

Thang Le. I would like to thank my family and friends. With their support and encouragement, I am able to become the artist I am today.

ARTIST BIOS

SPECIAL THANKS